3

The Manners and Customs
of the Police

D1561441

The Manners and Customs of the Police

Donald Black

Center for Criminal Justice
Harvard Law School
Cambridge, Massachusetts

ACADEMIC PRESS

A Subsidiary of Harcourt Brace Jovanovich, Publishers

New York   London   Toronto   Sydney   San Francisco

ACADEMIC PRESS, INC.
111 Fifth Avenue, New York, New York 10003

United Kingdom Edition published by
ACADEMIC PRESS, INC. (LONDON) LTD.
24/28 Oval Road, London NW1 7DX

Library of Congress Cataloging in Publication Data

Black, Donald J.
    The manners and customs of the police.

    Bibliography: p.
    Includes indexes.
    1. Police——United States——Addresses, essays,
lectures. I. Title.
HV8138.B5   363.2'0973   80–1675
ISBN 0–12–102880–1 (Cloth)
ISBN 0–12–102882–8 (Paper)

PRINTED IN THE UNITED STATES OF AMERICA

80 81 82 83   9 8 7 6 5 4 3 2 1

To Herman and Anne Elizabeth Black

Contents

Sat.

Sun.

mon.

Tues.

Preface

Archaic though it may seem, the title of this volume expresses the spirit and content of the pages that follow. It recalls anthropological works of a century ago, reports of expeditions into the hinterland and encounters with little-known tribes viewed as exotic or even savage. Like those earlier works, the present volume is based primarily upon observations in the field, and—despite its considerably more scientific character—there are similarities in the purpose, mood, and presentation as well. Its subject is the behavior of the police in modern America. No effort is made here to survey all of the "manners and customs" of the police, however, but only those pertaining to their role as legal officials. The book is intended to be a contribution to the study of law as a natural phenomenon.

The first chapter introduces police work as an instance of law, discusses how it may be predicted and explained by the sociological theory of law, and illustrates the relevance of that theory in a variety of settings where the police have been studied, including patrol, investigation, and the handling of vice, juveniles, skid row, traffic, and rebellion. The second chapter examines how cases come to the attention of the police and other legal officials, and some of the implications of these patterns for the larger process of social control through law. The next three chapters report findings from a three-city observation study of patrol officers on their daily rounds, and pertain to the social conditions under which the police define incidents as crimes and make arrests, and to the patterns by which they handle disputes between people who know each other (such as husbands and wives, parents and children, and neighbors). The closing chapter, co-authored with M. P. Baumgartner, explores techniques by which people might be encouraged to handle their own conflicts instead of relying upon the police and other legal officials. Finally, appended to the volume is a note on law as a problem in scientific measurement (first published in a West German journal), and also an example of the observation forms used during the three-city study.

It should be recognized from the beginning that this volume includes several previously published essays, and for this reason has shortcomings of which the reader might be forewarned. A degree of repetition is unavoidable, for instance, and, because the various essays were written over a period of years (1970–1979), the analytical strategy, its execution, and even the writing style are not perfectly consistent from one chapter to the next. This may be especially noticeable when the introductory chapter and Chapter 5 ("Dispute Settlement by the Police"), written most recently and expressly for this volume, are compared to the other chapters. Another limitation should also be mentioned: The field observations on which the essays are based took place a number of years ago (the three-city study in 1966), so the facts reported may not be entirely representative of police behavior as it appears today. From a theoretical standpoint, this has no importance—the data would be pertinent to the theory of law were they even older—but the reader with a practical interest in the findings should proceed with caution. (A brief assessment of subsequent research—particularly in regard to the question of racial discrimination by the police—is attached as a "postscript" to Chapter 4.) The findings are nonetheless given in the present tense, a convention known in anthropology as the "ethnographic present." For all of this, it is hoped that the volume retains a degree of symmetry and that it has some practical as well as theoretical value.

The publication of this work brings to a conclusion a project that began in the early 1960s under the direction of Albert J. Reiss, Jr., at the Center for Research on Social Organization, Department of Sociology, University of Michigan. I joined this project as a graduate student in the summer of 1964, first developing a technique for analyzing telephone calls to the Chicago police (of which we had tape recordings), then observing patrol and juvenile officers in Detroit (1964–1965), and ultimately collaborating with Professor Reiss on a field study of patrol work in Boston, Chicago, and Washington, D.C., conducted under the auspices of the President's Commission on Law Enforcement and Administration of Justice (1966–1967). Several chapters in the present volume (2–4) derive from my doctoral dissertation, which was based upon the three-city study and was completed in 1968. In the following years, I continued to devote time to this material, initially as a Russell Sage Fellow at Yale Law School (1968–1970)—in a program directed by Stanton Wheeler and Abraham S. Goldstein—and later as a member of the Department of Sociology at Yale University (1970–1979). The volume was completed at Harvard Law School's Center for Criminal Justice, a research facility directed by James Vorenberg and Lloyd E. Ohlin.

A number of individuals and organizations are acknowledged at the beginning of each chapter for their suggestions and support, as are the journals where several of the chapters were originally published. In addition, I am grateful to have been awarded a grant by Yale University's Behavioral Sciences Publication Fund to complete the volume itself. Suggestions for improving the volume as a whole were made by Malcolm M. Feeley, Peter K. Manning, and Lawrence W. Sherman. The manuscript was typed by Arlene Bernstein, Anna Coyle, Kathy Keating, and Mary Markiza. The people at Academic Press added their skills as well. Finally, I take this opportunity to thank Maureen Mileski for her important contribution to this project and to acknowledge the enormous help and stimulation given to me over a period of years by M. P. Baumgartner, presently my assistant and colleague at Harvard.

Introduction*

1

Like anything else in the natural world, the behavior of the police may be understood from a variety of perspectives. Police work is an occupation, for instance, with its own subculture and modes of recruitment, socialization, stratification, and mobility (see, e.g., Wilson, 1963; 1964; Westley, 1970; Van Maanen, 1974). Police departments are organizations, typically bureaucracies, and this too provides a topic for study in its own right (see, e.g., Peabody, 1964; Skolnick, 1966; Reiss and Bordua, 1967). Policing involves politics (see Wilson, 1968; Muir, 1977), human relations (Preiss and Ehrlich, 1966; Sykes and Clark, 1975), and even drama (Manning, 1977). Indeed, police work might be studied from the standpoint of practically any field in social science. There is nonetheless one dimension by which this phenomenon is most readily identified: It is a kind of social control, a system of authority that defines and responds to deviant behavior. The police are legal officials who handle complaints from citizens and who proceed against conduct that they themselves define as offensive. Police work is arguably the most visible species of legal life, it touches the most people, and it is probably the most controversial. Even so, little scientific theory has been developed to predict and explain how policing varies from one setting to another.

* * *

The purpose of this chapter is to show how the sociological theory of law applies to the behavior of the police. The chapter begins with a discussion of the sense in which police work may be understood as an instance of law and,

---

*M. P. Baumgartner commented upon an earlier draft of this chapter.

accordingly, as a phenomenon that varies with its location and direction in social space. The remaining pages are then devoted to a survey of police work in modern American cities, touching upon patrol, investigation, and the handling of vice, juveniles, skid row, traffic, and rebellion. Each of these illustrates a major activity of the police and, beyond this, poses its own questions for the sociological theory of law. Such a survey also provides a beginning for the volume as a whole: Although the chapters that follow pertain primarily to the routine work of patrol officers, it is important to recognize that this is only one context in which the police exercise social control through law.

Police Work as Law

Law may be understood as a quantitative variable, known by the degree to which people define or respond to conduct as deviant within the framework of a state (see Black, 1976:2–3; 1979b).[1] The more this occurs—whether in a single case or in a larger setting such as community or society—the more law there is. In a civil matter, for example, a lawsuit is an increment of law, since it defines the conduct of a person or group as somehow undesirable. If the plaintiff (or complainant) wins, this further increases the quantity of law, since the decision of the court constitutes an official endorsement of the complaint. If the court awards compensation for damages to the plaintiff, law is increased still more, and the greater the award, the greater is the quantity of law. Similarly, in a criminal case, law increases with prosecution, conviction, and the severity of punishment.

In a number of ways the police determine the quantity of law as well, since they have the capacity to exercise more or less social control from one setting to another. When a citizen telephones the police to make a complaint, for example, the officer who answers may or may not dispatch a patrol car to handle it. If a car is sent, this by itself introduces law into the situation, since it accords official recognition—if only tentatively—to the complaint that was made.[2] Upon arriving at the scene, the officers assigned to the case further increase the quantity of law if they write an official report of an alleged crime, thereby notifying the

---

1. For these purposes, conduct is taken to be deviant if it is designated as undesirable in any way, whether as "wrong," a "nuisance," a "disturbance," "dangerous," "negligent," "sick," or whatever.

2. A perspective on law and social control ignores police work that does not pertain to deviant behavior as such. Assistance with medical problems, for example, when these are unrelated to conflict, should not be construed as the distribution of law, even though a substantial amount of police time is used in this way. The same is true of help for lost children and stranded motorists, the handling of safety hazards such as fallen trees or electrical wires, and other service work. Such activities would more properly be studied in a sociology of helping behavior.

detective bureau of the matter and creating the possibility of a more extensive investigation and possibly even an arrest. Where an alleged offender is present when the police arrive, they may themselves decide to make an arrest—a substantial increment of law—or they may exercise their authority in lesser ways through an interrogation, search, threat, or admonishment of one or more individuals. Whenever the police act in an official capacity, every kind of social control they exercise, including forms of punishment considered brutal by some, is understandable as law. Accordingly, the most law the police ever apply is the taking of a person's life on their own authority.

It should also be noted that law varies in style as well as quantity (see Black, 1976:4–6). The style of social control ordinarily associated with the police is penal in character, since they so often relate to people as offenders who have violated the prohibitions of criminal law and who therefore deserve punishment. In some cases, however, they exercise other styles of social control. One of these is the conciliatory style, in which the emphasis is upon the restoration of social harmony rather than punishment of a wrongdoer. The police frequently employ conciliation when they encounter conflicts between people who have an ongoing relationship, such as members of the same family or neighborhood (see Chapter 5 of the present volume). Occasionally the police employ a therapeutic style of social control, treating the deviant as someone who needs help instead of punishment. This happens when they define a person as mentally ill. Finally, from time to time the police even employ a compensatory style of social control, asking the deviant to pay damages, or restitution, to the person who was allegedly victimized. In short, then, neither the quantity nor the style of law involved in police work can be taken for granted, and variation in each must be explained.

The Relevance of Social Space

The sociological theory of law predicts and explains legal variation with its location and direction in social space (see generally Black, 1976). Social space has a number of dimensions, and each of these is relevant to the prediction and explanation of every expression of law. These include a vertical dimension, arising from an uneven distribution of wealth; a horizontal dimension, described by the distribution of people in relation to each other; a cultural dimension, pertaining to the symbolic aspect of social life; a corporate dimension, referring to the capacity of people for collective action; and a normative dimension, determined by the distribution of authority and social control (see Black, 1979c). It is possible to predict and explain the quantity and style of law according to whether it is higher or lower in vertical space, for example, or according to whether its direction is downward or upward, invoked by a wealthy person against someone with less wealth, or vice versa. Law also varies with its location and direction in the structure of interaction, as, for example, with the relational distance between the parties involved in a dispute or the degree to which they are integrated into social life, and it varies with its location and direction in the cultural space delimited by ethnic enclaves or lifestyles. It varies within and between differing degrees of organization, and with its location and direction in the normative order defined by other kinds of social control, such as authority within a family, school, church, or other institution.

The sociological theory of law predicts, for instance, that the quantity of law will be greater when a higher-status person complains against a lower-status person than when a complaint is made in the opposite direction (Black, 1976:21, 50, 65, 92, 114). This implies that a downward lawsuit is more likely to be brought than an upward lawsuit, that an upward crime will be punished more severely than a downward crime, that a higher-status person is more likely than a lower-status person to win a reversal of a court's decision, and so on. In the case of lateral complaints—between people equal in status—the theory predicts that law will increase as the status of the parties is greater. As regards the relationship between law and relational distance, or intimacy, the theory predicts that— within the same community or society—the quantity of law will vary directly with relational distance, increasing as people are less intimate.[3] Thus, a person is more likely to bring a lawsuit against a stranger than against a friend or relative, courts are more severe toward those who offend strangers than toward those who offend their intimates, and so on. Still another proposition from the theory of law is the following: Law varies inversely with other social control (Black, 1976:107). This implies that where nonlegal authority is strong, such as between parents and children, husbands and dependent wives, or employers and employees, there will be relatively little recourse to law. And if a person subject to considerable nonlegal authority is brought to court, it may be expected that the outcome will be relatively lenient (which explains, for instance, why juveniles and women generally receive less severe dispositions than adults and men). These and other formulations of like kind predict and explain variation in law across all social settings. Along with who brings lawsuits against whom, they predict who wins in court, who receives more or less compensation, mediation, or help (such as psychiatric care), and, in a criminal process, who is handled in what way, with what degree of severity. The same theory tells us whether a community or

---

3. Here relational distance is measured by the scope, frequency, and duration of interaction between people, and by the nature and number of links between them in a social network (Black, 1976:41). It might be added that, strictly speaking, the relationship between law and this type of social distance is curvilinear rather than direct, since there is little or no law between people who are separated by the greatest distances, such as those who live in different societies or tribes (Black, 1976:41–43).

society will have any law at all, and, if so, how much there will be and the styles in which it will appear. This theory may also be applied to police work.

The sociological theory of law implies that police work will vary with its location and direction in social space. This means, for example, that how the police handle a particular case will depend upon the social characteristics of the alleged offender and of the complainant or victim, and with the nature of the relationship between the parties. It also will depend upon the characteristics of the police officers themselves and upon their relationship with the citizens involved. The direction of a complaint to the police may be upward, downward, or lateral in vertical space, for instance, and it may cross a greater or lesser distance in relational space. The police officers handling the matter may be higher, lower, or equal in status to each of the citizens, and may be more or less intimate with each. Variables such as these predict and explain how the police will deal with each case they handle and also, more generally, how they will respond to an entire class of conduct—whether and to what extent they will allocate their resources to combat it by, for example, assigning undercover or other specialized units to it or, conversely, leaving it alone. Similarly, the social characteristics of a neighborhood or community predict and explain the nature of the police work—if any—that it will have (see, e.g., Carroll and Jackson, 1979).

In all of these settings it is possible to understand how police work varies across social space itself, higher or lower in a distribution of status, downward or upward, among and between structures of intimacy, organizations, and subcultures, in the presence or absence of other social control. Since the sociological theory of law assumes that the behavior of the police obeys the same principles as legal life in general, a study of the police may be informed by knowledge about law of other kinds, and, in turn, it may itself contribute to this larger body of knowledge. It can do so by providing its own range of conditions under which the theory of law may be tested and, if necessary, refined, and by suggesting formulations that may be generalized to other legal phenomena. In fact, each variety of police work—patrol work, detective work, vice work, etc.—offers unique opportunities of this kind. First consider patrol work.

Patrol

Patrol officers are the rank and file of a police department, the men (and increasingly women) in uniform who ride in radio-equipped cars or walk their beats among the public, handling diverse incidents that they or others deem worthy of police attention. (A bibliography on patrol and other police work is provided by Manning and Van Maanen, 1978: Appendix; for a review of quantitative studies, see Sherman, 1980b). The great majority of the cases handled by patrol officers are brought to their attention by ordinary citizens who use the telephone to request their services (see Black, 1968:45; 1973). Since a police car ordinarily is dispatched in response to these requests,[4] the social location and direction of patrol work is to a large degree decided by citizens rather than police officers. This means that most often it is citizens rather than police who initially decide what is to be regarded as a "crime" or, at least, what is to be a candidate for this official designation. It might be added that a call to the police is itself an increment of law, and so the pattern by which these cases are selected is understandable in terms of the principles comprising the sociological theory of law in general (see Black, 1976; 1979a; compare Gottfredson and Hindelang, 1979). For example, since law varies inversely with the relational distance between people in a community, it follows that people will be more likely to call the police when they have a grievance against a stranger than when the offending party is a friend or relative. And, since law varies inversely with other kinds of social control, it follows that people in patriarchal families will be less likely to call the police about their domestic conflicts than those in more egalitarian families (see Chapter 5 of the present volume, pages 124–128). In this way it is possible, in theory, to predict and explain every call to the police.

That the police comply with the great majority of requests by telephone de-

---

4. This generalization is based upon the present author's analysis of telephone calls made to the Chicago Police Department on April 21, 1964, and the response of the officers who handled these calls on the switchboard at the communications center. (Tape recordings of the conversations were played back and their content coded for purposes of the analysis.) Of the 6172 calls made during this 24-hour period, 58% were complaints about what the caller considered a crime or other social disruption, 23% were requests for assistance concerning matters such as medical emergencies and automobile accidents, 11% were requests for information such as questions about the law or legal procedures, 4% involved information for the police such as reports about the return of a missing person, and 3% were complaints about the police themselves, usually because of their failure to appear after an earlier call. (For further details, see Reiss, 1971b:70–72; see also Bercal, 1970.)

In 82% of the cases the caller apparently wanted the police to dispatch a patrol car, and, among those, they did so in 84% of the cases. In response to another 8% of these requests the police told the caller that the problem would be referred elsewhere, though it could not be ascertained whether or not this actually was done. In 4% the caller was told to seek help somewhere else, such as a precinct station or other government agency. In 2% the caller was told, in so many words, that the request was not legitimate, and in a few more cases (.5%) he or she was convinced to withdraw the complaint altogether. In another 1% the officer, without elaboration, simply told the caller that the problem was a "civil matter" and "not police business." Finally, in 1% the officer rejected the request by cutting off the caller on the switchboard while he or she was still talking.

It should be recognized, however, that police responses to calls may vary significantly from city to city (see Manning, 1980b). Within a city officers also respond with varying degrees of urgency, sending cars immediately in some cases but not in others. The response of the patrol cars themselves varies as well, with urgency in some cases, moderate speed in others, and even intentional dallying in still others (see, e.g., Chapter 5 of the present volume, page 117).

For an overview of the communications system of a modern department, including the responses of officers to telephone calls and to radio dispatches, see Rubinstein (1973: Chapter 3).

serves emphasis in its own right, particularly in light of the considerable degree of variation found in other aspects of police work. Nevertheless, from the standpoint of the sociological theory of law this uniformity in their behavior is not surprising, since the officers who handle the calls know little or nothing about the social characteristics of the people involved; in other words, they have little social information at their disposal (see Black and Baumgartner, 1981:forthcoming). All that the police typically learn is the name of the caller, the address of the incident, and the voice of the caller over the telephone. These elements provide a few clues about the social characteristics of the caller, such as the status of his or her neighborhood (if the person is calling from home) and possibly his or her ethnicity or race, but a great deal about the social nature of the case always remains unclear. Often, for example, little or no information is given about the characteristics of the alleged offender. Furthermore, in many cases the caller is not directly involved in the incident itself, and so even superficial characteristics of the parties are also unknown.

The flow of social information to officers in face-to-face encounters with citizens is far greater than in their telephone encounters. The police dispatched to an incident immediately become aware of the race and often the ethnicity of the citizens involved, and because they generally see how and where the people live, they are also able to assess their social class and lifestyle. As the encounter proceeds, they may learn a great deal more about the location and direction of the incident in social space, including the nature of the relationship between the parties, the relative status of each, whether the people are parents, dependents, jobholders, residents of the neighborhood or community, past offenders, and so on—all facts that predict and explain how the case will be handled (see, e.g., Black, 1970; 1971; Chapter 5 of the present volume). Imagine, for example, a complaint by someone that he or she has been struck in the face, along with some of the conditions under which this might occur: The complainant might be a wealthy white stranger accosted on the street by a lower-class black youth, for instance, or a dependent wife beaten by her husband because she did not have dinner ready when he returned home from work, or a young man struck by a friend in an argument over a gambling debt, or a child hit by a parent for disobedience, or a police officer attacked by a citizen on the street, or a citizen attacked by a police officer. The response of the police would vary dramatically across these cases. At one extreme the alleged offender would very likely be arrested (if the victim were a wealthy white stranger or a police officer), while at the other extreme the complaint itself would probably be treated as an offense (if the victim were a child struck by a parent or a citizen struck by a police officer). Or imagine some of the conditions under which a rape might occur: between a man and wife, friends, strangers, equals, people of different social status, etc. Again it is not difficult to hypothesize how the response of the police might vary. One rape would elicit concern and sympathy for the victim, another indifference or even contempt. In one case the alleged offender would be treated as a serious criminal, in another, merely scolded, ignored, or even given a knowing wink. Similar patterns occur in cases of all kinds, so that any generalization about police behavior must be stated in terms of the social setting in which it occurs.

Patrol work is different for middle-class people in the suburbs than for lower-class people in the inner city, for intimates than among strangers, for blacks than for whites (unless they are, say, Mexican Americans or Puerto Rican Americans), adults than for juveniles, organizations than for individuals, and so on. A complaint in the suburbs is also handled with more care and, other things equal, is more likely to be defined as a criminal case (see Black, 1970:745). On the other hand, conflicts between people of low status, such as poor blacks and juveniles, are taken relatively lightly, and so are those between intimates.[5] Violence such as a stabbing or severe beating is typically dismissed as "family trouble" when it involves a husband and wife (see Chapter 5), and an expropriation of property by stealth is rarely considered a "theft" if the victim is a friend, neighbor, or relative of the perpetrator.[6]

A dispute between blacks—especially lower-class blacks—is likely to be viewed as trivial even if violence is involved or threatened. In a case observed by

---

5. The same variables are relevant to citizens as well. In one case observed by the author, for example, a black man complained that someone had taken his valuables from him as he was having an epileptic seizure. When asked by an officer whether he would sign a complaint if the offender were apprehended, however, he replied as follows:

MAN: *Well, sir, now I don't know about that. I guess that depends upon who he is. All I'm interested in right now is getting my things back.* [His sister supported him in that position.]

OFFICER: *You mean to say that you don't care about him stealing from you as long as you get your stuff back?*

MAN: *Well, like I say, that depends upon who it is. You find out who did it and then I'll tell you what I want to do about it.*

OFFICER: *You mean you want to know first whether he's friend or foe, is that it?*

MAN: *Yeah, yeah, you might say that.*

Everyone chuckled, and we left. [author's field notes].

The above example derives from the author's observations of police work in Detroit during the years 1964–1965. Officers were accompanied during their routine round of activities on 24 occasions, usually for the bulk of an 8-hour shift, and ultimately observations were assembled from police work in eight different precincts. These precincts included a wide range of socioeconomic areas, from among the poorest to the wealthiest in the city. Most of the field work was done with the patrol division (19 of 24 observation periods), and the remainder with the department's division for juvenile offenders (the "Youth Bureau"). Field notes prepared after each visit provide a number of the illustrations given in the remaining pages of this chapter.

6. It should be apparent that patterns of this kind undermine the validity of crime rates as a measure of police work across social space (see generally Black, 1970; compare Kitsuse and Cicourel, 1963). Perhaps it goes without saying that crime rates are a still worse measure of human conduct in the population at large, since citizens fail even to notify the police of numerous incidents that might otherwise be viewed as crimes.

the author, for instance, a black man hailed the police to complain that another black man had caused an auto accident with him but was denying responsibility. The men were on the verge of a fight and a crowd was gathering, but the officers showed little interest. They simply told the parties to exchange names, waited until this was done, and then left them arguing on the street:

A fight was clearly imminent, but that did not seem to bother the officers; they just wanted to get out of there. Ted [one of the officers] even remarked that the older black man [the alleged offender] was drunk and feeling "big." When I say a fight was imminent, I mean I thought they were going to start swinging while we were right there. As we drove off, Frank [Ted's partner] turned to me and said, "Did you hear them? Just like a bunch of chimpanzees" [author's field notes].[7]

When dispatched to a call involving blacks, officers may try to avoid handling the incident at all. For example, in a case described by the dispatcher as "family trouble" (and involving people known by the officers to be lower-class blacks), the police knocked extremely softly at the door, apparently intending that the people who had called for help would not hear that they had arrived:

As we walked to the door of the run-down brick house, Harold [an officer] said, "I was here a month or so ago, and the husband came out with a shotgun." Gene [Harold's partner] said nothing. Of course, none of us stood directly in front of the door. Gene tapped lightly at the storm door. There was no answer, but we could hear music inside and a light was on. Nevertheless, Gene didn't knock again, but said, "Well, if they don't want to answer, that's fine with me. Let's go." So we did [author's field notes; compare this to a case reported in Chapter 5:146].

Another officer made the following comment about blacks:

The kind of people I like to do business with the most are working people— like myself. The main ones I don't like to do business with are the niggers —I would rather stay clear of them [author's field notes].

Even less important to the police than a conflict between blacks is a complaint by a black against a white. The officer just quoted, for instance, characterized one interracial case he was assigned to handle as follows:

---

7. It should be recognized from the beginning that this example—and many more that will be presented in the following pages—was selected only in order to illustrate the kind of variation in police work that is implied by the sociological theory of law. It should not be thought that the examples necessarily portray typical police behavior in the situations that are described; rather, often the examples were chosen because they are extreme instances of more general patterns.

We got a run [dispatch] *one time—someone had been threatened . . . So when we get there we find this nigger kid about 16, and he says he went to see his* [white] *girlfriend at her house and her old man* [father] *told him if he ever came around again he would shoot him. My God, that's just what I would have said! And don't think I* wouldn't *shoot him if that was a daughter of mine* [author's field notes].

Had the complaint been made in the opposite direction, however, by the white man against the black youth, the officer's response surely would have been quite different.

The same pattern may be seen in matters involving juveniles in general, regardless of race. A conflict between juveniles, whether a robbery of one newspaper boy by another, a fight, a threat, or property damage, is treated as unimportant. A complaint by a juvenile against an adult is accorded yet less concern, and may be dismissed or even condemned in its own right. On the other hand, a complaint by an adult against a juvenile is likely to be considered a serious matter (see Chapter 5:152–155).

The characteristics of the police officers handling a case, and the nature of their relationship with each citizen involved, also predict and explain the police response. If a woman complaining about her husband's violence is known to be the sister of a fellow officer, for example, they might be more concerned about her problem, whereas if the offending party is himself an off-duty officer, they would be less willing to take action on the complainant's behalf (see Chapter 5:174). Whether the police are of the same race, ethnicity, and sex as each party is relevant as well: They are more inclined to sympathize with the citizens who are most like themselves (see Chapter 5:174–175).

Patrol officers who are not busy responding to calls are free to do largely as they please. Although many use this time primarily for relaxation and recreation—including sleeping and drinking in the patrol car, visiting friends, or watching sports events—most officers do police work during at least part of these periods. Some officers are vigilant and aggressive nearly all of the time, continually watching for situations that they might deem worthy of their intervention, while others seem to avoid police work at every opportunity. Most fall between these extremes, exercising a moderate degree of surveillance from time to time, usually in a relaxed fashion (see generally Rubinstein, 1973: Chapters 4–6; Kelling, Pate, Dieckman, and Brown, 1974: Chapter 11). Those assigned to relatively affluent neighborhoods generally have the most free time for patrol work of this kind. In slum areas, officers often complain that their territories (or "beats") are so "active" that they have no time to do anything but answer calls, whereas officers in suburban areas are likely to complain that their territories are so "dead" that they become bored. It should be recognized, however, that this difference is partly a result of the policy by which police departments assign their patrol cars: People in more affluent areas receive more patrol cars in relation to their rate of calls for service, and so their police have more time for free patrol *(Yale Law Journal* Editors, 1967b:822). This allows the police in such a neighborhood to protect its inhabitants better (though it also allows them more time to avoid work altogether). They are able to watch more carefully for "suspicious circumstances" and "crimes in progress," for instance, and in some areas they have time to provide special services when requested, such as visits to check houses that are temporarily unoccupied while the owners are away on vacation. In a slum, such a request would be viewed as preposterous. In all areas, however, people are occasionally stopped on the street for questioning and possibly a personal search ("frisk") when an officer decides that they look "suspicious." Young men, blacks in white neighborhoods, and lower-class people in higher-class settings are particularly likely to be seen in this way (see, e.g., Werthman and Piliavin, 1967; Sacks, 1972).

The police also devote some of the time they have when not answering radio dispatches to recurrent "problems" that have come to their attention. Often such a "problem" consists of young people who continually congregate or make "noise" on a street corner or at a place of business. In fact, juveniles are the primary target of aggressive patrol work of this kind, perhaps because nearly any of their conduct that annoys adults is viewed as a proper subject for police action (see Baumgartner, 1981b:forthcoming). Thus, in a typical instance the owner of a drive-in restaurant had complained that teenagers were circling his parking lot (a major form of sociability for American youths who drive automobiles, but known as the "idiot parade" to many police). Two officers thereafter made it a point to discourage this activity, and were provided with free meals by the owner in return. As one of the officers explained:

Sometimes you get half off or a quarter off [the price of the meals], *but you almost never get free meals the way we do at that place. That's the way it is there because we did that guy a big favor. We cleared the punks out of there, and now his business is up 100%. You know what the idiot parade is? Well, we used to park behind that place, and every time some guy would go parading around that place and drive out, we'd ticket him* [write a traffic citation] *for driving through private property. That's how we cleaned the place up, and that guy is really grateful. We went out of our way for him, now he goes out of his way for us* [author's field notes].

In a similar instance, two other officers were at pains to take special measures against a group of black children as they went home from school:

About a block down we saw several black kids scrambling in several directions, in obvious response to the sight of our wagon [patrol vehicle]. *Ted* [an officer] *said, "Let's chase them around for a while—make them run." Then, to me: "On days* [8 A.M. to 4 P.M. shift] *we have to come over here every day after school lets out to watch these little burr-heads* [blacks]. *We have to herd them down this alley like a bunch of animals—that's what they are—right out of the jungle"* [author's field notes].

The most common patrol work pertaining to juvenile "problems" involves ordering young people to move from where they are standing (usually a street corner). For example:

Officer C. pulled the car to the curb near four teenaged boys, 16 to 17 years old, who were apparently just standing and talking on the corner near a small grocery store. Officer C. said to Officer P., "There's your boy, Roy." Officer P. glared sort of fiercely at the boys, then he called one of their names and said firmly, "All right . . ., what are you doing standing here today? . . . Huh?" One of the boys answered in a snotty manner, "Nothing." Officer P. then bellowed, "Get out of here! Get on home out of sight!" They paused. Even more firmly Officer P. said, "Now! Get going!" They took off, swaggering around the corner. We moved on, and Officer P. told me, "Them kids are always hanging around that same corner being a nuisance—the man who owns that store is always calling about them. They don't do nothing special— they just make remarks to passing girls, and stand on the corner drinking pop [soft drinks] *getting in the way of everybody. We'd take them in for loitering but I know the judge would throw it out"* [author's field notes].

Much aggressive patrol work is directed at people in automobiles as well. Apart from routine traffic work (discussed on pages 32–36), this also often involves harassment of juveniles and others viewed as "suspicious," including blacks of all ages:

As we were pulling up to a stop sign at a main street, we paused next to a big sedan where four black adults were sitting, three in the back and one in the front. Bob shined his flashlight into their car and said, "Waiting for someone?" One of them snarled a "yeah" at him. He replied, "O.K.," and we drove on. The blacks were obviously displeased with the incident, but they said nothing. They only glared at us [author's field notes].

Mixed couples—black and white—are especially vulnerable. An officer recounted the following incident:

One time I saw this parked car in a funny place, so I thought I'd just better check on it. So I drove up next to it, and there was a nigger and a white girl in it. She only looked about 16 years old! So I walked up to the car and asked if everything was all right, you know, and I asked for the guy's driver's license and registration. He acted like I had no right to be checking on him—you know, like there was nothing at all unusual about it. The girl was real good looking, and he was just like any other nigger—big thick lips, black as hell—I mean, he was ugly. I don't know for the life of me what that girl could see in him . . . Well, there was nothing I could do, so I just left [author's field notes].

(It might also be noted that many officers take pleasure in quietly approaching and shining their flashlights into cars that they suspect may contain a young couple engaged in sexual activity. Asked by the author what is done when such a situation is discovered, one officer replied, "Oh, we don't do anything—there's nothing we *can* do, unless they're queers. We just do it for laughs. It's like watching skin movies.")

Whether initiated by citizens who call the police or by the police themselves, then, patrol work varies with its location and direction in social space. When a citizen calls for help, how the police respond depends upon who is involved, and when the police are free to select their own cases, only a limited segment of the population is vulnerable. This raises the issue of "discrimination" or "bias" by the police. If discrimination in the application of law is taken to occur when the police systematically handle similar cases in different ways, and when this is related to the social characteristics of the people involved, it should be apparent that discrimination is ubiquitous in police work. Indeed, the sociological theory of law assumes that law simply does not occur without discrimination, and takes it for granted (see generally Black, 1976). Nevertheless, the specific nature of this phenomenon is not entirely obvious.

Racial discrimination, for example, ordinarily refers to a pattern of greater overall severity toward blacks than toward whites, but this is not precisely what the sociological theory of law predicts, and it oversimplifies how the police actually behave. Instead, the theory predicts that the handling of alleged offenders who are black will depend upon the social characteristics of their victims. Should an offense be upward in direction, against a wealthier white, greater severity is predicted, as it is for a black approached by white police on their own initiative, where no victim is involved. Wealthier whites who offend blacks are expected to be treated leniently, while poor blacks who offend other poor blacks are expected to be handled with less severity than whites (see pages 4–5). It should be remembered that the theory of law also predicts discrimination according to such variables as the integration, respectability, and organization of the parties, their intimacy, the amount of nonlegal social control that is available, and so on (see pages 3–5). And it predicts such discrimination not merely in patrol, but in every kind of police work.

Investigation

For the most part, criminal investigation, or the effort to identify offenders in "crimes known to the police," is the work of detectives. Although relatively little research has focused upon investigation (but see Skolnick, 1966: Chapter 8; Sanders, 1977), the sociological theory of law implies how the behavior of detectives is likely to vary across social space.

Detectives learn about most alleged crimes from "crime reports" filed by patrol officers who first handle the complaints. Thus, just as ordinary citizens decide which among a large pool of incidents are initially to be defined as crimes and brought to the attention of the police, so patrol officers further select from among the cases they encounter those that will become known to detectives.[8] In turn, by deciding whether and how much to investigate these cases, and whether and when to make an arrest after a suspect is identified, detectives narrow still further the number of people who will be subject to prosecution. In so doing, they participate in the distribution of law.

The crime reports that are forwarded to detectives provide information not only about alleged crimes as such but also about their location and direction in social space, including various characteristics of the victim and the nature of his or her relationship with the alleged offender. Detectives learn whether the victim was a person or an organization, for instance, as well as the status of the neighborhood in which the incident occurred, the victim's race, sex, age, occupation (if any), and possibly some of these facts about the alleged offender (for an example of a form used in reporting a crime, see Sanders, 1977:54).[9] The nature of this social information predicts and explains the initial response of the detectives who receive the report. Some cases are viewed as potentially "big" or "important"; others are "little" or "insignificant" (see Sanders, 1977:95–96). If the incident was a burglary, for example, it is likely to be defined as "bigger"—and to receive more immediate attention—if the victim was a business firm rather than a household, or, in the case of a household, if the event took place in a wealthy suburb rather than in a black ghetto or other lower-class area. In some cases detectives begin their investigation as soon as they are notified, in others they are more casual, and in still others they do nothing at all, so that the victim never hears anything from the police after the initial visit by the patrol officers. If the offense was committed against someone of sufficiently high status, a large num-

---

8. Patrol officers exercise discretion of this kind in most of the cases they handle, since usually the alleged offender is not present when they arrive to handle a complaint. This is true of 77% of the cases that might be classified by a lawyer as "felonies" (i.e., subject to more than one year of imprisonment) and of 51% of the "misdemeanors" (Black, 1970:737).

9. In many cases, the identity of the offender is obvious from the beginning. (This applies to many assaults and rapes, for instance.) Such cases are known to detectives as "walk throughs," since they require so little investigative work (see Sanders, 1977:276).

ber of detectives might be assigned to the case, and they might even be directed to work around the clock until a suspect is found and charged with the offense. (Though rare, this is the kind of case so often portrayed in movies and television.) Thus, the murder of a prominent politician, businessman, or socialite is likely to be handled with great diligence and fanfare, whereas that of a homeless man on "skid row" is apt to be classified merely as a "death by misadventure" (or a similar label) and accorded no investigation of any kind. Offenses against police officers are treated as "big" cases as well (see pages 36–40).

How much time and energy detectives devote to the investigation of a case (known as "working" the crime) is predictable not only from the social information they first receive in the crime report, but also from that which unfolds as the investigation itself proceeds. When the victim is interviewed, for example, they acquire a more detailed knowledge of the social location of the incident, deciding in some cases to end the investigation at that point and in others to expand it. If, for example, detectives infer that the likely offender in a burglary is a former spouse or friend of the victim, they may decide to pursue the matter no further. Or they might abandon an investigation after learning that the victim has a criminal record, is a prostitute, homosexual, former mental patient, or is in some other way disreputable (see Black, 1976:113–117). Beyond this, the credibility of each person interviewed—whether victim, witness, suspect, or whatever—directly depends upon the social status of each, so that detectives are more likely to disregard what they are told by those who are poor, black, young, transient, uneducated, and so on (see Black, 1979c:157–159). Some complainants are unable to convince the officers that what they allege has occurred at all, and their complaints are classified as "unfounded" or merely as "suspicious circumstances" (instead of a crime of some kind); others find that their reports are completely trusted from the beginning. A sociologist who observed detectives in the field reports the following:

> The detective is allowed wide discretion in the filing of burglary complaints as "suspicous circumstances." Not only does he record a complaint as a suspected offense (rather than an actual offense) when one or more of the elements of the alleged crime appear to be missing, but he also may list a complaint as a suspected offense when he believes—even in the absence of hard evidence to support his suspicion—that the complaint is unfounded [Skolnick, 1966:197].

The same investigator then describes the kind of robbery complaint that is likely to be questioned:

> A Negro delivery boy claims to have been robbed of the money he was supposed to deposit for his employer. He shows a lump on his head and holds to his story, but the detective does not believe him. Such a complaint is filed as a suspicious

circumstance, and as such does not fall into the category of "offenses reported."
. . . Usually the detective concentrates on "actual" offenses and ignores further
investigation of "suspicious circumstances" [Skolnick, 1966:172].

Thus, those whose complaints are considered questionable may never hear from
the police again; more credible people, on the other hand, may receive frequent
visits and telephone calls about the progress of the investigation. Who receives
what response is predictable from the sociological theory of law.

Patrol officers effectively create the "crime rate" of a community ("crimes
known to the police") by writing official reports about some of the cases they
handle (see Black, 1970; Pepinsky, 1976b). Detectives are said to "clear" these
crimes when they successfully investigate them by "solving" them to their own
satisfaction (regardless of whether an arrest is made). The proportion of crimes
known to the police that detectives clear in this way is their "clearance rate," and
it is widely taken as a measure of their efficiency (see generally Skolnick, 1966:
Chapter 8). Such a clearance rate is based only upon the cases that detectives
regard as "actual" crimes, however, with any reports that they decide are unfounded or merely suspicious not figured into this measure of their efficiency.
Moreover, detectives are not equally concerned with every case that does affect
their clearance rate; they are particularly anxious to "break" the "big" ones, and
the bigness of a case, it will be recalled, is predictable from its location and
direction in social space.

In a big case, such as a robbery, rape, or murder of a prominent citizen by a
stranger presumed to be of low status, detectives may go to great lengths to clear
the case by an arrest. They may seek physical evidence such as fingerprints, tire
tracks, and hair samples at the scene of the crime, interview large numbers of
potential witnesses and informants, and conduct extensive interrogations, poly-
graph ("lie detector") tests, and "line-ups" (sessions at which suspects are
viewed by victims or witnesses through a one-way mirror). If a case is not
big—if the victim in question is, say, a poor black or Mexican American—such
steps are unlikely to be taken.[10]

Also relevant to the social nature of investigation is a method—little known to
the public—by which detectives clear many crimes, particularly burglaries. This
is to persuade suspects to take responsibility for offenses other than those with
which they are charged. Confessions of this kind are treated by the police as
confidential, and immunity from prosecution is tacitly granted for all of the
offenses involved (Skolnick, 1966:174–175). Suspects are often willing or even
eager to make such confessions, since detectives will reward them with relative

---

10. It should be noted that the bigness of a case may be increased substantially if the victim
receives the sponsorship of someone higher in status. A newspaper might give a case publicity, for
example, and interested individuals or organizations might pressure the police to do all they can to
find the offender. In cases of this kind, the status of the sponsors predicts what the police will do.

leniency in regard to the offenses for which they were originally arrested (e.g., by lowering a charge from burglary to larceny). Suspects who help the police improve their clearance rate are thus given special consideration, so that, in effect, admitted criminality is rewarded. The following case illustrates this process:

> Arthur C was arrested as an auto thief and cooperated with the police by confessing to the commission of two additional thefts of autos and five "classy" burglaries. In return for this cooperation, Arthur received several assets. First, the police agreed to drop the two counts of auto theft and to charge Arthur with only one count of burglary. Secondly, Arthur's formal confession as given to the court showed that he had committed only one burglary [Skolnick, 1966:174].

A detective sergeant explained why the case was handled in this way:

> *We had him cop out* [plead guilty] *to only one charge because we don't really want it made public that he committed the other burglaries. If it were made public, then the question might be raised as to why we didn't charge him with the other burglaries, and the public doesn't understand these things* [174–175].

Since the practice of multiple clearance (or mass clearance) of crimes benefits suspects, it should not be surprising that in an unknown number of cases people admit to crimes that they have not actually committed. In one case, for example, two men charged with a single burglary were willing to admit to hundreds of past offenses:

> Over a period of about ten days after the arrest, burglary police from neighboring cities frequently visited the Westville jail, since, between the two of them, Jerome and James could account for more than five hundred burglaries. James himself provided the police with more than four hundred clearances. I witnessed several interrogations of James regarding burglaries he had presumably committed and, in my opinion, it was relatively simple for him to "fake" clearances. One need not have been exceptionally shrewd—and James was—to sense the detectives' pleasure at writing off old cases. . . . When he expressed vagueness of memory as to those two or three years old, he thereby created a situation in which the police would have either to be extremely scrupulous, and thus forego potential clearances, or "feed" him information to refresh his recollection (which, to this observer, appeared to be rather easily renewed) [Skolnick, 1966:178].

The two suspects cooperated with the police in other ways as well, and each was ultimately charged with only a single misdemeanor. One spent 4 months in custody, while the second was free after 30 days.

Since a mass clearance involves only a minimal application of law on behalf of the victims, the sociological theory of law predicts that detectives will reserve the strategy primarily for criminal complaints that in other respects are predicted to attract the least attention. These include cases with victims of relatively low social status. Burglaries in a poor neighborhood such as a black ghetto, for example, are surely more likely than those occurring in a higher-status area to be solved in this way. The latter would be more apt to receive individual attention and to be solved by authentic investigation and arrest.[11] What it means to say that a crime has been solved thus depends upon its location and direction in social space.[12]

Vice

The police in modern America devote considerable time and energy to a range of conduct known to them and many citizens as "vice." The activities so labeled are also called "crimes without victims"[13]—usually by people who do not view them as immoral—in that people generally engage in them by mutual consent and have no wish for the intrusion of law into their affairs. A large police department normally has a special division to handle vice (a "vice bureau" or "morals squad"), and this may itself be further differentiated into units concerned with specific varieties of prohibited conduct. A substantial part of vice work, perhaps most, pertains to the possession and sale of certain mind-altering drugs, such as heroin, cocaine, lysergic acid diethylamide (LSD), and marijuana, and is typically the responsibility of a "narcotics squad." Vice also includes such offenses as gambling, prostitution, homosexuality, the sale of pornography, and the sale of alcoholic beverages in violation of local regulations. The police seek out and proceed against most of this conduct on their own initiative rather than relying upon specific complaints from citizens,[14] and in this sense vice work is primarily "proactive" rather than "reactive" (see Black, 1973). Hence, the police employ a number of enforcement tactics not usually seen in the handling of other offenses.

---

11. Skolnick (1966:176) speculates that the police may have looked upon the original case in the illustration above as "unusually important" partly because the victim was a "leading citizen" of the community.

It might also be added that, unlike some crimes of violence, burglaries in lower-class areas seldom receive newspaper publicity or other sponsorship of the victims by organizations or higher-status citizens. This further enhances their suitability for inclusion in a mass clearance.

12. For this reason, comparisons of clearance rates across socioeconomic areas may obscure differences in the behavior of detectives from one setting to another.

13. It is unclear when this phrase came into being, but one of the first to use it in the scholarly literature was Schur (1965).

14. Although individual vice cases are seldom initiated and pursued by citizens, people occasionally call or write the police with information, or "tips," about patterns of vice in a particular neighborhood or other location. In Chicago (during a period of 1964), for example, the great majority of anonymous letters to the police commissioner involved complaints of this kind (Reiss, 1971a:85–86). The degree of police concern with vice of various kinds also reflects the demands of the larger public, as expressed in newspaper stories and editorials, statements and protests by organizations, and pressures brought to bear upon politicians who have the capacity to influence police administrators.

One striking feature of narcotics work, for instance, is the enormous effort invested by officers simply in learning about violations.[15] A major technique employed for this purpose is the development of a network of informers, composed for the most part of people who are themselves known to be narcotics users and who agree to help the police in exchange for immunity from arrest, leniency after they have been arrested, or money (see Skolnick, 1966: Chapter 6; Rotenberg, 1967: Chapter 19; Gould, Walker, Crane, and Lidz, 1974:72–76). Other people may also be willing to provide information in exchange for consideration of one kind or another:

> Non-addicts [such as proprietors of taverns and hotels in "vice districts"] cooperate because they want to avoid difficulties with the police or, more importantly, with "official" agencies that inspect and license. If the police were to report that their places were "hangouts" for undesirable characters, they might be closed down . . . . In addition, it is not uncommon for bartenders to be fences for stolen merchandise and for police to overlook this activity in exchange for information leading to the arrest of addicts. Consequently, hotel owners and bartenders are a regular source of information for police . . . . Hotel managers will [also] give keys to policemen that permit them to make searches while the occupant is out of the room, and some hotel owners will permit the vice control squad to tap into their switchboards [Skolnick, 1966:123].

In addition to the use of informers, the police uncover violations by going "underground" to infiltrate networks of narcotics users and sellers. This generally involves some degree of participation in the prohibited behavior itself, such as offering to purchase drugs or using them for purposes of deception. Officers on narcotics squads also learn about violations through their close ties with colleagues in other jurisdictions, including state and federal police with whom they work cooperatively on some cases. These ties may even reach across international borders, as occurs when American agencies ask the help of the Mexican government in the destruction of marijuana or the Turkish government in the control of opium. Finally, narcotics officers may enlist the assistance of dogs specially trained to detect the odor of drugs in suitcases or behind closed doors.

The police also devote much energy and resourcefulness to the detection of other kinds of prohibited conduct. In one city, officers watch suspected prostitutes from afar with fieldglasses, for example, and informers are used as well. In addition, many arrests result from undercover work by officers or their temporary employees who pose as customers and actively encourage women to solicit their business (Skolnick, 1966:100–102; see also Rotenberg, 1967: Chapter 16). Undercover officers do whatever they can to convince the women that they are

---

15. The following remarks about narcotics enforcement pertain primarily to the work of specialized plainclothes officers (known in the drug subculture as "narcs"). For an overview, see Manning (1980a). A discussion of narcotics enforcement by uniformed patrol officers is provided by Coates and Miller (1974).

true customers, in some instances even removing their clothing in seeming preparation for a sexual transaction (see, e.g., Rotenberg, 1967:219–220). Similarly, in order to attract and identify homosexuals, the police employ a strategy known to some (interviewed by the author) as "trolling for queers." A major tactic involves an officer exposing himself in a public restroom and feigning interest in homosexual contacts (see, e.g., Rotenberg, 1967: Chapter 17, especially 234–235).

It should be noted that officers in vice enforcement engage relatively often in activities that many people might deem improper if they were to learn of them. In narcotics work, for instance, officers routinely make arrests that a lawyer or judge would view as illegal (see, e.g., Gould et al., 1974:79). Some of these arrests are based upon false, or "planted," evidence. Thus, one officer told an investigator the following:

> *Some guys plant dope on addicts when they think they have to, but I won't do it . . . . If you're in an apartment you can drop a bag* [of drugs] *someplace on the floor and feel pretty sure that one of the other* [officers] *is going to find it later. If no one else does, you can always find it yourself. I've thought about doing that a lot of times. It isn't hard, and some cops do it . . .* [Gould et al., 1974:82–83].

Women suspected of prostitution are highly vulnerable as well. In one city an investigator found that so-called whore squads account for nearly half of the total arrests in a particular precinct. Most of the women involved—who number from 40 to 50 a night—are arrested simply because the police believe them to be prostitutes, not because they have been observed soliciting customers or doing anything else ordinarily viewed as illegal (La Fave, 1965:451, 453). Known as "Disorderly Person Investigations" (or D.P.I.s), such arrests are made for purposes of harassment rather than prosecution:

> If a woman is found in an area in which prostitution is practiced and it is known or thought that she has a past record of arrests for accosting and soliciting or D.P.I.s, she will be taken into custody . . . . Prostitutes may be arrested [despite the fact that] they are in a restaurant or on the street for some other purpose at the time of their arrest. Other women, even in the absence of any knowledge on the officer's part as to a past record, will be arrested when found late at night in areas with a high incidence of prostitution. In such an area, the mere fact that a woman is slowly walking down the street, standing on a street corner, or standing in a doorway may be the basis for arrest [La Fave, 1965:454].[16]

In fact, at the time of the study (1956–1957), any woman in the area seen talking to men who she was unable to prove were her relatives, or to men of another

---

16. For a fictional description of a mass arrest of this kind (based upon the author's experiences as police officer), see Wambaugh (1970:78–86).

race, was subject to arrest (La Fave, 1965:455). All of these practices, the investigator notes, "undoubtedly" result in the arrest of some women who are not actually prostitutes (La Fave, 1965:455).

Arrest for purposes of harassment is also used against transvestites (usually men dressed as women). In at least one city the police simply arrest any transvestite they see in public, hold him overnight in jail, and release him the next day (La Fave, 1965: Chapter 23). In addition, such a person is "often subjected to ridicule at the time of arrest and usually is made to dispose of at least some of his female garb when he is booked [entered into police records]" (La Fave, 1965:469).[17] Arrest is also frequently used to harass people who patronize establishments where gambling and illegal liquor sales occur. In one Detroit precinct, for example, the so-called cleanup squads made 592 gambling arrests in a 6-month period, of which only 24 resulted in prosecution. In the same period 420 arrests were made for violations of the liquor laws, with 36 cases prosecuted (La Fave, 1965:473).

A few words might also be said about how the police sometimes conduct searches in the field of vice enforcement. In a study of narcotics work in a city on the West Coast ("Westville"), for example, it was found that "the practice of making an unlawful exploratory search of the room of a suspected criminal is . . . accepted by both the Westville police and the state police" (Skolnick, 1966:144). One of the officers is quoted as follows:

> Of course, it's not exactly legal to take a peek beforehand. It's not one of the things you usually talk about as a police technique. But if you find something, you back off and figure out how you can do it legal. And if you don't find anything, you don't have to waste a lot of time [Skolnick, 1966:144].

An officer interviewed by sociologists in another city also made a comment about narcotics searches:

> As a general rule I don't worry very much about whether or not I have a [search] warrant when I go into a house. Sometimes you take a little flack from the people in the house about not having a warrant but usually not much. If you find something, they can't argue that you weren't justified in going in. If you don't find anything they're so relieved that they're usually willing to forget the whole incident. Besides, addicts are not very likely to complain about that sort of thing. They know they're guilty and what they want most is to stay out of the limelight. What good does it do for them to have a big stink made about one cop and then have the rest of the squad out trying to bust [arrest] them? [Gould et al., 1974:79; see also 77–78].

In addition to property searches, narcotics officers frequently conduct personal searches, or "frisks," which would be viewed as illegal (see Skolnick, 1966:145–

---

17. An interesting feature of these arrests is that at the time of the observations, transvestism was not explicity prohibited in the written law (La Fave, 1965:469).

148). They also readily use coercion of various kinds. If someone is present in a room or an apartment they want to search (without a warrant), for instance, they may break down the door and tackle or threaten anyone who is present. As one officer commented:

> You've got to be tough about it. If you hear a lot of movement on the other side of the door you don't wait until somebody comes and opens the door, you've got to kick it in. Once you get in you've got to stop them quick. If you tackle them and have them on the floor fast, you may not have an all-out fight on your hands [Gould et al., 1974:79].

Such searches are often conducted late at night, giving officers the benefit of surprise and adding an element of degradation and possibly terror for the citizens involved.

Lastly, it should be noted that officers in vice work may occasionally apply their own punishments to those they regard as offenders. As one officer remarked:

> It is true that sometimes we have to beat people up. It comes down to this. When I have a choice of whether I'm going to punch somebody in the nose or wait for him to punch me, I hit him. . . . What's more, if some guy takes a swing at me, I'm not going to let it drop when I hit him back. I've got to teach him a lesson. People have got to learn that they can't hit cops. Three weeks ago I arrested some guy and he tried to hit me over the head with a chair. We beat the living hell out of him. I don't apologize for that, I think we had to do it. Three days later, the guy's lawyer got up in court and started talking about what a brutal beating this bastard had gotten from the cops. It's true, we stomped him, but he deserved it. He started it. If we don't do that, every two-bit punk is going to think that he can get away with hitting a cop [Gould et al., 1974:81–82].

It should not be thought that all officers in vice work routinely engage in practices such as those described in the preceding pages, but it is important to recognize that policing of this kind is distinctive in some respects, particularly in its intrusiveness and severity. In fact, vice officers undoubtedly have one of the highest rates of arrest per person among the members of police departments in American cities.[18] Perhaps it would be pertinent to consider how they select these cases, and also why they devote so much time and energy to vice at all.

Conduct regarded as vice involves unconventional recreation, that is, pleasure-

---

18. This arrest rate would be even higher were it not for the so-called protection from arrest that many otherwise vulnerable people are able to purchase directly from officers who know about their involvement in vice (see generally Sherman, 1978).

It should be noted that uniformed patrol officers also contribute significantly to the total number of vice arrests, especially for drug violations. Manning reports that patrol officers account for the great majority of drug arrests, and that these usually occur in the context of "routine traffic stops" (1980:119). It seems unlikely that these are actually "routine," however, since most people stopped for traffic violations are not subjected to a search. For a study of arrest patterns specifically in marijuana cases, see Johnson, Petersen, and Wells (1977).

seeking of a kind pursued by only a minority of the population. Those handled as offenders may be the suppliers of these pleasures, the consumers, or both. In any event, it appears that the mere fact of an act's unconventionality, by itself, attracts legal repression (see Black, 1976:69–73; Baumgartner, 1981a). Nevertheless, it also seems clear that the police direct their attention to only a limited range of the conduct that outwardly qualifies as vice. In the case of narcotics enforcement, for instance, they show little or no interest in the use of illicit drugs by people who are in other respects conventional in lifestyle. Thus, although physicians as a group have an exceptionally high rate of opiate addiction, the police do not develop informers within the medical profession. Furthermore, even when they learn of a physician who is an addict, they rarely make an arrest or subject the individual to the other indignities that "street addicts" so often experience (see generally Winick, 1961). The same largely applies to the use of marijuana and cocaine among professionals of all kinds. Narcotics enforcement is aimed primarily at those for whom the use of drugs is part of an entire lifestyle that departs substantially from that of the cultural mainstream. In America, many of these people are young black men who are openly contemptuous of the dominant values of the society, preferring instead their subculture of "cats, kicks, and color" (Finestone, 1957), which is antithetical to the so-called Protestant ethic (see Becker, 1963:135–146). The police are also likely to take action against those with a bohemian lifestyle. Undercover work by the police occurs overwhelmingly in subcultural locations such as these, as do midnight raids, personal searches, harassment, and beatings. In this light it is even understandable why the police would "plant" narcotics where none exist: It justifies legal action against people whose principal offense is their way of life. Theoretically speaking, then, drug arrests based upon planted evidence have much in common with other drug arrests.

The same patterns can be seen in the control of prostitution, homosexuality, gambling, and after-hours drinking, all of which attract the most law when they occur in a larger context of unconventionality. The prostitutes who most interest the police are those who inhabit the world known as "the life," a subculture of "pimps" and their "hustlers," of colorful attire and exotic automobiles (called "pimpmobiles" by the police). The homosexuals who most interest the police are those of the "gay world," and the gamblers, those of the "underworld." The recreation of social elites, even when unconventional and technically illegal, rarely is subject to the enforcement techniques found in vice work.

Juveniles

In the past, police have sometimes been established to deal exclusively with persons inhabiting a single location in social space. In early America, for example, there were "stranger police" in the East, "Indian police" in the West, and "slave police" in the South (see, e.g., Bacon, 1939; Hagan, 1966). Similarly, modern American police departments in larger cities have divisions especially established to handle young people, or "juveniles" ("juvenile divisions," "youth bureaus," etc.). The officers in these units (as well as ordinary patrol officers in their dealings with juveniles) relate to young people in a distinctive fashion: In some respects they treat them more severely than adults, and in other respects more leniently.

On the one hand, juveniles are subject to more prohibitions, surveillance, harassment, and degradation than adults. They may get into trouble with the police simply because they are on the streets late at night (past "curfew"), while standing on a streetcorner ("rowdiness"), because they have a conflict with an adult such as a teacher or parent ("incorrigibility"), because they are drinking alcoholic beverages ("underage drinking"), and so on. If standing on a street corner, they may hear a shout or growl from a police officer, telling them to "break it up," "get going," or just to "move." In general, they are watched closely by the police and may at any time be, in effect, raided. A boy interviewed in San Francisco described the following incident:

> We was standing there on the corner bullshitting like we always do, and there was only four of us. Then this cop on a motorcycle pulled over and walked over to us. I seen him before. He rides around the neighborhood a lot. He didn't say nothing. He just zipped down his jacket and there was his big old billy club. And then he started asking questions, identification, what we were doing, and all like that. And he searched us and got our names down in the book and everything . . . . They do anything to get our names on that book. You know. They want us to know they in charge [Werthman and Piliavin, 1967:62].

Teenagers in other public places, too, may be stopped, questioned, and searched at any time, and if they show hostility or indifference they may be threatened, arrested, or beaten. Another boy gave this example:

> One day we were standing on the corner about three blocks from school and this juvenile officer comes up. He say, "Hey, you boys! Come here!" So everybody else walked over there. But this one stud [young man] made like he didn't hear him. So the cop say, "Hey punk! Come here!" So the stud sorta look up like he hear him and start walking over real slow. So the cop walk over there and grab him by the collar and throw him down and put the handcuffs on him, saying, "When I call you next time, come see what I want!" So everybody was standing by the car, and he say, "All right you black mother fuckers! Get your ass home!" Just like that. And he handcuffed the stud and took him to juvenile hall [a detention center] for nothing. Just for standing there and looking at him [Werthman and Piliavin, 1967:90–91].

In fact, a failure to show deference to a police officer in a public encounter is a major predictor of when a juvenile will be arrested and referred to court (Piliavin and Briar, 1964; Black and Reiss, 1970:74–75; Lundman, Sykes, and Clark, 1978:86–87; Chan, 1980:6–8).

Most police encounters with juveniles arise as a result of telephone complaints by citizens (see Black and Reiss, 1970:66–67), and in these cases too a juvenile's primary offense may be a failure to show deference to an adult. Thus, for instance, during the author's observation of juvenile officers in Detroit (see page 8, note 5), a school janitor commented that he calls the police only when he has problems with young people who are "nasty" or "hard to handle," and not when they are apologetic about their misconduct (in this case, stealing from lockers in the school's gymnasium). One of the juvenile officers also mentioned that he is "constantly getting calls" from school principals and that usually these pertain to "smart-alecky" boys:

> *I hate to say this, but sometimes they'll call us about a boy just because they don't like him for some reason. But then some really bad kid who needs help they'll think is a good boy just because he soft-soaped them . . . . Just because the kid says "sir" to the principal and another doesn't can mean whether or not the boy will get a record with the police* [author's field notes].

Most calls about juveniles appear to be made by women who call about young people in their neighborhoods, but a significant number also come from business people such as managers of drive-in restaurants and drugstores. Only rarely do parents call about their own children (see Chapter 5:152–155). Hence, it seems that the policing of juveniles arises primarily when adults have complaints about the deportment of young people but do not themselves have the capacity to exercise the amount of social control they view as appropriate. Most often this pertains to the conduct of juveniles in public places, where they are away from the authority to which they are usually subject.

Although patrol officers initially handle the great majority of complaints about juveniles, and are also responsible for most of the harassment of juveniles in public places (see generally Black and Reiss, 1970; Lundman *et al.*, 1978), when an arrest is made the case is transferred to a juvenile officer. At this stage, juveniles often have further experiences that are largely reserved for them. Juvenile officers tend to be moralistic toward young people, for instance, frequently lecturing them about their misconduct and seeking to show them the selfishness and foolishness of their behavior.[19] In one case, a 15-year-old boy who was caught with a stolen bicycle had the following exchange with a juvenile officer:

---

19. This may be especially common when officers are socially similar to the juveniles they handle. There is some evidence, for instance, that white officers are more moralistic toward white juveniles than toward black juveniles, though their formal dispositions of blacks may be more severe (see, e.g., Suttles, 1968:204, note 10).

OFFICER: *"How come you took it?"*
BOY: *"I needed a ride home."*
OFFICER: *"You needed a ride home? Don't you think maybe the boy who owns it wanted a ride home, too?"*
BOY: *"I guess so, sir."*
OFFICER: *"You* guess *so?"*
BOY: *"Yes, sir, he did."*
OFFICER: *"When are you going to learn to leave other people's property alone?"*
The boy lowered his head.

[author's field notes; see also Chapter 5:152–155].

Juvenile officers also commonly subject the young people in their custody to humiliations and degradations beyond those experienced by most adults. In one such case, for example, three boys were brought to the station because they had fled when two patrol officers noticed them looking into an abandoned automobile. This was defined as "tampering" with the car, and they were accused of planning to steal something from it. After making this allegation, which was strongly denied by the boys, the officer continued as follows:

> *"Come over here and empty your pockets,* punks," *motioning them to come to his desk. After they had complied, they started back to where they had been sitting, but the officer ordered them to remain standing. Next, he proceeded to pick carefully through each boy's belongings. Only one of them had a billfold, and the officer didn't leave an item untouched. He became very sarcastic, almost fiendish, as he commented upon each item. He found a letter which a girl had written to this boy–it amounted to a love letter– and the officer read almost all of it aloud, then commented,* "Nice girl *she must be, chasing after you like that. Humph!"* [author's field notes].

Throughout the encounter the officer made it clear that he did not believe the boys, and at one point he asked this question:

> *Which of you would be willing to bend over and get a good swat with a paddle in order to pay for what you did? Who thinks he deserves it, huh?* [One of the boys said he would take it. The others were quiet.] *Well, at least one of you is willing to stand up like a man and own up for what he did. You other two make me sick* [author's field notes].

Next he called each boy's home, speaking to the parent who answered as follows:

> *His tone was that of a charming smart aleck. For example: "Mrs. X? Do you have a son by the name of Y? You do? Do you know where he is this evening? . . . No, I'm afraid he isn't. Your son is at the Sixteenth Precinct police*

station. Isn't that nice?" Then he told her what the boy had done and requested that she pick him up [author's field notes].

As a final expression of his contempt, the officer ordered the three boys to sit on the floor until their parents arrived to take them home. In another case, the same officer sought to humiliate a boy (whom he also called "punk") by having him squat on the floor and walk around the room like a duck: "You look awfully comfortable in that chair all slouched down. Maybe you need some exercise, huh? Why don't you duck-walk around the room for awhile, huh?" (The boy said that he had a "bad knee," however, and could not comply.)

Even if the examples above are extreme, the available evidence indicates that juveniles are more likely than adults to be subjected to violence, though generally not of a severe nature. According to one officer interviewed by the author, complaints by parents about what they view as physical mistreatment of their children by the police are "very common." In addition, a lieutenant noted that an official at the detention center for juveniles had complained that one of the boys arrived with "welts" from a "paddling" he had received while in police custody. The juveniles interviewed in another study also reported that physical violence by the police was frequent, and described several instances (see, e.g., Werthman and Piliavin, 1967:92–98). One boy added that "they don't never beat you in the car. They wait until they get you to the station [p. 92]."

Even though juveniles often experience harshness on the street and in the police station, officers are relatively restrained in the ultimate disposition of their cases. A juvenile who is arrested is far more likely to be released at the station without further action than is an adult under the same conditions. This seeming contradiction, a blend of unusual severity with unusual leniency, reflects the peculiar world of social control that juveniles inhabit. One the one hand, when abroad in public places young people are largely free of adult authority. On the other hand, for the rest of the day, at home and at school, they are subject to an enormous amount of social control by their parents and teachers. This means that in their everyday lives juveniles experience extreme degrees of social control by adults—other than law. Moreover, since law varies inversely with other kinds of social control (Black, 1976:107–111), it follows that the conditions of juvenile life attract law in one respect but repel it in another. In public places, the police effectively fill the normative vacuum created by the absence of parents and teachers:

> Because behavior in the public spaces of the city tends to be structured around exigencies of adult life, . . . the mere conspicuous presence of young people can cause concern. They are, as it were, off the reservation and, lacking justification for being abroad, they are subject to preventive regulation . . . . Policing juveniles is not a task created by or for the police; it merely devolves upon the police when juveniles are, or are thought to be, beyond the reach of primary supervisory control [Bittner, 1976:84, 74].

Once in the police station, however, juveniles are most likely to be spared further action, since they can simply be returned to the jurisdiction of home and school. As noted earlier, in fact, the normal procedure is for the juvenile officer to ask parents to retrieve their children at the station, a kind of transfer of custody or extradition. When they arrive at the station, parents commonly glare and snarl at their children, in some cases striking them as well, and the police seem pleased when parents indicate that their children will be punished when they get home. Indeed, juveniles sometimes seek to escape from the police in order to avoid having to face their parents.

The specific nature of authority in a juvenile's home further predicts how an officer will handle a case. A juvenile subject to relatively little parental authority— such as a child in a fatherless home whose mother has a full-time job—is more likely to be sent to court and to be incarcerated in a public institution (see Black, 1976:7). Similarly, a severe disposition is more likely to be the lot of a juvenile who no longer attends school, since this results in a normative vacuum during part of the day.[20] Juveniles of all kinds, however, are subject to greater amounts of nonlegal social control than are adults—especially adult men—and this explains the leniency they generally enjoy at the police station.[21] But when they are on the streets, they have no such immunity. To the contrary, unless and until information about their subordination to adults is forthcoming, few people are more vulnerable to the police.[22]

---

20. Greater severity toward juveniles from fatherless homes and toward those who do not attend school is reflected in official statistics (such as police and court records). These in turn support theories of "juvenile delinquency," popular as well as academic, that hold that a "broken home" and a lack of school attachments make a child more prone to misconduct (e.g., Hirschi, 1969). However, these statistics can be explained with the sociological theory of law as well as with the theory of juvenile delinquency (see Black, 1976:9–10; see also Cicourel, 1968: Chapter 2). For that matter, the theory of law provides a radically different explanation for all facts addressed by theories designed to explain who engages in conduct subject to law (i.e., theories of crime, delinquency, etc.). This is the case because the distribution of deviant behavior—understood as conduct subject to social control—is the same as the distribution of social control itself, and so a theory of one effectively predicts the facts addressed by the other (see Black, 1976:9–10, 30–31, 54–55, 79–80, 99–101, 117–118).

21. Women who are economically dependent upon their husbands are in a position similar to that of juveniles, and enjoy a similar leniency at the hands of the police: They are often allowed to remain in the custody of their husbands (see Kruttschnitt, 1979: Chapter 7).

22. Bittner suggests that juveniles in public experience special surveillance because it is known that they are subject to so much adult authority at other times:

> The presumption of total parental control colors the meaning of a young person's presence everywhere in society. The question, "Do your parents know where you are?" is never wholly impertinent. Both the assumption of functioning parental control and the suspicion that it may have lapsed create a peculiar asymmetry in the dealings between young people and adults [1976:74].

One can imagine that the position of slaves in a slave society would not be so different from that of juveniles: If away from the master's home, they would probably be subject to surveillance by everyone.

Skid Row

Police work involving homeless men—people variously known as "vagrants," "bums," "tramps," "derelicts," etc.— provides a study in the degree to which law may concentrate upon a single location in social space (see generally Bittner, 1967b; Pastor, 1978). Although many cities have a specific place called "skid row" where such men gather, sociologically skid row is not so much a matter of geography as of lifestyle, involving nomadism, unemployment, heavy consumption of alcoholic beverages, foraging, begging, and a principled rejection of conventional modes of existence (see generally Wallace, 1965; Spradley, 1970; Wiseman, 1970). Moreover, skid row is largely illegal: Its inhabitants are subject to a level of police attention rarely seen anywhere else in modern society.

In one American city, for example, 80% of the people jailed in the course of a year are "chronic alcohol offenders," overwhelmingly men of skid row (Spradley, 1970:9). Most homeless men have been arrested so many times that they have lost count; for some, the number of arrests reaches into the hundreds (Spradley, 1970:80). Most arrests of these men are made by ordinary patrol officers, although some cities have officers in civilian clothes specially assigned to skid-row districts. (The police who deal with them are known to skid-row men by such names as "bulls" and "rag pickers.") Homeless men are frequently arrested when they are observed sleeping, drinking, showing signs of intoxication, or begging in a public place, but many are also taken into custody merely upon being recognized by the police, regardless of their conduct. As one man explained:

Once they pick you up drunk, they know you and will pick you up whenever they need you [to fill the police wagon]. *They will just say, "Come on, let's go"* [quoted in Wiseman, 1970:79].

Another made the same point:

After a man has been arrested several times, he gets picked up automatically if he happens to be around during a regular cleanup [mass arrest]—*he's picked up whether he's drunk or not, just as a matter of course* [quoted in Wiseman, 1970:79].

Some men even report having been arrested only moments after their release from jail, before they have had a drink or have done anything else that might normally be construed as an offense (e.g., Spradley, 1970:112; Wiseman, 1970:80). As one of the men quoted above noted, a skid-row man may be caught in a police "round-up" in which everyone in sight is arrested (see also Bittner, 1967b:704, note 24; Spradley, 1970:124; Wiseman, 1970:68). Or he may be arrested because he just happens to be present when someone else is being taken away:

Sometimes drunk arrests are made mainly because the police van is available. In one case a patrolman summoned the van to pick up an arrested man. As the van was pulling away from the curb the officer stopped the driver because he sighted another drunk stumbling across the street. The second man protested saying that he "wasn't even half drunk yet." The patrolman's response was "O.K., I'll owe you half a drunk" [Bittner, 1967b:713].

The so-called revolving door pattern, whereby the same men repeatedly enter, leave, and reenter jail, may be related to their chronic drinking, but it clearly is a pattern in the behavior of the police as well. It is therefore understandable that homeless men often move from neighborhood to neighborhood or city to city, seeking to spend some time on the street before they become known to the police and subject to immediate arrest (Spradley, 1970:179).[23] But they are caught in a "double bind" to some extent, since transiency itself tends to attract law, and is part of the reason these men are so vulnerable in the first place (see Black, 1976:49–52; on double binds, see Bateson, Jackson, Haley, and Weakland, 1956). In any event, it may not be an exaggeration to say, as did one student of the subject that "law occupies the very center of the skid rower's life [Wallace, 1965:92]."

Arrest is only one kind of social control exercised by the police on skid row. In various other ways, they pursue a strategy of total domination. Officers warn homeless men to get off the street, question them about their personal affairs, enter their hotel rooms unannounced, search them, and ridicule them (see, e.g., Bittner, 1967b:708–709). Many police address them with epithets such as "bum," "wino," "drunk," and "tramp." One man, for instance, remembered being told that he was "just a wino and a bum that wasn't worth being tossed in a shit ditch" [Spradley, 1970:141]. Those homeless men who are also members of a minority group may experience special hostility, such as that shown to an American Indian who remembered being told by an officer that he was a "fucked-up chief" and that, in general, the "fuckin' Injuns" never should have been given "liquor rights" (Spradley, 1970:142; see also Lundman, 1974b:133). If a man is carrying a bottle of wine or liquor, an officer may break it with his nightstick, though some prefer to pour the contents over the individual's head or into his trousers (Spradley, 1970:126; Wiseman, 1970:81). Homeless men are also frequently divested of their money and valuables by the police, both on the street and at the police station. One investigator heard many stories about officers "rolling drunks" (taking their money), but did not believe the reports until after he conducted the following experiment:

---

23. Spradley (1970:177–178) further notes that the sentencing patterns of judges have a similar effect: Since skid-row men know that they generally receive longer sentences in jail in direct relation to the number of times they have been brought to court, they are ever more motivated to leave town as their records grow longer. In the case of Seattle, men start with a clean slate if they can avoid arrest for 6 months, and so they often leave that city when their risk of longer sentences increases, only to return in 6 months qualified for leniency as first offenders.

The author . . . pretended to be drunk, "passed out" on the street, and had himself arrested. Deposited along with two other drunks in the city jail, he was promptly relieved of his money by the police officers on duty, one of whom he heard to remark: "'They'll never know the difference, and nobody will believe 'em anyhow" [Wallace, 1965:97; see also Spradley, 1970:144–147, 152; Sherman, 1978:163–164].

Violence by the police is common as well. In fact, it appears to be a major tactic used by officers in banishing homeless men from their patrol districts. Frequently the men are kicked in the buttocks as an encouragement to go elsewhere —indeed, this appears to be a customary practice of many police. In one study, experiences of this kind were reported by about one-third of the homeless men interviewed $(N=94;$ Spradley, 1970:125; see also Chevigny, 1969:116–121). The following account seems to be typical:

I was eating in a cafe when this bull noticed me. I had been home for two months and just got off the bus. He said, "I'm tired of seeing you around here–keep off my beat!" He aimed his kick for my rear end but kicked me in the thigh instead and I limped for three or four days [Spradley, 1970:125].

A similar incident occurred in the presence of an observer:

[The police] were told to investigate two drunks in a cemetery. On arriving they found two white men "sleeping one off." Without questioning the men, the older policeman began to search one of them, ripping his shirt and hitting him in the groin with a nightstick. The younger policeman, as he searched the second, ripped away the seat of his trousers, exposing his buttocks. The policemen then prodded the men toward the cemetery fence and forced them to climb it, laughing at the plight of the drunk with the exposed buttocks. As the drunks went over the fence, one policeman shouted, "I ought to run you fuckers in!" The other remarked to the observer, "Those assholes won't be back; a bunch of shitty winos" [Reiss, 1968a:13].

Violence not only encourages homeless men to leave a particular area, but seems in some cases to be levied for its own sake, perhaps as a kind of punishment for being in the wrong place at the wrong time. A man found sleeping or intoxicated in an alley, for instance, should expect to be kicked, clubbed, or otherwise injured as a matter of course. Some of this police behavior is properly understood as torture. An officer might twist a man's arm, pull his hair, step on him, or whatever. In one case (described by an observer in the three-city study reported in Chapters 3–5 of this volume), a patrol officer applied what the observer called a "painful finger lock" in order to awaken an intoxicated man, and in another case an officer intentionally pushed smelling salts up a man's nostrils until blood began to flow.

Violence also seems to be frequent when skid-row men are arrested and jailed (see Spradley, 1970:124–125, 148–149). But the most extreme violence seems to occur when a man refuses to submit totally to an officer's authority. Thus, in one case a man protested when an officer appropriated $11 from his wallet during a street search: "Since when do you look for a gun or knife in a man's wallet?" For this he was beaten severely and required four stitches to close a wound on his head (Spradley 1970:150). Certainly not all police officers are as harsh toward these men as those described above, but then most other people in society have little or no fear of ever being treated with severity of this degree.

The treatment of homeless men illustrates the fate of those who occupy simultaneously a number of social locations, each of which is, by itself, a favorable climate for law. Men on skid row are at once poor, unemployed, unmarried, unconventional, uneducated, unorganized, unrespectable, transient, and subject to comparatively little social control other than law. Beyond all of this, they are often the objects of complaints by people of higher status, especially merchants (Wiseman, 1970:66–67), and they are viewed with distaste by members of the public at large. They are also lower in status and culturally distant from the police themselves. All of these conditions increase the likelihood and magnitude of law (see generally Black, 1976). Only a certain intimacy that sometimes develops between the officers and these men—a result of police harassment itself—operates to restrain law to some degree, but this is absent in many cases, and in any event seldom endures for long.

Traffic

The movement of people and vehicles is another major concern of the police, and this too illustrates in its own way the relevance of the sociological theory of law. In particular, traffic enforcement reveals dramatically the degree to which legal variation depends upon a flow of social information.

Like telephone calls to the police (see page 7), motor vehicles in themselves generally provide little information about the social characteristics of their owners or operators. The economic value of a vehicle is not a reliable indicator of the driver's social status, and its general appearance and registration plate typically add little information either. It is therefore understandable that in a large city, citations ("tickets") for parking violations are distributed for the most part independently of the social characteristics of the people involved, since only the vehicle is present when they are issued. Even parked cars can sometimes be identified with low-status people, however, such as prostitutes and their associates ("pimpmobiles") and teenagers (cars with raised or lowered rear ends), and these may be more vulnerable. It is also likely that in a small town or village, where the police have more social information about the automobiles they encounter, selective ticketing is more frequent: Cars of strangers are probably more vulnerable than those of local residents, for example, and the area's leading citizens may enjoy a degree of immunity.

The regulation of automobiles that are occupied is somewhat more complex. Anyone who has ridden in a police car knows that officers ignore many incidents normally viewed as traffic violations (see Lobenthal, 1970). Their usual policy is to ticket only as many drivers as their supervisors demand, and to relax after this so-called quota has been filled (see Petersen, 1971; Lundman, 1979). As one police chief explained, "Policemen write as many traffic tickets as you encourage them to write [Gardiner, 1969:88]." In effect, then, police supervisors act as the complainants in most traffic work, but, within limits, they leave to the officers the selection of cases to be treated as offenses. The quota itself varies from city to city[24] and, within a department, from one division to another, with the most tickets being expected of officers who specialize in traffic control. In addition, officers among themselves tend to enforce a maximum number of tickets that any individual should write—apparently to prevent their supervisors from changing the standard of a reasonable day's work (Petersen, 1971: especially 357–358). Among patrol officers observed by the author in Detroit, it was understood that a single ticket a day should be written, and the men often remarked that "One a day keeps the lieutenant away." A common practice was to write a ticket at the beginning of their shifts so that they could forget about traffic violations for the next 7 hours (see also Petersen, 1971:359). Officers frequently explained their failure to act upon seemingly egregious violations with such comments as "I've got mine for the night," or "I don't need it, I've already got one." In another city, it was found that officers had a tendency to write more tickets toward the end of each month—since their quotas had to be met only on a monthly basis (Lundman, 1979:164). It might be added that many officers fill the ticket quota by going to a location with features known to produce a large number of violations, even by the most careful drivers. Such a place is called a "duck pond" (also noted by Van Maanen, 1974:108). In one precinct in Detroit, for example, a number of officers favored an intersection where it was unusually difficult for drivers to see the sign reading "no left turn." A good duck pond such as this will yield a ticket within a few minutes. Another technique for filling the quota with little effort is to write a ticket for a safety defect that is widespread but that is not ordinarily handled as a violation, such as a missing headlight (known as a "one-eye").

It should not be inferred, however, that ticket quotas are filled without regard to the social characteristics of the drivers. On the contrary, many officers speak openly about taking these into account in traffic enforcement. Just as people with children, for instance, are treated more leniently if they are convicted of a crime (see Black, 1976:49–52), so they are less vulnerable to traffic tickets when they drive automobiles—as long as their children are present and visible to the police.

---

24. There is some evidence that in smaller cities and towns police supervisors are less ticket-oriented than their counterparts in larger cities, and that they may reprimand officers who are overly zealous in this regard (see, e.g., Gardiner, 1969:56, 85).

Thus, in one case observed by the author, a white woman "ran" a stop sign and nearly collided with the patrol car:

> *Earl* [the officer driving] *slammed on his brakes just in time. It was a woman with several kids in the car. When Earl talked to her he found that she didn't have her driver's license with her—that's an automatic trip to the station. But, instead, he decided to follow her home where her license was.*
>
> *He talked to her on the front stoop. Meanwhile, Bob* [Earl's partner] *said to me, "You know, we're supposed to take people in when they don't have their licenses. But here's a lady with kids and everything—it's one of those times when we* bend *the law. A policeman can never follow the law right down the line . . . ."*
>
> *Earl was gone about five minutes. When he got in the wagon* [patrol vehicle] *he said, "Boy, this is just not my night—no luck at all. The broad* [woman] *has five kids. They were yelling and everything and it distracted her. I told her I have two kids and you have five—I know how those kids can make noise . . . . I just wrote a warning. I couldn't see giving her a ducat"* [ticket] [author's field notes].

Another officer reported to the author that during his 9 years on the police force he had never given a ticket to a driver with a family in the car. Still another said that he will not even stop a car with children in it:

> *I like to get them when they're alone. I make it a point not to stop cars with whole families in them. I can't take it when the kids say, "Is he a real policeman?" and I'm writing a ticket for Daddy. Daddy can do no wrong, so I don't like to embarrass him in front of the kids* [author's field notes].

If the police learn that a driver is himself an officer, this too discourages them from writing a ticket. As one officer explained:

> *If a guy is a police officer, he'll mention it to me—if he has any brains. If he doesn't mention it, then he deserves the ticket* [author's field notes].

People with other ties to the police also have a degree of immunity. This is true, for example, of friends and acquaintances of the officer handling an incident, of relatives of another officer, and of ex-officers. In one case the police stopped a man who had disobeyed a red traffic signal, but released him without a ticket when it was learned that the driver's wife (who was not present in the car) had been a cook at a recent police banquet that they had attended.[25] Taxi drivers,

---

25. In many cities, people with "connections" to the police who have nonetheless received tickets are able to have them "fixed," or nullified, at a later time (see Gardiner, 1969:118–126).

truck drivers, fire fighters, government officials, and clergymen—all respectable people who also work on the streets or who serve the public—are among those who are likely to receive special consideration as well. But leniency is not the only form of selective enforcement: Drivers may also be singled out for special severity.

At the time of the author's field research, some officers made an effort to give tickets only to black people. Upon one occasion, the police being observed decided to look specifically for one-eyes, the easily identifiable cars with a missing headlight. It soon became apparent, however, that they would stop only those driven by blacks. When the first such car—occupied by a black couple—approached, one of the officers said, "Is he the right color? Yep!" and then stopped the driver and wrote a ticket. His partner remarked that the observer would think that they were "prejudiced," and laughed heartily. Shortly thereafter, the officers passed another one-eye that they seemed to notice, but it was occupied by whites and was not stopped. The third car with one headlight they encountered was driven by a black man, and the officer again asked rhetorically whether he was the "right color" before stopping him and writing a ticket. The behavior of these officers may not be representative of most police who enforce traffic regulations, but it is noteworthy that it occurred at all, especially in the presence of an observer.

Many police also tend to be more aggressive and severe toward young people, often stopping them as a means of harassment (see also pages 11–12, 24). As one investigator reports:

> Even when no particular violation can be charged against a teenager, Massachusetts policemen frequently write traffic tickets and ask the Registry of Motor Vehicles (not the courts) to suspend licenses. Registry files contain many tickets citing no violation but simply stating "improper operator," "drag racing," "obscene language," "noisy," or "driving to a riot" [Gardiner, 1969:151].

The young people who most attract the attention of the police—besides blacks and other minorities—are those who drive vehicles expressing youth itself, such as cars or vans with distinctive decorations or equipment (e.g., figures painted on the bodies, loud mufflers, oversized tires, altered rear ends) and motorcycles of any kind (see Skolnick, 1966:94–96).

Cars bearing unconventional slogans on their bumpers ("bumper stickers") may also be subject to harassment or selective enforcement. For instance, it was found in a California experiment involving college students that drivers of cars with stickers of a militant black political organization, the Black Panther Party, were considerably more likely to be stopped and given traffic tickets by the police (Heussenstamm, 1971). Even though social information on the streets is limited, then, enough is available to result in an uneven distribution of traffic tickets across social space (compare Ross, 1960:232–235).

When the police stop an automobile, whether they give a ticket may depend not only upon who the driver is but also upon how he or she behaves: All else constant, the likelihood of a ticket varies inversely with the degree to which the driver cooperates with the police. A driver who protests innocence, or in any other way resists or criticizes an officer's definition of the situation, is more likely to receive a ticket. As one student of ticketing notes, "Persons who have been abusive to officers . . . are more likely than others to receive a ticket and are also ineligible to fix tickets" (Gardiner, 1969:151; see also Skolnick, 1966:94; Lundman, 1979:164, 166). Any failure to show respect toward an officer increases the likelihood of a ticket, whereas an exceptionally deferential driver is the least likely to be ticketed. In a study of patrol work in three cities, only 11% of the "antagonistic" drivers were released without being ticketed or arrested, whereas this proportion rose to 35% of the drivers who were "civil" and to 49% of those who were "very deferential" (Black, 1968:256).[26] This pattern, however, is not peculiar to traffic enforcement. The relationship between the legitimacy accorded the police and their behavior is the focus of the next (and last) section of this survey.

Rebellion

A number of investigators have found that the police are unusually severe when people rebel against their authority. Just as an argumentative driver is more likely to receive a traffic ticket, so an uncooperative juvenile or adult—in any kind of incident—is more likely to be arrested (Piliavin and Briar, 1964; Black and Reiss, 1970:74–75; Black, 1971:1100, 1103, 1108; see also Chapter 5 of the present volume, pages 169–172). In addition, a person who fails to defer to the police is more likely to be subjected to violence (Westley, 1953; Reiss, 1968a:18; Chevigny, 1969:51–83). In some cases, people not only fail to defer or cooperate but also seek to exercise social control against the police themselves. In so doing, they may use violence, physically assaulting or even killing an officer as an act of punishment or retribution. When this occurs, the police tend to retaliate with extreme severity, using tactics rarely applied in other cases. This pattern appears dramatically in the context of "political crime," as seen during riots, revolutions, and other popular uprisings.

In the late 1960s, for example, large numbers of blacks rebelled against the police during the course of riots in many American cities. Running through the streets, destroying and confiscating property, the crowds repeatedly ignored orders to disperse, threw rocks and debris, and in some instances fired guns at the officers and military personnel involved. In response, the police and the troops

---

26. There were 37 drivers judged by observers to be "antagonistic," 156 who seemed "civil," and 43 who seemed "very differential." All in this subsample were adults (at least 18 years old) and were "predominantly blue-collar" in social-class status. They included both blacks and whites, and, it might be added, the pattern reported in the text applied to both (Black, 1968:256).

tended to relate to all blacks as offenders, regardless of their conduct. Thousands were arrested, and many were subjected to beatings and to occasionally fatal shootings. Thus, during the Newark riot of July 12–17, 1967, "general and deliberate violence [was directed] against the whole [black] community . . . . People were stopped indiscriminately in the streets, shoved, cursed, and beaten and shot [Hayden, 1967:47–48]." Some of the blacks shot and killed were not participating in the riot in any way. For example:

> On Saturday before darkness fell, three women were killed in their homes by police fire. Rebecca Brown, a twenty-nine-year-old nurse's aide, was cut nearly in half as she tried to rescue her two-year-old child by the window. Hattie Gainer, an elderly twenty-year resident of her neighborhood, was shot at her window in view of her three grandchildren. Eloise Spellman was shot through the neck in her Hayes apartment with three of her eleven children present [Hayden, 1967:48–49].

Another woman who went outside to look for her children was killed when the police fired into a crowd. A man was killed as he stepped out of a restaurant where he had just finished eating: The police stopped their car, shot him, and then drove on. Another man was shot while fixing his car. In yet another instance, a man who told police that he had been shot in the side was knocked to the ground by an officer and kicked in the ribs (examples drawn from Hayden, 1967).

Blacks were addressed as "niggers" and harassed and abused with a variety of techniques. For instance, in one case a man walking peacefully on a sidewalk with two women was "stopped by the police who told him to strip, ripped off his clothes, and forced him to run naked down the street [Hayden, 1967:48]." In another case, a black professional worker was arrested while driving on a quiet street after the 10 P.M. curfew that had been declared during the riot. He was "beaten unconscious, and then forced to perform what his lawyer describes as 'degrading acts' when he revived at the police station [Hayden, 1967:48]." In addition to their use of violence against individual blacks, the police destroyed or damaged many black-owned places of business that had been left unharmed by the crowds (Hayden, 1967:49). In general, the tendency of the police to treat all blacks as offenders increased as the riots continued: A statistical study of deaths in the Newark riot, as well as in similar riots in Los Angeles and Detroit, indicates that "officials become increasingly indiscriminate, random, and personal in their killing as the riot progresses [Bergesen, 1980:153]." It may even be appropriate to speak of the reaction as a "police riot" (see Stark, 1972).

In cross-cultural and historical perspective, the police response to rebellions and other political crime may be viewed as an extreme instance of the phenomenon of collective responsibility—or, more precisely, collective liability—in which all members of a particular social category are held accountable for the conduct of any of their fellows (see, e.g., Moore, 1972; Koch, 1981). In many tribal societies, for example, a person's relatives are liable for his or her offenses against people in other families (for African illustrations, see Evans-Pritchard,

1940: Chapter 4; Lewis, 1961: Chapter 6; Peters, 1967). Conflicts between members of different communities and societies often entail collective liability as well: A war or feud proceeds in this way, and the same phenomenon may be seen when one society invades and occupies another (see, e.g., Gross, 1979:207–209).[27] It seems that a system of collective liability is especially likely when the parties in conflict are members of corporate groups or are separated by a relatively great distance in social space. Evidence such as that given above, however, suggests that this strategy of social control may also be precipitated by a rebellion against authority. In turn, this may be more pronounced when those involved have other characteristics associated with collective liability, such as when they are members of different racial or ethnic groups (see, e.g., Enloe, 1977).

It might be added that collective liability tends to be reciprocal, so that people who are held accountable for their fellows' conduct by members of another group generally relate to the individuals in that group in the same way. Hence, just as many police in the 1960s held all blacks liable for the conduct of a few, so many blacks did the same in regard to the police: Frequently the police officers chosen as targets of violence by blacks during the riots previously discussed had done nothing themselves to offend blacks, and some might well have been sympathetic to their side. Under normal circumstances, too, many cases of violence against the police, including so-called random attacks and killings, are actually expressions of social control meted out within a framework of collective liability, in retaliation for the misconduct of other officers.[28]

---

27. Much so-called terrorism is also an expression of collective liability: Members of a particular social category—a nationality, religion, ethnicity, social class, or whatever—are injured, killed, or taken hostage in retaliation for what the "terrorists" define as deviant conduct by other members of that social category.

The concept of terrorism usually is applied to the violence of rebellious groups, but similar conduct may occur on the part of legal officials (see, e.g., Jakubs, 1977).

28. It has been suggested by the anthropologist Sally Falk Moore that wherever a system of collective liability is found, those who become accountable for a fellow member's conduct will hold that individual responsible within their own group, and will not accept unquestioningly the burden that his or her actions place upon them:

> It is my hypothesis that where every member of a corporate group has the power to commit it . . . to a collective liability, a corollary rule always exists whereby the corporation may discipline, expel or yield up to enemies members who abuse this power or whom the corporation does not choose to support in the situation in which he has placed them . . . . There is no doubt that within a group or aggregate bearing collective liability, in the long run individuals are held individually responsible for their actions. Collective responsibility does not exclude or substitute for individual responsibility. Both can and do operate simultaneously at different social levels [Moore, 1972:89, 93, italics omitted].

The system of collective liability that operates between the police and a rebellious group would seem to depart from the pattern Moore describes in her formulation. Thus, during the riots discussed in the text, neither blacks nor the police appear to have held their fellows responsible to any significant degree for the conduct that made the entire group vulnerable to sanctions. For that matter,

How the police respond to rebellion varies not only with the degree of resistance they meet but also with how they themselves are constituted. For example: Since the quantity of law varies directly with the organization of its administration (see Black, 1976:95–97), it may be expected that police who are more organized—those with more centralization and coordination—will deal more severely with rebellion. The size of a police force is relevant as well, in that, other things being equal, a larger number of officers involves a greater degree of organization. Accordingly, a national police system will generally respond more severely than a local system such as that in the United States, where each city and state has its own police force, and the most severe will be a very large, national system such as that in the Soviet Union.[29] More organized police will also define more conduct as political crime, and they will define more people as their enemies (see Bergesen, 1977). Extremes of severity were seen, for example, in the activities of the Soviet police in the years following the Russian Revolution of 1917. Millions of people were arrested as political criminals (in a program known as "social prophylaxis"), arrest quotas were specified for every city and district, informers were widely employed, and a refusal to serve as an informer was itself treated as an offense (see Solzhenitsyn, 1973: Chapter 2). Collective liability for political crime extended across social class, ethnicity, nationality, religion, occupation, association, kinship, and friendship:

> Arrests rolled through the streets and apartment houses like an epidemic. Just as people transmit an epidemic infection from one to another without knowing it, by such innocent means as a handshake, a breath, handing someone something, so, too, they passed on the infection of inevitable arrest by a handshake, by a breath, by a chance meeting on the street. For if you are destined to confess tomorrow that you organized an underground group . . . , and if today I shake hands with you on the street, that means that I, too, am doomed [Solzhenitsyn, 1973:75].

---

even on a day-to-day basis, rather little internal social control of the kind Moore describes can be found among the segments of a population in a modern city, though collective liability may occur under these conditions. An example can be seen in the "random punishment" of Poles—in response to the offenses of other Poles—during the German occupation of Warsaw (Gross, 1979:207–212). The association between collective liability and internal social control would appear to be related to such factors as the size of the groups involved, the anonymity of the members, and their relational distance from one another (see Gross, 1979:209).

29. Factors other than their organization may also operate to increase the severity of national police systems. In contrast to local systems, the officers are likely to be recruited from outside the regions to which they are assigned, to maintain their permanent residences elsewhere (living in barracks while on duty), and to be rotated from one locality to another—all factors that widen the social distance between police and citizens, and that correspondingly increase their severity (see page 4). National police are also more likely to represent a single ethnic group, a factor that may increase their severity still further (see Enloe, 1977).

It might be added that the conditions increasing the severity of national police in comparison to local police would seem to be even more extreme in the case of military systems, resulting in a still greater degree of severity.

Rebellion stimulates the police to a level of activity rarely seen at other times. In some cases *agents provocateurs* employed by the police encourage people to participate in conduct defined as political crime so that they can be arrested (see Marx, 1974). The police may even execute those who oppose them, a practice found throughout the world, now and in the past. Those who are highly organized seem to be the most repressive in this regard, but police everywhere take a special interest in anyone who questions their authority.

*   *   *

In sum, every kind of police work is understandable with the sociological theory of law. The dispatch of a patrol car, the writing of a crime report, the pursuit of an investigation, the admonition, ticketing, arrest, or beating of a citizen—all of this and more is law. The police thus appear as so many mechanisms by which law is distributed in greater or lesser quantity, in one style or another, across social space. Every kind of police work encounters its own social conditions, and these predict and explain what happens—which events are defined as crimes, which are treated as serious or trivial, who goes to jail, who is hit with a club or shot with a gun, and so on.

Although police behavior in any given setting may be predicted and explained with the sociological theory of law, it is important to recognize that both the police themselves and law in general are exotic phenomena, not seen in most societies across human history (see, e.g., Schwartz and Miller, 1964). They are found only where the conditions are right—where there is a substantial degree of inequality among the population, for example, where many relationships are distant and impersonal, where lifestyles struggle for dominance, where unemployment, homelessness, and isolation are widespread, and where people have few alternatives by which to handle their conflicts (see generally Black, 1976). The police and law therefore flourish in modern society, since it has these conditions in abundance. But neither the police nor any other species of legal life should be taken for granted. As society evolves, some or all of these conditions may decline or disappear, undermining the value of legal officials such as the police, making it difficult for them to maintain their present level of development and possibly endangering their very survival.[30] The police and law may prove to be nothing more than transitory phenomena, found only during the stage of social evolution through which we are now passing.

---

30. This does not necessarily mean that the many emergency services the police now perform would go out of existence (see Bittner, 1974), but only that social control by the police might ultimately be reduced.

The Mobilization of Law*

2

A theory of social control seeks to understand patterns of normative life and their relation to other aspects of social organization. Little theory of this type can be found in social science, although over the years several self-conscious efforts in this direction have been made in sociology and social anthropology (for examples of earlier works, see Ross, 1901; Malinowski, 1926; Mannheim, 1940; Hollingshead, 1941; Llewellyn and Hoebel, 1941). Sociological thought about social control has been too broad for some purposes, too narrow for others. The subject matter has been defined as the conditions for social order—a subject matter some would give to sociology as a whole—while the detailed study of social control has centered upon how official reactions to deviant behavior affect individual motivation (e.g., Goffman, 1961; Andenaes, 1966; Scheff, 1966; Chambliss, 1967). Focusing thus upon the relationship between constraint and individual adaptation, sociology has neglected the character and integrity of social control as a natural system (but see, e.g., Schwartz, 1954; Piliavin and Briar, 1964; Black, 1970; 1971). In the anthropological work on social control, more emphasis has been placed upon systems of social control and dispute settlement than upon the influence of these systems at the level of individual motivation. Unfortunately, however, anthropologists tend to stress concrete description and have shown little interest in the development of general theory (but see, e.g., Bohannan, 1965; Pospisil, 1971).

*This chapter is reprinted with minor revision from the *Journal of Legal Studies* 2 (January, 1973):125–149.

For comments on an earlier draft the author is indebted to John Griffiths, Jerrold K. Guben, Robert Kagan, Richard Lempert, Michael E. Libonati, Maureen Mileski, Albert J. Reiss, Jr., David M. Trubek, and Stanton Wheeler. Support was provided by the Russell Sage Program in Law and Social Science and by the Law and Modernization Program, both of Yale Law School.

Law may be defined, very simply, as *governmental social control* (Black, 1972:1086). Although its social characteristics are highly complicated, writ large in law are properties and processes that inhere in all forms of social control but that escape our notice in systems lacking its formalization, scale, and intrusiveness. Hence, it seems likely that theoretical tools for understanding social control in general will be fashioned in the sociological study of law. In the following pages, I discuss a single dimension of legal life: the *mobilization of law*,[1] or the process by which a legal system acquires its cases.[2] The day-by-day entry of cases into any legal system cannot be taken for granted. Cases of alleged illegality and disputes do not move automatically to legal agencies for disposition or settlement. Without the mobilization of law, a legal-control system lies out of touch with the human problems it is designed to oversee. Mobilization is the link between law and the people served or controlled by law.

The literature of jurisprudence shows little evidence of interest in the problem of mobilization, although here and there an exception is encountered. A century ago, for instance, Rudolph von Jhering appealed to the citizenry to call the law to action in every case of infringement of their legal rights (1877). He argued that without continual mobilization law would lose its deterrent power, and claimed that legal mobilization is the moral obligation of every citizen whose rights are offended. Roscoe Pound, too, warned that the effective power of law requires a citizenry ready and willing to activate the legal process (1917). Pound's point is occasionally repeated by contemporary legal critics and scholars (e.g., Jones, 1969:21–26), but the problem of mobilization more often is entirely ignored.

Likewise, legal sociology rarely deals with the problem of mobilization. Usually the study of law as a social-control system concerns the process of legal

---

1. While this use of the word *mobilization* is hardly standard, it is not utterly unknown. For instance, Bronislaw Malinowski speaks of the "judicial machinery" being "mobilized" (1942:1250). Nevertheless, I have misgivings about the appropriateness of the word *mobilization* in this context. Colleagues have commented that it has a militaristic flavor and that it is too heavy for these purposes. I agree with these criticisms and would add that *mobilization* is a word ordinarily used in the analysis of larger-scale social phenomena, as in the mobilization of a society for war or the mobilization of a political movement. Still, I have been unable to find an adequate substitute. *Invocation* is too narrow, for instance, while *activation* seems even more awkward than *mobilization*. It is to be hoped that someone will eventually improve upon my choice. In the meantime I console myself with the thought that this problem with words reflects the lack of scholarly attention to the analytic problem itself.

2. Perhaps more specification is required: By *legal system* I mean any governmental organization involved in defining or enforcing normative order. Thus, I speak of a total governmental apparatus as a legal system—the American legal system—but I also refer to a specific legal agency such as the police as a legal system. By *case* I mean any dispute or instance of alleged illegality that enters a legal system. A breach of contract, for instance, becomes a case only when a suit is filed; a burglary becomes a case when it is reported to the police. A mobilization of law, then, is a complaint made to or by a legal agency. Mobilization occurs at several stages in some legal processes, for example, at a detection stage, an evidentiary or prosecutorial stage, and an adjudicatory stage.

prescription or policymaking, such as legislation, or of legal disposition or dispute settlement, such as we see in judicial decisionmaking or police encounters. Legal mobilization, however, is a process that mediates between the prescriptions of law and the disposition of cases, between rules and their application. Although most social scientists focus upon rules or their application, a few theoretical references to the problem of mobilization can be found (e.g., Bohannan, 1965; Aubert, 1967; Mayhew, 1968:15–16), and there is also a valuable body of empirical research relevant to a theory of mobilization, revolving primarily around the questions of when and why people go to law to solve their problems (e.g., Gulliver, 1963; Kawashima, 1963; Macaulay, 1963; Nader and Metzger, 1963; Macfarlane, 1970).

In the present discussion I slight the social conditions under which law is mobilized. Instead, my concern is *how* law is set into motion. I try to show that whether or not the state selects the legal cases it handles makes a critical difference in the character of law as a social-control system. I examine the organization of legal mobilization as it relates to other aspects of legal control, including *(a)* legal intelligence, *(b)* the availability of law, *(c)* the organization of discretion, and *(d)* legal change. In so doing, I show how mobilization systems influence diverse aspects of legal life, such as the kinds of cases a legal system handles, the accessibility of the population to law, the degree of particularism in law enforcement, and the responsiveness of law to moral change in the citizenry.

The Structure of Legal Mobilization

A case can enter a legal system from two possible directions. A citizen may set the legal process in motion by bringing a complaint, or the state may initiate a complaint upon its own authority, with no participation of a citizen complainant. In the first sequence a legal agency reacts to a citizen, so we may refer to it as a *reactive* mobilization process. In the second sequence, where a legal official acts with no prompting from a citizen, we may speak of a *proactive* mobilization process.[3]

Across societies, history, and substantive areas of law there is enormous variability in how law is mobilized, whether by means of citizens, the state, or both. Some legal processes are organized to allow the government to take action on its own; in others no such route is provided. In the United States, for example,

---

3. In psychology, the concepts *reactive* and *proactive* have been used to classify individual actions in terms of their origins, the former referring to actions originating in the environment, the latter to those originating within the actor (see Murray, 1951). The usefulness of these concepts in the context of legal life—specifically in the analysis of the police—was first suggested to me by Jerrold K. Guben.

Instead of reactive and proactive legal systems we could also speak, respectively, of passive and active legal systems (see Selznick, 1969:225–228).

the government has no responsibility for mobilizing what is traditionally called "private law," such as contract law, tort law, and property law. There are no government organizations or offices empowered to bring a private-law case on behalf of a private citizen. There are only the courts, where citizens, assisted by attorneys, can make their own claims on their own behalf.[4] American public law presents an entirely different appearance. Here the government is authorized to initiate cases independently of the grievances of private citizens.[5] The major examples are criminal law and the regulatory laws enforced by federal and local government agencies such as the Federal Trade Commission, the Internal Revenue Service, city health departments, and local licensing agencies. The government is organizationally as well as legally equipped to initiate public law cases, since there is a network of government agencies that routinely carry out investigations concerned with detecting illegality. Most visible are the federal, state, county, and city police forces, but numerous government agencies outside the operational jurisdiction of the police are also engaged in proactive enforcement of public law. In the Soviet Union, owing in good part to the office of procurator, considerably more state-initiated legal cases arise than in the United States. The Soviet procuracy is the prosecuting arm in criminal cases but also watches over all civil proceedings and may initiate or enter any lawsuit at any stage on either side of the dispute (a description is provided by Berman, 1963:239). In earlier historical periods, the proactive capacity of the state in the American system was considerably less than it is now, but never was the American government so passive in the mobilization of law as was, for example, the government of republican Rome, to cite an extreme case where proactive enforcement was almost wholly absent (see generally Lintott, 1968).

But legal agencies with the capacity to initiate cases do not necessarily use that capacity to its limits, if they use it at all. For instance, in legal theory and in the popular mind, American criminal justice is a process in which the government is

---

4. This is not to deny that the state can and often does initiate private-law cases on its own behalf as a private party, such as when the government is the victim of a breach of contract. The point is that the government cannot bring a private-law case on behalf of a private individual as it does, in effect, in many criminal cases. Neither does the participation of a legal-aid lawyer in a private action constitute government initiative analogous to a criminal prosecution, since legal aid implies no partisanship on the part of the state itself.

5. In fact, mobilization provides a useful way to distinguish between public law and private law, although it corresponds only roughly to traditional usage. We can define public law as law that the state is authorized to enforce upon its own initiative, private law as law in which the initiative is granted exclusively to private citizens. By this definition a legal process formally may be part of public law whether or not in practice the state acts upon the authority vested in it.

This distinction is very close to one advanced by A. R. Radcliffe-Brown:

In the law of private delicts a dispute between persons or groups is brought before the judicial tribunal for settlement; in the law of public delicts the central authority itself and on its own initiative takes action against an offender [1965:219].

highly aggressive in ferreting out illegality and bringing actions in court, but in fact the criminal-justice system resembles a private-law system far more than is generally recognized. The typical criminal case comes to the attention of the authorities not on account of police initiative but through the initiative of a private citizen acting in the role of complainant (see Reiss and Bordua, 1967:29–32). Among the uniformed patrol force of a large police department, where the heaviest part of the police workload is carried, the vast majority of citizen contacts arise at the instigation of citizens who mobilize the police (see Black, 1971:1090–1092). The police do initiate most cases of vice and narcotics enforcement and are very aggressive in traffic and crowd control. These patterns disproportionately influence the police image in the community, but, again, they are exceptional. Recent studies of other public-law systems, such as antidiscrimination commissions and housing-code enforcement agencies, reveal a similar dependence upon citizen complainants for the influx of cases (see Berger, 1967; Mayhew, 1968; Mileski, 1971b:60–65).

Like any analytic distinction, the reactive–proactive distinction encounters occasional difficulties when it confronts the empirical world. One marginal situation, for example, occurs when legal cases are brought to court by paid citizen informers. In England the use of common informers who make money from the misdeeds of their fellow citizens has a long history. These informers were a primary source of cases in some areas of English law—notably economic regulation—in the sixteenth and seventeenth centuries (Beresford, 1957). Informers also were frequently put to use in the early American legal process (Bacon, 1939), and they are still widely employed by the police in narcotics work, vice enforcement, and political surveillance. Similarly, the Internal Revenue Service offers financial incentives to informers against tax evaders. As an actor in the legal-control process, the informer mixes the roles of citizen complainant and public official. Another marginal pattern is voluntary surrender and confession by a law violator. In most areas of early Chinese law a citizen was rewarded with complete immunity if he or she confessed to an offense before it had been detected (Rickett, 1971). Voluntary confession still holds an important place in Chinese legal practice, and it is by no means unknown or unrewarded in Western legal systems.

I move now to several aspects of law for which the structure of legal mobilization carries significant implications, each being an important topic in its own right in the study of legal control. The first is legal intelligence.

Legal Intelligence

By legal intelligence I mean the knowledge that a legal system has about law violations in its jurisdiction. How the mobilization of law is organized has profound consequences for the discovery of illegality. A reactive system lodges the responsibility for detection of violations in citizens, thereby blinding the control process to whatever citizens are unable to see, fail to notice, or choose to ignore. Thus, private-law systems, such as the law of contracts or torts, remain ignorant of that vast number of breaches of law about which the citizenry is silent.[6] On the other hand, a citizen-based system of legal intelligence receives much information about legal cases that would otherwise elude its attention. From a sociological standpoint, however, there is no "proper" or even "effective" system of legal intelligence, since the adequacy of any aspect of legal control is not a scientific question (see Black, 1972).

ACCESS TO CASES

The proactive strategy of mobilization often appears in legal systems where a reactive strategy would fail to uncover illegality of a particular kind. A reactive strategy would be almost useless in traffic control, for example, and impracticable in vice or "morals" control. Frequently those few among the citizenry who would make vice complaints do not have access to the violative situations, so they cannot inform the police, and most of those with access do not complain. Hence, if detection in these cases is to occur at all, it requires a government-initiated mobilization system. Apart from crimes under the authority of the police, numerous forms of illegality—such as income-tax evasion and violations of health and safety standards by businesses—are unlikely to be known or recognized by ordinary citizens; enforcement in these cases generally necessitates a system of inspection carried out by government agencies. To facilitate its enforcement program the government may, for instance, require self-reports from citizens and organizations, as is seen in tax enforcement, antidiscrimination surveys, and wage and price control. Totalitarian regimes employ self-report systems extensively. Registration and licensing systems similarly assist the government in learning about the population and its activities. It might be added that the more differentiated a society becomes, the more illegality tends to arise in specialized domains of social life where the offenders are encapsulated beyond the reach of a citizen detection system. Accordingly, as the process of social

---

6. Perhaps it is apparent that my concept of illegality is broader than many American lawyers might deem proper. I treat an act as illegal if it falls within a *class* of acts for which there is a *probability* of official sanction, resistance, or redress after the fact of detection. Put another way, an act is illegal if it is *vulnerable* to legal action. A concept of this kind is required if a breach of private law not responded to as such is to be understood as illegality. By contrast, the American lawyer tends to view a breach of private law as illegality only if a complaint is made or if it is defined as such in a court of law. From this legalistic view it is impossible to consider the mobilization of private law as a problem for investigation, since where there is no mobilization there is by definition no illegality. From a sociological standpoint, however, unenforced private law is perfectly analogous to unenforced public law; in both cases the mobilization of law is problematic.

differentiation continues, notably in the economic sphere, we see an ever-enlarging battery of administrative agencies involved in proactive enforcement (see Durkheim, 1893:221–222).

The location of law violations is another factor conditioning the access of a legal process to its cases. Thus, most illegality arises in private rather than public settings, making access to much illegality difficult for a government enforcement system. In part this is because of legal restrictions protecting private places from government intrusion (see Stinchcombe, 1963), but the impact of the law of privacy on legal intelligence can easily be exaggerated. Even if privacy law were totally eliminated, opening every private place to government intrusion at any time, still the sheer unpredictability of illegal behavior would bar the government from knowledge of most illegality. Unless it were to go to the technological lengths fictionalized in George Orwell's *1984*, a government could not possibly achieve the surveillance necessary to detect even a minute proportion of all the illegal conduct. Police officers on patrol in public settings, for instance, rarely discover any but the relatively trivial varieties of criminal behavior. The more serious violations, such as homicide, burglary, and grand larceny, take place behind closed doors. The police therefore depend upon ordinary citizens to provide them with information about crimes that have been committed. Of course much illegality escapes the knowledge of citizens as well. Nevertheless, the latent power of a hostile or alienated citizenry to undermine the capacity of the government to locate violations is undeniable and is amply demonstrated in the history of colonial and other kinds of authoritarian legal systems (see, e.g., Massell, 1968). Unpopular law-enforcement programs such as these often use paid informers.

The power of the citizenry is all the greater in private law, where enforcement without the initiative of citizens is impossible, making the location of illegality a moot question. People can entirely ignore domestic law or the law of negligence, for example, and the government can do nothing short of redefining these areas as public law. It is popularly believed that written laws fall into disuse on account of government indifference or indolence, but in fact the demise of laws is more likely to result from citizens who fail to mobilize courts or other legal agencies. One by one, citizens may lose interest in a law, and, in private, it may die a slow death.

LIMITS ON LEGAL INTELLIGENCE

Any legal system relying upon the active participation of ordinary citizens must absorb whatever naiveté and ignorance is found among them. Such people may make occasional errors when they apply what they take to be legal standards to their everyday lives, not only because of their lack of legal training but also because many social situations have a legally ambiguous character. In complex legal systems, miscalculations by citizens are continually routed away from the courts by legal gatekeepers of various kinds. In private law, for example, a major gatekeeping burden is carried by the private attorney (see Parsons, 1954). In the process of advising their clients, attorneys serve the larger legal process as intelligence agents, sorting through and narrowing the raw input of cases moving toward the courts from day to day. In public law, others screen out the legal dross: police, government prosecutors, and the many enforcement officers attached to administrative agencies, such as health officers, food and drug inspectors, and internal revenue agents. Without these gatekeepers, intelligence gaps in the citizenry would reappear in the legal system.

Other intelligence losses greatly overshadow those resulting from the errors of citizens, however. It is clear, in particular, that much illegality is unknown because so many citizens fail to call upon law when they experience violations. The reluctance of citizens to mobilize law is so widespread, indeed, that it may be appropriate to view legal inaction as the dominant pattern in empirical legal life. The number of unknown law violations probably is greater in private law than in public law, although only speculation is possible. The outline of legal inaction is just now beginning to be known through surveys of the citizen population (see, e.g., United States President's Commission on Law Enforcement and Administration of Justice, 1967:17–19), and other relevant research is afoot. A recent study of dispute settlement in a Swedish fishing village, for instance, indicates that communities can passively absorb an enormous amount of illegal behavior, even when it continues for many years and includes numerous well-defined victimizations (Yngvesson, 1970). In fact, legal mobilization sometimes is more socially disruptive than the illegal behavior that gives rise to it.

Gradually a research literature is collecting around the question of when people mobilize law, given illegality. The nature of the social relationship enveloping a legal dispute or violation emerges as an especially powerful predictor of legal mobilization. Thus, we know that resort to a government court occurs primarily in legal conflicts between relative strangers or persons who live in different communities (see, e.g., Gulliver, 1963:204, 263–266; Kawashima, 1963), whereas persons in intimate relationships tend to use extralegal mechanisms of dispute settlement when quarrels arise. However, those who are intimately related do not hesitate to call upon law to settle their disputes when extralegal social control is unavailable (a pattern seen, for example, in the loosely structured barrios of Venezuela—Peattie, 1968:57–59). The likelihood that extralegal control will be available in a social relationship nevertheless tends to be a function of the intimacy of the relationship, as measured by such indicators as its duration, the frequency of interaction, the intensity of interaction, the degree of interdependence between the parties, and the number of dimensions along which interaction between the parties occurs. Accordingly, we expect that the mobilization of law will be infrequent in what Gluckman in his classic study of the Barotse of Zambia calls "multiplex" relationships, those in which individuals are tied together by more than a single interest or bond (1967:18–19).

Much of this may be summarized in the following proposition: *The greater the relational distance between the parties to a dispute, the more likely is law to be used to settle the dispute* (see Black, 1970:740–742; 1971:1107–1108). With formulations of this sort we can easily anticipate many empirical patterns, such as the finding that breach of contract rarely leads to a court case when it takes place between business people who have a continuing relationship with recurrent transactions (Macaulay, 1963). We may observe, then, that a reactive legal system acts to reinforce the tendency of citizens to use law only as a last resort, since it allows them to establish their own priorities. Because citizens use law reluctantly, they help to make law a conservative enterprise that for the most part leaves the status quo to its own designs. Social research eventually will reveal the extent and context of legal inaction in numerous areas and across societies, thereby making possible a comprehensive theory of the mobilization of law.[7]

A legal-intelligence system resting upon the initiative of citizens involves another kind of limitation, one that occurs regardless of the rate at which citizens mobilize the law. It inheres in the simple fact that reactive systems operate on a case-by-case basis (Mayhew, 1968:159). Cases enter the system one by one, and they are processed one by one. This creates an intelligence gap about the relations among and between cases. It is difficult to link patterns of illegal behavior to single or similar violators and thus to deal with the sources rather than merely the symptoms of these patterns. To discover these patterns, a systematic search for similarities across cases is needed.

Police systems do some pattern-oriented analysis of the cases coming to their attention through citizen complaints, but most patterns of illegality escape their detection net. One consequence may be a higher chance of survival for professional criminals (Bittner and Messinger, 1966). Some patterned criminality is uncovered through modus operandi files, and other areas where the government does its own investigations, strategies for finding patterns of violation

---

7. As noted earlier, I make no effort here to survey the many social factors that predict the mobilization of law. My discussion of relational distance above is intended only to introduce this issue and to illustrate how it may be approached with general theory. A more comprehensive treatment would include, for example, the seriousness of the dispute or illegality, measured by the nature of the sanction or restitution or by its effects upon the ongoing social order; the organization and integration of the community context; the resources required for the mobilization of law; the social status of the parties; the cultural context, including the degree of normative integration between the parties; and the organization of the dispute-settlement process itself, whether adversarial or conciliatory, formal or informal. The concern of this chapter—the organization of mobilization—also relates to the probability of mobilization.

can likewise be used, although illegality varies in its amenability to pattern detection. One case of processed food contamination, for instance, can lead to an inspection effort covering all businesses producing and distributing that particular variety of food, and the inspection may expose one business routinely violating health standards or a number of businesses involved in the same category of violative behavior. In fact, frequently one case of illegality by a business enterprise implies a pattern of illegality, since much business activity is by its nature programmed and repetitious. One violation of safety requirements by an automobile manufacturer, for example, usually means that numerous cases are at large in the community, and government inspections may unveil similar violations by other manufacturers. Likewise, in some cities housing-code enforcement officers inspect the whole of an apartment building when they learn, by complaint, of one violation in the building; they assume that the landlord may fail to meet code specifications in all of the units (Mileski, 1971b). In the criminal-justice system, single complaints about narcotics or vice can provide the police with opportunities to penetrate offense networks and markets and discover large numbers of interrelated violations.

The enforcement of private law contrasts sharply with these illustrations from public law. A case in point is contract law, where it is not unusual to find patterns of breach emanating from a single individual or business or from members of a broader category of legal actors, such as real estate agents, mail-order businesses, or insurance companies. Apart from patterns involving a recurrent breach, one act by a single business may involve numerous breaches of contract with individuals dispersed in the population, as when a holiday tour or an entertainment event is ended prematurely and the promoters do not make a monetary refund to the many victims. Private-law violations such as these can be remedied through "class actions," single legal suits covering a number of complaints of the same kind, but their frequency is far behind the rate at which patterns of multiple private-law violation apparently occur and would be much greater if the government were involved in enforcement. The government would learn of more patterns of illegality, if only because information about all known violations would pass through one central processing system similar to a police system. At present, the only official information on private-law cases is generally to be found in court records. Since no record is made of private-law cases that do not reach the court, there can be no legal intelligence about them analogous to police records in the criminal realm. And even the court records on file are presently irrelevant to the ongoing process of legal control.[8]

---

8. I make no effort in this chapter to review the extragovernmental controls operating in response to illegal behavior. Some pattern-oriented control of private-law violations, for instance, occurs through credit bureaus, informal reputational networks, and blacklisting systems.

Also eluding any case-by-case legal process is the larger pattern by which legal problems are distributed in the population of citizens. Owing to social conditions beyond the reach of any case-oriented mobilization system, legal trouble is differentially visited upon the citizenry. Crimes of violence and inter-personal conflicts of all kinds disproportionately afflict the lower social strata (family-related violence, for example, may be particularly common among poor blacks), and property matters often create a demand for law among the higher-status segments of the population. These structurally embedded patterns cannot be a direct concern of reactive control systems, although case records may be useful to social engineering efforts of other kinds. Because these patterns cannot be confronted by single legal officials dealing with single cases of so many isolated victims and violators, their job is very much a matter of picking up the social debris deposited by larger social forces. Apart from its deterrence effect, the extent of which is unknown, a reactive legal system ever listens to the troubles of the citizenry, while the larger principles and mechanisms by which these troubles come into being escape it. In this sense, a case-oriented legal process always begins too late.[9]

While a proactive system also is unable to attack the broader social conditions underlying law violations, it does have an ability to intervene in social arrange-ments that reactive systems lack. It can, for instance, destroy an illegal business operation, such as a gambling enterprise or crime syndicate, that may be the source of thousands of violations a week. Police control of automobile traffic, too, involves prevention through social engineering of a kind impossible in a legal process relying solely upon citizen complaints. A proactive system also has the power to prevent illegality in specific situations. While it cannot reach the many forms of illegality occurring in private places, a proactive system can prevent some violations in public places. The degree of prevention is difficult to assess, however, and in any case the forms of illegal behavior subject to situational prevention are likely to be minor. In a reactive process, prevention of this kind occurs only in the rare case when a citizen contacts a legal agency concerning an illegal act that is imminent or in progress and the agency intervenes. The heavy reliance of legal systems upon citizens thus assures that prevention will not be a major accomplishment. This is a more concrete sense in which a reactive sys-tem begins too late. And to the inherent sluggishness of any citizen-based sys-tem, private law adds the delay involved in gaining a hearing in court: No civil police are available for immediate aid and advice to people involved in private-law problems. This will probably come with further legal evolution and differen-

---

9. This is not to deny that a legal agency can respond to pressures built up in a reactive mobiliza-tion process. For instance, a high rate of purse-snatching complaints may lead the police to institute patrol or undercover operations to deal more effectively with the problem. In this way, the caseload of a citizen-based mobilization system can be an important source of intelligence to legal admin-istrators and policymakers.

tiation, but in the meantime private-law systems lag far behind in the wake of the problems they are established to control.

In sum, a mobilization system implies a particular organization of knowledge about law violations. A reactive system places responsibility in the citizenry and thereby brings law to the private place, with its numerous and serious forms of illegality. A proactive system can discover violations that citizens are unable or unwilling to report but misses much private illegality. In a reactive system, the kinds and rates of cases are a function of the kinds and rates of complaints by private citizens. In a proactive system, the kinds and rates of cases result from the distribution of official resources by the control system itself. Because of the reactive system's reliance upon citizens and its case-by-case schedule of operation, it involves certain intelligence weaknesses, such as a near incapacity to identify patterns of illegality necessary to prevention. The proactive system can deal with patterns rather than mere instances of illegality, which gives it a strong preventive capacity, but it is limited largely to marginal and minor forms of illegality. The legally more important problems, then, are the responsibility of a mobilization system that cannot prevent them.

The Availability of Law

The previous section concerned the access of a legal system to the cases within its jurisdiction. Now we reverse our viewpoint and consider the access of citizens to law. We must view legal life from below as well as from above (Nader and Yngvesson, 1973:892), since every instance of legal control is also an instance of legal service. The availability of law to citizens varies markedly across and within legal systems and cannot be taken for granted in a sociological theory of law. Access to law is a function of legal organization.

TWO MODELS OF LAW

The reactive mobilization system portrays an *entrepreneurial model of law*. It assumes that citizens will voluntarily and rationally pursue their own interests, with the greatest legal good of the greatest number presumptively arising from the selfish enterprise of the atomized mass. It is the legal analogue of the market economy.

Indeed, it has been argued that the organization of private law as a reactive system is not merely the analogue of a market economy; it is also the legal substructure essential to a market economy. Historically the system of "private rights" in contract, property, and tort law emerged and flourished with capitalism (see Trubek, 1971:65–70). Here, however, I am suggesting only that a citizen-based system of mobilization—whatever the type of law—operates according to the same behavioral principles as a market system of economic life.[10] In their primordial forms, both are self-help systems. The proactive system, by contrast, involves a *social-welfare model of law*, with the legal good of the citizenry being defined and then imposed by government administrators, albeit with some influence by interest groups in the citizen population. In the pure type of the social-welfare model of law, however, no role is provided for members of the citizenry in the determination of legal policy, just as in the pure type of welfare economy the will of the population need not be systematically introduced into the decision process. We might say, then, that a proactive system does not merely make law available; it imposes law.

Legal systems that operate with a reactive strategy often employ mechanisms assuring that mobilization will be truly voluntary and entrepreneurial, although this may not be the motive behind their implementation. One American illustration is the ethical prohibition against aggressive solicitation by attorneys. Were attorneys authorized to gather legal cases through solicitation, the input of legal business surely would change, since many otherwise passive victims of illegality undoubtedly would be persuaded to mobilize law.[11] The already great influence that lawyers exert on the input of cases would also be increased. In the American system, where attorneys stand to profit from some cases, the same incentives that

---

10. This claim has also been made for the common-law system in general, since, like an economic market, it is highly decentralized, competitive, largely private, and generates strong pressures for efficient performance among individuals (Posner, 1972:49). Posner also notes that the mobilization of negligence law is literally an economic market system:

> The motive force of the system is supplied by the economic self-interest of the participants in accidents. If the victim of an accident has a colorable legal claim to damages, it pays him to take steps to investigate the circumstances surrounding the accident; if the investigation suggests liability, to submit a claim to the party who injured him or the party's insurance company; if an amicable settlement cannot be reached, to press his claim in a lawsuit, if necessary to the highest appellate level. The other party has a similar incentive to discover the circumstances of the accident, to attempt a reasonable settlement, and, failing that, to defend the action in court. By creating economic incentives for private individuals and firms to investigate accidents and bring them to the attention of the courts, the system enables society to dispense with the elaborate governmental apparatus that would be necessary for gathering information about the extent and causes of accidents had the parties no incentive to report and investigate them exhaustively [1972:48].

11. It may be useful to distinguish between mere advertising and active solicitation, since the former has recently gained acceptance in the United States. Mere advertising is a process by which the legal consumer is simply informed of available legal services, while active soliciting involves an attempt to persuade an already informed consumer. Mere advertising would appear to be consistent with an entrepreneurial legal process since, unlike solicitation, it does not fly in the face of the assumptions of voluntariness and rationality in the entrepreneurial decision-making model. But then it is also arguable that even active solicitation does not disturb *assumptions* of voluntariness and rationality. Honest advertising and solicitation of all kinds are usually understood as consistent with a market economy.

entice private citizens to bring suits, such as treble damages in private antitrust actions, might entice attorneys to solicit business. Insofar as attorneys create their own business through solicitation, they in effect become private prosecutors, diluting the purity of the legal market. The legal doctrine of "standing" is another device that buttresses the entrepreneurial organization of law. This doctrine holds that before parties may complain in lawsuits, they must show that their interests are directly affected in the matters at issue. Here it is uninvolved citizens rather than attorneys who are barred from influencing the mobilization of law, again protecting the purity of the legal market.

There are few mechanisms, however, to accommodate citizens who have occasion to mobilize law. This is not surprising, since, like any entrepreneurial process, a reactive legal system assumes that those wanting to pursue their interests are able to do so.

LIMITS ON LEGAL AVAILABILITY

The cost of litigation is a widely recognized limitation on the availability of private law. While services such as legal-aid programs and small-claims courts have been established to reduce the financial burden for low-income citizens, the fact remains that the ability of citizens to pursue their legal interests often is affected by their wealth. In the criminal-law domain, on the other hand, the quality of legal representation does not depend upon a complainant's wealth. This is not to deny that wealthy and socially prominent complainants may receive better service from the public authorities, a form of discrimination in their behalf. But criminal justice is not organized so that wealthy complainants can secure better attorneys in court, since all complainants are represented by a public prosecutor.

A variety of other circumstances can also lessen the availability of law, whether public or private, for some segments of the community. Sheer physical proximity to legal institutions can be a highly significant factor in premodern legal systems, owing to the meager communication and transportation systems in these societies. In nineteenth-century China, for example, the farther complainants lived from a court, the less likely it was that they could pursue their cases. This was especially noticeable in civil matters, but it was also true in criminal matters. If the plaintiff resided in a city containing a court, his or her civil suit would reach a final disposition in 60% of the cases, while the corresponding figure was only 20% for plaintiffs living 71 to 80 li, or roughly 24 to 27 miles, away (Buxbaum, 1971:274–275). Some modernizing nations now employ so-called popular tribunals at the neighborhood level, thereby providing law to the common people and, at the same time, a mechanism of social integration important to the modernization process itself. Other premodern societies, however, are characterized by a high degree of legal availability. In seventeenth-century Massachusetts, for instance, each town had its own court of general jurisdiction, easily accessible to all. In fact, the ease of access to these courts seemingly tempted the citizenry to great litigiousness, resulting in a high rate of trivial, unfounded, and vexatious suits (Haskins, 1960:212–213), whereas back home in England the law had not been nearly so available to the common people. In tribal societies the availability of law also tends to be quite high.

Another force that sometimes interferes with the operation of a reactive legal process is a countervailing normative system: Informal norms among some pockets of the citizenry prohibit citizens from mobilizing the official control system. Generally it seems that people are discouraged from mobilizing social-control systems against their status equals. With respect to the police, for instance, some citizens are subject among their peers to norms against "squealing" or "ratting." This morality appears rather clearly in the American black subculture. We also see strong antimobilization norms in total institutions such as prisons, concentration camps, mental hospitals, and basic training camps in the military. Similarly, these norms appear among the indigenous population in colonial societies, in schools, and in factories. Even in the traditional family, children enforce a rule against "tattling." Antimobilization norms seem to be particularly strong among the rank and file wherever there is a fairly clear split in the authority structure of a social system.[12]

In light of the foregoing, we may propose that *whenever there is comparatively open conflict between an authority system and those subject to it, reactive legal systems will tend toward desuetude and there will be pressure for greater use of the proactive control strategy.* We should therefore expect to find that governments disproportionately adopt proactive systems of legal mobilization when a social-control problem primarily involves the bottom of the social-class system. It appears, for instance, that the emergence of a proactive police in early nineteenth-century England reflected the elite's fear of growing class consciousness among the lower orders (see Silver, 1967). In cross-national perspective, we see that police authority and political power are generally concentrated at the same points and that every police system is to some extent an instrument of political control. This is especially noticeable in the underdeveloped world; in most of Asia, Africa, and the Middle East the roots of proactive police systems are to be found in earlier colonial policies (see Bayley, 1971). Similarly, it appears that proactive control in republican Rome was routinely exercised only upon slaves and that urban throng sometimes known as the riffraff (Lintott, 1968:102, 196). The common forms of legal misconduct in which upper-status

---

12. While I am emphasizing here the role of *informal* norms against the mobilization of law, it might be noted that one of the hallmarks of social oppression is a formal incapacity to mobilize the law. For instance, in early medieval England a woman could not bring a felony complaint unless the crime of which she complained was violence to her own person or the killing of her husband. Women were excluded from other aspects of the legal process as well, such as jury service, with the result at that time that they were largely unable to give evidence (Pollock and Maitland, 1898:Volume 1, 484–485).

citizens indulge, such as breach of contract and warranty, civil negligence, and various forms of trust violation and corruption, are usually left to the gentler hand of a reactive mobilization process.

In theory law is available to all. In fact, the availability of law is in every legal system greater for the citizenry of higher social status, while the imposition of law tends to be reserved for those at the bottom. Thus, the mobilization of law, like every legal process, reflects and perpetuates systems of social stratification. In contemporary Western society the availability of law is nevertheless greater for the mass of citizens than in any previous historical period, and the trend is toward ever greater availability. And yet it appears that the scope and depth of legal imposition is also greater than ever before.

The Organization of Discretion

Students of law often comment that legal decision-making inevitably allows the legal agent a margin of freedom or discretion. Sometimes this margin does not much exceed the degree of ambiguity inherent in the meaning of the written law, an ambiguity resulting in uncertainty about how the law will be interpreted under variable factual circumstances. Because of this ambiguity and factual variability, a degree of slippage is unavoidable in legal reasoning (Levi, 1948). Sometimes the decision maker's margin of freedom is so great, as in much of administrative law, that more of the person than the law determines the decisions made (see Davis, 1969).

MORAL DIVERSITY

The organization of a legal system allocates the discretion to decide when legal intervention is appropriate. A reactive system places this discretion in the ordinary citizen rather than in a legal official. This has far-reaching consequences for legal control. It allows the moral standards of the citizenry to affect the input of cases into the legal system. Much of the population's power lies in their ability *not* to invoke the legal process when they are confronted with illegality; this gives them the capacity to participate, however unwittingly, in a pattern of selective law enforcement. Citizens determine for themselves what within their private world is the law's business and what is not; each becomes a kind of legislator beneath the formal surface of legal life.

The anthropologist Paul Bohannan suggests that law functions to "reinstitutionalize" the customary rules of various social institutions, such as the family, religion, and the polity (1965:34–37). According to this view, law is an auxiliary normative mechanism that comes into play to lend needed support to nonlegal rules. This notion of "double institutionalization" is an extension of the older and simpler view that law enforces the common morality. A conception like this may have serious shortcomings as a way of understanding modern legislative and judicial behavior (see Diamond, 1971), but it has some relevance to an analysis of legal mobilization. When citizens call law to action according to their own moral standards, they in effect use law as supplementary support for those standards. The functional relationship between the individual and law is an analogue of the relationship proposed by Bohannan at the level of the total society. But this individual pattern cannot be generalized to the level of the total society, since the moral standards of the citizenry are not homogeneous across social classes, ethnic groups, the races, the sexes, generations, and other such aggregates. On the contrary, the reactive system makes it possible for members of these social segments and enclaves to use law to enforce the rules of their own moral subcultures. From this standpoint, when law is reactive it does present a pattern of double institutionalization, but it is a doubling of multiple institutions, as multiple as the moral subcultures we find in modern society. Thus, law perpetuates the moral diversity in the mass of citizens (for a comment on this pattern in police work, see Black, 1971:1105). This may seem a strange role for some government agencies such as the police and for other predominantly reactive control systems, but the law and morality relationship is very complicated and is bound occasionally to disagree with common sense. In societies characterized by moral heterogeneity, it is only through proactive control that one morality can be imposed on all. [13]

DISCRIMINATION

Discretionary authority often carries with it the possibility of particularistic law enforcement or, more simply, discrimination. From a sociological standpoint, legal discrimination provides an interesting problem in the relation between law and social stratification. The liberal fear of a proactive legal system has long been part of a fear of discriminatory enforcement. But whether a system of mobilization is reactive or proactive does not determine the probability of discriminatory enforcement; rather, it organizes that probability. A reactive system deprives state officials of the opportunity to invoke the law according to their own prejudices, but it creates that opportunity for the average citizen. When a legal system is brought into operation by citizen demands, its direction follows the whims of the unmonitored population, whether they are universalistic or not. Each citizen has the discretionary power to decide which people, of those who

---

13. Proactive control sometimes emerges under conditions of moral diversity in a population and serves to integrate the larger system. The same may be said of law itself (see Fortes and Evans-Pritchard, 1940). Proactive law seems particularly likely to arise when moral diversity in a population includes a high degree of normative conflict among the diverse elements, as we see, for instance, among tribal and ethnic groups in new nations. We might go further and suggest that normative conflict is an important predictor of authoritarian law in general.

are legally vulnerable, deserve official attention. The white citizen has the power to be more lenient toward the white than the black, and vice versa; the bourgeois can discriminate against the bohemian, the older against the younger, the rich against the poor. Even if we assume, *arguendo,* that citizens do what their consciences dictate, what they think is right, the aggregative result of all these individual decisions surely distributes legal jeopardy unequally across the population of law violators, especially when we consider decisions *not* to mobilize the law (Black, 1970:739). The possibilities of government surveillance over this kind of discrimination seem minimal. Reactive mobilization is no more accessible to surveillance than many of the illegal acts in private settings that a reactive system uncovers. The amenability of a proactive legal system to surveillance and control is far greater, if only because a proactive system by its nature involves an organizational base that can be penetrated. Proactive control is itself subject to proactive control while reactive control is dispersed in the citizen mass and is therefore extraordinarily difficult to reach. In short, patterns of legal discrimination in reactive systems—the more democratic form of legal process—are more elusive, and consequently they are more intransigent than are similar patterns in proactive mobilization systems.[14] And yet it remains likely that a government-initiated mobilization system contributes more to the maintenance of the existing forms of social stratification than does a system geared to the demands of the citizenry. Discriminatory decision making by citizens to a degree cancels itself out in the citizen mass, while discriminatory behavior by legal officials mirrors their own biases, and these are apt to flow in only one direction.

Besides accommodating discrimination by citizens, a reactive legal system permits individuals to expropriate law for functions that lawmakers may never have anticipated. People may mobilize law in order to bankrupt or destroy the reputations of their competitors (see, e.g., Cohn, 1959), to delay transfers of property or payments of debts (see, e.g., Lev, 1971:64), or for revenge (see, e.g., Mileski, 1971b:66–68). Within the limits imposed by law itself and legal officials, then, the discretion accorded to citizens by a reactive control process lets them do with law what they will, with little concern for the long-range social results.[15]

---

14. Just as it organizes the possibility of discrimination and its control, a system of mobilization organizes the possibility of legal corruption. We discover corruption, like discrimination, where it is easier to control, namely, in proactive systems of law enforcement. In police work, for example, we hear about corruption in vice control and traffic control rather than at the level of the citizen complainant, where it is probably most frequent.

15. The diverse input of requests made upon reactive legal processes can teach much about the internal dynamics of a community. We learn about aspects of male–female interaction, for instance, by looking at who brings whom to court (see Nader, 1964). Likewise, the fact that citizens implicate the police in so many noncriminal disputes suggests that American urban life lacks the battery of extralegal mechanisms of dispute settlement often seen among preliterate peoples. The police find themselves playing conciliatory as well as adversarial roles in dispute settlement (see Chapter 5 of the

Legal Change

Students of legal change have traditionally occupied themselves with changes in the substance of legal rules. Legal scholars have paid particular attention to changes in legal rules occurring by accretion in the judicial decision making process (e.g., Holmes, 1881; Cardozo, 1921; 1924; Levi, 1948), whereas recent work in social science has been concerned more with legislative change (e.g., Gusfield, 1963; Mayhew, 1968; Lemert, 1970). There has also been some interest in changes in legal organization (e.g., Weber, 1925; Schwartz and Miller, 1964; Moore, 1970). Yet in modern societies nearly every aspect of legal life is in a state of flux. Apart from changes in legal rules and organization, continuous shifts are taking place in the kinds and rates of cases that enter the legal process through mobilization, in modes and patterns of disposition, in legal personnel, and in the interchange between legal control and other aspects of social life, such as status hierarchies, informal control mechanisms, the cultural sphere, political movements, and, as Durkheim noted (1893), the ever increasing degree of social differentiation.

MORAL CHANGE

As changes occur in the kinds of legal problems citizens have, and in their definitions of legal problems as such, changes follow in the workload of a legal system organized to respond to the citizenry.[16] A reactive system by its nature absorbs every such change that comes about in the population.[17] The police, for example, who are notorious for their conservatism, will nonetheless change their workload to adapt to moral changes in the citizenry. Because they are organized to respond to citizen calls for service, they are organized for change, and they are organized to provide different police services to the various segments of the population. Hence, whatever the police attitude toward the status quo may be, the citizen-based mobilization process renders them eminently pliable.

The legal work that government officials do on their own initiative is not

---

present volume). These roles are sometimes wholly differentiated in tribal societies (see, e.g., Gibbs, 1963).

Like reactive control, systems of proactive mobilization can be put to a variety of uses. These may be public or private. A proactive enforcement campaign, for example, can augment the government treasury through the collection of fines, such as traffic fines, or it can advance or subvert the interests of political figures or political organizations, as is sometimes seen in vice crackdowns and corruption scandals.

16. I make no assumption that citizens will see their own problems as those problems are defined by law, nor that they will necessarily be willing or able to act upon what they experience as their problems. When they do act upon their grievances, however, the reactive system can listen in a way that the proactive system cannot.

17. It has been suggested that democratic organization in general—of which the reactive system is an instance—is especially suited to accommodate social change (Bennis and Slater, 1968:4).

nearly so adaptable to the felt needs of citizens. Although citizens can and often do affect the course of proactive legal work by a kind of lobbying, the fact remains that it is possible for attitudes of officials that may not be shared by many or even most citizens to influence the selection of cases. A proactive system therefore displays a potential rigidity under conditions of moral change in the citizen population. Beyond its potential rigidity, a proactive control process can aggressively enforce a legal policy upon a resistant population, as has been strikingly illustrated by the political police of authoritarian regimes. It is just this kind of aggressiveness that may be essential to the implementation of law in a modernizing society, where the population is likely to be legally flaccid or apathetic, if not hostile, toward official innovations. Still, because there is no mechanism by which the sentiments of the citizenry are routinely recorded or sampled, as we find in reactive systems, it is always difficult to ascertain whether a proactive control process is following, repressing, or leading moral change in the mass of citizens.

PLANNED CHANGE

While a citizen-based system may be more attuned to moral shifts in the population, it may be recalcitrant in the face of attempts at centrally directed planned change. Just as the discretionary authority of citizens in a reactive system creates the possibility of discrimination and provides no sure means of controlling it, so in general the citizenry is beyond the reach of other kinds of intentional legal reform. In a reactive process there is no way to intervene systematically in the selection of incidents for legal disposition; hence, public policy may be redefined and public purpose invisibly attenuated (Selznick, 1969: 228). The proactive system, by comparison, is a willing instrument of planned change, for it is under the authority of the planners themselves.

Questions about legal change again call up the economic analogy. Because the reactive mobilization system is built around an entrepreneurial model, because it operates in accordance with the market for legal services, it registers legal changes just as changes appear in economic markets. The changes do not and cannot arise from a center; they arise by increments throughout the citizen population, following a plan no more tangible than the "invisible hand" of the market. Historical drift can express itself in market behavior, and it can similarly flow through the many channels of a citizen-based mobilization system (see Nader and Yngvesson, 1973:907–908). Proactive mobilization, resembling as it does a social-welfare system, in its pure form involves a central plan with intentional changes and constancies that may or may not take the expressed wishes of the citizenry into account.

Even in a proactive system oriented to the felt needs of the population, individuals may not come forth to make known their wishes, since only in isolation from their fellows are individuals likely to pursue their interests with positive action (see Olson, 1965). In a mobilization system geared to the initiative of citizens, each individual is in fact isolated and must pursue his or her interest, or no one will. Where a government system is concerned, on the other hand, aggregates of individuals typically share concerns realizable through law, but for that very reason individuals by themselves can assume that someone else will look after the legal policies that benefit them. When others use the same calculus, they do not act to influence legal policy either, and the outcome is an unknown relation between the changing interests of the citizenry and the selection of cases through the initiative of the state. Where planned legal change is possible, then, there is no mechanism to learn the felt requirements of the population. Where there is such a mechanism, there is no way to plan.

LEGAL EVOLUTION

Perhaps the clearest trend in legal evolution over the past several centuries has been the increasing role of law as a means of social control, a development closely related to the gradual breakdown of other agencies of control such as the kinship group, the close-knit community, and the religious organization (Pound, 1942). This trend continues along a number of dimensions of the legal world, including the ever greater volume and scope of legislation and adjudication by the state. There almost seems to be an historical drift toward a state monopoly of the exercise of social control (see Diamond, 1971:124).

An examination of the role of mobilization systems in legal evolution shows that this trend is proceeding in part at the bidding of the citizenry. With the continuing dissolution of extralegal social control, these atomized citizens more and more frequently go to the state to help them when they have no one else. One by one these individual citizens draw upon law to solve their personal troubles, although one by one they would probably agree that the larger outcome of their many decisions is an historical crisis. And yet to deprive these individuals of the initiative they now possess may do nothing more than to substitute a plan for what is now unplanned, while their fate would remain the same.

Conclusion

How deviant behavior and disorder come to meet resistance is a problem for investigation, whatever the social context and form of social control. Some societies have managed very well with almost no social control beyond that brought to bear by the complainant and his or her kinfolk (see, e.g., Karsten, 1923:1–32; Evans-Pritchard, 1940:150–191). In others, systems of proactive mobilization emerge and disappear in rhythm with the collectivity's involvement in corporate action; during warfare or a hunt in some earlier societies, proactive control would arise, only to recede during less eventful times. (This was common, for example, among many Indian tribes of North America—see Lowie, 1948). Another pattern occurs in coercive institutions, such as prisons or mental hospitals, where it seems that proactive strategies are used almost exclusively in the everyday maintenance of the official order. At still another extreme are face-to-face encounters among social equals, where social control is more diffuse and there appears a kind of orderly anarchy with no mobilization at all (see Goffman, 1956a). We see variation expressing the texture of life from one setting to the next, and it is apparent that law makes visible a process found in every system of social control.

One kind of scientific advance consists in raising the level of generality at which the empirical world is understood. A relationship once seen as unique is shown to be one of a set; that set may in turn be revealed as a member of a still more general class. My observations on the mobilization of law are very general, since they cut across substantive areas of law, societies, and history. This is both the strength and weakness of the observations. Any reader can find exceptions to the generalizations, and perhaps some overgeneralizations were made as well, where the number or exceptions will eventually overturn the initial formulations. Yet even with this tentativeness, it is useful to point the direction of a still more general level to which we aspire in legal sociology. We may generalize about all of law, again without regard to substance, place, or time, but now also without regard to a particular dimension of the legal process.

What consequences follow when law is arranged reactively so that ordinary citizens can direct its course? What should we expect if law is proactive, the responsibility of government officials alone? These questions have guided my analysis of legal mobilization. Yet citizen participation in legal life is a problem for study not only in the mobilization of law, but also in other legal processes such as legal prescription and legal disposition. The ultimate issue is: How democratic is law? Legal rules and policies may arise at the direction of the citizenry, as by plebiscite or by a representative legislature, or at the direction of state officialdom alone, as by dictum or edict. Like the mobilization of law, the degree to which the prescription of law is democratic, then, varies across legal systems. Likewise, the disposition of law, or dispute settlement, may be more or less democratic, as is clear when we compare, for instance, the popular tribunals of some socialist countries (see, e.g., Berman, 1969) to the lower courts of the United States, with their powerful adjudicatory officials (see, e.g., Mileski, 1971a). In modern America, the grand jury and the trial jury are well-known mechanisms by which the citizenry is introduced into legal decision making. A sociological theory of law should tell us what difference such democratic organization makes.

Patterns in the mobilization of law suggest several propositions about democratic law in general. Consider, for example, the following:

1. *The more democratic a legal system, the more it perpetuates the existing morality of the population.* Democratic law perpetuates moral diversity as well as moral homogeneity among the citizenry.
2. *The more democratic a legal system, the more the citizenry perpetuates the existing system of social stratification.* Where law is democratic, legal discrimination is practiced by citizens more than by government officials and is therefore more difficult to detect and eliminate.
3. *The more democratic a legal system, the more law reflects moral and other social change among the citizenry.* Democratic law accommodates social change by historical drift more than planned change.

These propositions about democratic law are preliminary and in need of much refinement. But primitive propositions of this kind give us a necessary starting place. With each unexplained exception comes the possibility of creative reformulation, the heart of theoretical development. With each successful application we have the satisfaction of explanation, even as unsophisticated as it may presently be.

Production of Crime Rates*

3

Sociological approaches to official crime rates generally fail to make problematic the production of the rates themselves. Theory has not directed inquiry to the principles and mechanisms by which some technically illegal acts are recorded in the official ledger of crime while others are not. Instead, crime rates ordinarily are put to use as data in the service of broader investigations of deviance and social control. Yet at the same time it has long been taken for granted that official statistics are not an accurate measure of legally defined crime in a community (e.g., Beaumont and Tocqueville, 1833; Morrison, 1897; Sellin, 1931).

The major uses of official crime statistics have taken two forms (see Biderman and Reiss, 1967); each involves a different social epistemology, a different way of structuring knowledge about crime. One employs official statistics as an index of the "actual" or "real" volume and morphology of criminal deviance in the population. Those following this approach typically consider the lack of fit between official and actual rates of crime to be a methodological misfortune. In any event, the measurement of crime has long been the dominant function of crime rates in social science. The second major use of official statistics abandons the search for "actual" deviance, either by defining deviance with the official

*This chapter is reprinted with minor revision from the *American Sociological Review* 35 (August, 1970):733–748.

The findings presented in this chapter derive from the larger project described in the Preface to the present volume. This project was supported by Grant Award 006, Office of Law Enforcement Assistance, U.S. Department of Justice, under the Law Enforcement Assistance Act of 1965. Other grants were awarded by the National Science Foundation and the Russell Sage Foundation. Preparation of this paper was facilitated by the Russell Sage Program in Law and Social Science at Yale Law School.

The author is indebted to the following individuals for their constructive suggestions: Sheldon Ekland-Olson, Abraham S. Goldstein, Maureen Mileski, Albert J. Reiss, Jr., and Stanton Wheeler.

reactions themselves—a labeling approach—or by incorporating the official rates not as an index of deviant behavior but as an index of social control (e.g., Kitsuse and Cicourel, 1963; Erikson, 1966; Wilson, 1968). In effect, this second range of work investigates "actual" social control rather than "actual" deviance. It thus encounters methodological problems of its own, since, without question, social-control agencies do not record all of their official attempts to counteract or contain what they regard as deviant conduct.[1] A striking feature of police work, for instance, is the degree to which officers operate with informal tactics, such as harassment and manipulative human-relations techniques, when they confront law-violative behavior (e.g., La Fave, 1965; Skolnick, 1966; Bittner, 1967b; Black, 1968; Black and Reiss, 1970). In sum, when official statistics are used as a means of measurement and analysis, they usually function imperfectly. This is not to deny that such methods can be highly rewarding in some contexts.

The present analysis employs an alternative strategy that arises from an alternative conceptual starting point. It makes official records of crime an end rather than a means of study (see Wheeler, 1967; Cicourel, 1968:26–28). It treats the crime rate as itself a social fact, an empirical phenomenon with its own existential integrity. A crime rate is not an epiphenomenon. It is part of the natural world. From this standpoint, crime statistics are not evaluated as inaccurate or unreliable. They are an aspect of social organization and cannot, sociologically, be wrong. From a perspective of this kind, it nevertheless remains interesting that social-control systems process more than they report in official statistics, and that there is a good deal more deviant behavior than that which is processed. These patterns are themselves analytically relevant aspects of crime rates.

An official crime rate may be understood as a rate of socially recognized deviant behavior.[2] Deviance rates in this sense are produced by all social-control systems that respond on a case-by-case basis to sanctionable conduct. This is not to say, however, that deviant behavior as a general category is synonymous with socially recognized deviant behavior. As a general category, deviance may be defined as any behavior in a *class* for which there is a *probability* of negative sanction subsequent to its detection (Black and Reiss, 1970:63–64). Whether or not an agent of social control detects or sanctions a particular instance of conduct is thus immaterial to the issue of whether or not it is deviant: Deviance is

---

1. An approach that operationally defines criminal deviance as that which the police record as criminal—and nothing else—is immune to these problems. This would be the most radical "labeling" approach. It would exclude from the category of crime, for example, a murder carried out so skillfully that it goes undetected. It would also necessarily exclude most "police brutality," since crimes committed by the police are seldom detected and officially recorded as such.

2. In his definition of law, Hoebel (1954:28) notes that the enforcement of law is a "socially recognized" privilege. In the same vein, a crime rate may be understood as a socially recognized product of law enforcement work.

Malinowski (1926:79–80) was among the first to stress the importance of the social recognition of deviant acts for the community as well as for the deviant person.

behavior that is *vulnerable* to social control. This approach generates three empirical types of deviance: *(a)* undetected deviance; *(b)* detected, unsanctioned deviance; and *(c)* sanctioned deviance. It should be apparent that, while every social-control system may produce a rate of socially recognized deviance, much unrecognized deviance surely resides in every social system.[3] By definition, undetected deviance cannot be recognized as such, whereas sanctioned deviance presumes that a social recognition process has taken place. The concept of social recognition of deviance is simply a more abstract way of stating what we mean by expressions such as invocation of the law, hue and cry, bringing a suit, blowing the whistle, and so forth. The concept of deviance should always be applied with reference to specific systems of social control, since different systems may respond to conduct in different ways. For example, deviance that is undetected from the standpoint of a formal legal-control system such as the police may be detected or even sanctioned in an informal control system such as a business organization, neighborhood or friendship group, or family. Accordingly, crime rates are rates of deviance socially recognized by official agencies of criminal-law enforcement. They are official rates of *detection* ("crimes known to the police") and of *sanctioning* (arrest rates and conviction rates).[4] The following analysis explores some of the conditions under which police officers produce official rates of crime detection in field encounters with citizens.

The Social Organization of Crime Detection

Detection of deviance involves *(a)* the discovery of deviant acts or behavior; and *(b)* the linking of persons or groups to those acts. Types of deviance vary widely according to the extent to which either or both of these aspects of detection are probable. Thus, some deviant acts are unlikely to be discovered, although discovery generally is equivalent to the detection of the deviant person as well. Examples are homosexual conduct and various other forms of consensual sexual deviance. Acts of burglary and auto theft, by contrast, are readily detected, but the offending persons often are not apprehended. These differential detection

---

3. The moral and physical organization of social life into public and private places guarantees contemporary society some volume of secret deviance (Schwartz, 1968; Lofland, 1969:62–68). As far as criminal deviance is concerned, other well-known factors are the failure of citizens to report victimizations to the police and the failure of the police to report what is reported to them.

Evidence from victimization surveys suggests that underreporting of crime in official statistics is more a consequence of police discretion than of the failure of citizens to notify the police: Citizens claim that they report far more crimes to the police than the police ultimately report, and this margin of unreported crime exceeds that which citizens admit they withhold from the police (Biderman, 1967).

4. The "clearance rate" is a hybrid form of crime rate produced in American police systems. It refers to the proportion of "crimes known to the police" that have been solved, whether through arrest or some other means (see Skolnick, 1966:164–181).

probabilities stem in part from the empirical patterns by which various forms of violative behavior occur in time and social space. In part they stem as well from the uneven climate of social control.

The organization of police control lodges the primary responsibility for crime detection in the citizenry rather than in the police. The uniformed patrol division, the major line unit of modern police departments, is geared to respond to citizen calls for help via a centralized radio-communications system, and, apart from traffic violations, patrol officers detect comparatively little crime through their own initiative. This is all the more true of legally serious crime. Hence, crime detection may be understood as a largely *reactive* process from the standpoint of the police as a social-control system. Far less is it a *proactive* process. (See Chapter 2 of the present volume.) Proactive operations aimed at the discovery of criminal behavior predominate in the specialized units of a large police department, particularly in the vice or morals division (including the narcotics squad) and in the traffic division. But most crimes, unlike vice offenses, are not susceptible to detection by means of undercover work or the enlistment of quasi-employed informers (see Skolnick, 1966). Unlike traffic offenses, furthermore, most crimes cannot be discovered through the surveillance of public places. Since the typical criminal act occurs at a specifically unpredictable time and place, the police must rely upon citizens to involve them in the average case. The law of privacy is another factor that presses the police toward a reactive detection system (Stinchcombe, 1963), but even without legal limitations on police detective work the unpredictability of crime itself would usually render the police ignorant in the absence of citizens. Most often the citizen who calls the police is a victim of a crime who seeks justice in the role of complainant.

Vice control and traffic enforcement generally operate without the assistance of complainants. It appears that most proactive police work arises when there is community pressure for police action but where, routinely, there are no complainants involved as victims in the situations of violative behavior in question. In the average case, moreover, proactive detection involves a simultaneous detection of the violative act and of the violative person. Proactively produced crime rates are therefore nearly always rates of arrest rather than rates of known criminal acts, so that the proactive clearance rate is, in effect, 100%. It might be added that crime rates produced in proactive police operations, such as rates of arrest for prostitution, gambling, homosexual behavior, and narcotics violation, directly correlate with police manpower allocation. Until a point of total detection is reached (holding all else constant), these vice rates increase as the number of police officers assigned to vice control is increased. On the other hand, the more important variable in rates of "crimes known to the police" is the volume of complaints from citizens.

Rates of known crimes do not, however, perfectly reflect the volume of citizen complaints. A complaint must be given official status in a formal written report before it can enter police statistics, and the report by no means automatically follows receipt of the complaint by the police. In fact, during the present investigation patrol officers wrote official reports in only 64% of the 554 crime situations where a complainant, but no suspect, was present in the field setting. The police decision to give official recognition to a crime ordinarily is an outcome of face-to-face interaction between the police and the complainant rather than a programmed response to a bureaucratic or legal formula. The content and contours of this interaction differentially condition the probability that an official report will be written, much as they condition, in situations where a suspect is present, the probability that an arrest will be made. (See Chapter 4 of the present volume.)

Whether or not an official report is written affects not only the profile of official crime rates; it also determines whether subsequent police investigation of the crime will be undertaken at a later date. Subsequent investigation can occur only when an official report is forwarded to the detective division for further processing, which includes the possibility of an arrest of a suspect. Hence, the rate of detection and sanctioning of deviant *persons* is in part contingent upon whether the detection of deviant *acts* is made official. In this respect justice demands formality in the processing of crimes. The present analysis considers the following conditions as they relate to the probability of an official crime report in police encounters with complainants: the legal seriousness of the alleged crime, the preference of the complainant, the relational distance between the complainant and the absentee suspect, the degree of deference the complainant extends to the police, and the race and social-class status of the complainant.

Field Method

Systematic observation of police–citizen transactions was conducted in Boston, Chicago, and Washington, D.C., during the summer of 1966. Thirty-six observers —persons with law, social science, and police administration backgrounds— recorded observations of routine encounters between uniformed patrol officers and citizens. Observers accompanied patrol officers on all work shifts on all days of the week for 7 weeks in each city. However, the times when police activity is comparatively high (evening shifts, particularly weekend evenings) were given added weight in the sample.

Police precincts were chosen as observation sites in each city. The precincts were selected so as to maximize observation in lower-socioeconomic, high-crime-rate, racially homogeneous residential areas. This was accomplished through the selection of two precincts each in Boston and Chicago and four precincts in Washington, D.C.

The data were recorded in observation forms similar in appearance to interview schedules. (See Appendix B of the present volume.) One form was used for each incident that the police were requested to handle or that they themselves noticed while on patrol. These forms were not filled out in the presence of the police, and, in fact, the officers were told that our research was not concerned with their behavior at all, but only with citizen behavior toward the police and the kinds of problems citizens make for the police. The study thus utilized a degree of systematic deception.

A total of 5713 incidents were observed and recorded. In what follows, however, the statistical base is only 554 cases, roughly one in ten of the total sample. These cases comprise nearly all of the police encounters with complainants in crime situations where no suspect was present in the field situation. They are drawn from the cases that originated with a citizen telephone call to the police, 76% of the total. Excluded are, first, encounters initiated by police officers on their own initiative (13%), since these almost always involve a suspect rather than a complainant (complainants usually must take the initiative to make themselves known to the police). Also excluded are encounters initiated by citizens who walked into a police station to ask for help (6%) or who personally flagged down the police on the street (5%)—both of which have peculiar situational features and should be treated separately. The great majority of citizen calls by telephone are likewise inappropriate for the present sample, since in almost one-third of the cases no citizen is present when the police arrive to handle the complaint, and even when a citizen is present the incident at issue pertains to a noncriminal matter in well over one-half of the cases. When there is a criminal matter, a suspect not infrequently is present, so that the major official outcome possible is arrest rather than a crime report. Finally, the sample excludes cases in which two or more complainants of mixed race or social-class composition participated. It may appear that much has been eliminated, and yet, perhaps surprisingly, what remains is the majority of crime situations that the police handle in response to citizen telephone calls for service. There is no suspect available in 77% of the felonies and in 51% of the misdemeanors that the police handle on account of a complaint by telephone. There is only a complainant. These proportions alone justify a study of police encounters with complainants. In routine police work, indeed, the handling of crime involves the handling of complainants more than criminals.

Legal Seriousness of the Crime

Police encounters with complainants where no suspect is present involve a disproportionately large number of felonies, the legally serious category of crime. This was true of 53% of the cases in the sample of 554. When a suspect is present, with or without a citizen complainant, the great majority of police encounters pertain only to misdemeanors (Black, 1968: Chapters 5–6). In other words, the police arrive at the scene too late to apprehend a suspect in serious crime situations more often than in those of a relatively minor nature.[5] (In police language, felonies more often are "cold.") A moment's reflection upon the empirical patterns by which various crimes are committed reveals why this is so. Some of the more common felonies, such as burglary and auto theft, generally involve stealth and occur when the victim is absent; by the time the crime is discovered, the offender has departed. Other felonies, such as robbery and rape, have a hit-and-run character, such that the police rarely can be notified in time to make an arrest at the crime setting. Misdemeanors, by contrast, are more likely to involve some form of "disturbance of the peace," such as disorderly conduct or drunkenness, crimes that are readily audible or visible to potential complainants and that proceed in time with comparative continuity. In short, properties of the social organization of crime make detection of felony offenders relatively difficult and detection of misdemeanor offenders relatively simple, given detection of the act.[6]

When the offender has left the scene in either felony or misdemeanor situations, however, detection and sanctioning of the offender is precluded unless an official report is written by the police. Not surprisingly, the police are more likely to write these reports in felony than in misdemeanor situations.[7] Reports

---

5. It is interesting to note that in ancient Roman law an offender caught in the act of theft was subject to a more serious punishment than an offender apprehended some time after detection of the theft. In the *Laws of the Twelve Tables* these were called, respectively, "manifest" and "non-manifest" thefts. The same legal principle is found in early Anglo-Saxon and other Germanic codes (Maine, 1861:366–367). It could well be that a similar pattern is found in present-day law-in-action, since what is formal in one legal system is often informal in another.

6. The heavier penalties that the law provides for felonies may compensate for a loss in deterrence that could result from the relatively low rate at which felons are apprehended. Likewise, the law of arrest seemingly compensates for the social organization of crime that gives felons a head start on the police, since in most jurisdictions the police need less evidence in felony than in misdemeanor situations to make a legal arrest without a warrant. By both penalty and procedure, then, the law pursues the felon with a special vengeance.

7. Crime situations were classified as felonies or misdemeanors according to legal criteria. These criteria were applied to the version of the crime that prevailed in the police–citizen encounter. The observation reports required the observer to classify each incident in a detailed list of categories as well as to write a longhand description of each (see Appendix B). The felony–misdemeanor breakdown, however, was made during the coding stage of the investigation.

The major shortcoming of this strategy is that the tabulation allows no gradations of legal seriousness within the felony and misdemeanor categories. This shortcoming was accepted in order to facilitate more elaborate statistical analysis with a minimum of attrition in the number of cases.

It should also be noted that the tabulations do not provide information pertaining to the kind of official reports the police officers actually wrote. Occasionally the police officially characterize a crime with a category that seems incorrect to a legally sophisticated observer, most commonly by reducing its legal seriousness. In addition, there are cases where the officer, sometimes through sheer igno-

were written in 72% of the 312 felonies, but in only 53% of the 242 misdemeanors. It is thus clear that official recognition becomes more likely as the legally defined seriousness of the crime increases. Even so, it remains noteworthy that the police officially disregard one-fourth of the felonies they handle in encounters with complainants. These are not referred to the detective division for investigation, and so the offenders unknowingly receive a kind of pardon.

Now the reader might protest an anlysis that treats as crimes some incidents that the police themselves do not handle as crimes. How can we call an event a law violation when a legal official ignores that very event? This is a definitional problem in the sociology of law as well as in the sociology of deviant behavior and social control. How is a violation of the "law on the books" properly classified if in practice it is not labeled as such? It is easy enough to argue that either of these criteria, the written law or the law-in-action, should alone define the violative behavior in question.

The question, however, is entirely a matter of the usefulness of one definition or another. Here a major aim is to learn something about the process by which the police select for official attention certain technically illegal acts while they bypass others. If we classify as crimes only those acts the police officially recognize as crimes, then what shall we call the remainder? Surely that remainder should be conceptually distinguished from acts that are technically legal and carry no sanctions. For that reason, the present analysis operates with two working categories, *crimes* and *officially recognized crimes,* along with an implicit residual category of non-crimes. Crime differs from other behavior by dint of a probability, the probability that it will be sanctioned in a particular administrative system if it is detected. The written law usually—though not always—is a good index of whether that probability exists. "Dead letter" illegal acts, that is, those virtually never sanctioned, are not classified as crimes in this analysis. Crime as a *general category* consists in a probability of sanction; official recognition in the form of a crime report is one factor that escalates that probability for a *specific instance* of crime. This provides a vocabulary that distinguishes *between crimes* on the basis of how the police relate to them, so that police invocation of the law in the face of a law violation can be treated as empirically and theoretically problematic. By contrast, if we were to define a law violation with invocation of the law, we would be left with the peculiar implication that enforcement of the

---

rance of the law or inattention, increases the legal seriousness of the crime. In one case observed by the author in Detroit, for example, a woman complained that two young men in an automobile had made obscene remarks to her as she walked along the street near her residence. She insisted that she was prepared to press charges. After leaving the scene, the officer filled out an official report, classifying the incident as an "aggravated assault," the felonious level of assault. Before doing so he asked the observer for his opinion as to the proper category. The observer feigned ignorance.

law is total or universal. We would definitionally destroy the possibility of police leniency or even of police discretion in law enforcement.

The Complainant's Preference

Upon arriving at a field setting, the police typically have very little information about what they are going to find. At best they have the crude label assigned to the incident by a dispatcher at the communications center. Over the police radio they hear such descriptions as "a B and E" (breaking and entering, or burglary), "family trouble," "somebody screaming," "a theft report," "a man down" (person lying in a public place, cause unknown), "outside ringer" (burglar alarm ringing), "the boys" (trouble with juveniles), and suchlike. Not infrequently these labels prove to be inaccurate. In any case, police officers find themselves highly dependent upon citizens to assist them in structuring situational reality, and complainants, biased though they may be, serve the police as their primary agents of situational intelligence.

What is more, complainants not infrequently go beyond the role of providing information by seeking to influence the direction of police action. When a suspect is present, the complainant may pressure the police to make an arrest or to be lenient. When there is no available suspect, it becomes a matter of whether the complainant prefers that the crime be handled as an official matter or whether he or she wants it handled informally. Many complainants, however, are quite passive and remain behaviorally neutral: During the observation period the complainant's preference was unclear in 40% of the encounters involving a "cold" felony or misdemeanor. There were 184 felony situations in which the complainant expressed a clear preference, and in 78% of these he or she lobbied for official action. Of the 145 misdemeanor situations where the complainant expressed a clear preference, the proportion favoring official action was 75%, roughly the same proportion as that in felony situations. It therefore seems that complainants are, behaviorally, insensitive to the legal seriousness of crimes when they seek to direct police action.

Police action displays a striking pattern of conformity with the preferences of complainants: In not one case did the police write an official crime report when the complainant manifested a preference for informal action. This pattern seen in legal perspective is particularly interesting, since felony complainants prefer informal action nearly as frequently as misdemeanor complainants. Police conformity with those complainants who do prefer official action, however, is not so symmetrical. In felony situations the police comply by writing an official report in 84% of cases, whereas when the complaint involves a misdemeanor their rate of compliance drops to 64%. The police thus follow the wishes of officially oriented complainants in the majority of encounters, but the majority is somewhat heavier when the occasion is a legally more serious matter. Citizen complainants have much to say about the official recognition of crimes, then, but the law seemingly screens their influence.[8]

Recall that the raw inputs for the official detection rate are generated by the citizenry who call the police. Hence, at two levels the operational influence of citizens gives crime rates a peculiarly democratic character. Here the servant role of the police predominates; the guardian role recedes. Since an offical report is a prerequisite for further police investigation of the crime, this pattern also implies that complainants are operationally endowed with an adjudicatory power: Their preferences can ultimately affect probabilities of arrest, prosecution, and conviction. While the structure of the process is democratic in this sense, it most certainly is not universalistic. The moral standards of complainants vary to some extent across the citizen population, thereby injecting particularism into the production of outcomes. Consequently, there appears a trade-off between democratic process and universalistic enforcement in police work. This is an organizational dilemma not only of the police but of the legal system at large. When the citizenry has the power to direct the invocation of law, it has the power to discriminate among law violators. Moral diversity in the citizen population by itself assures that some discrimination of this kind will occur, regardless of the intentions of individual citizens. When a legal system organizes to follow the demands of the citizenry, it must sacrifice uniformity, since the system responds only to those who call upon it while it ignores illegality that citizens choose to ignore. A legal system that strives for universalistic application of the law, by contrast, must refuse to follow the diverse whims of its atomized citizenry. Only a society of citizens homogeneous in their legal behavior would be able to avoid this dilemma.

---

8. Here two general remarks about analytical strategy seem appropriate. One is that the present approach abdicates the problematics of psychological analysis. The observational study does not provide data on the motives or cognitions of the police or the citizens whose behavior is described. However, the findings on patterns of behavior themselves make prediction of police behavior possible. They also offer opportunities for drawing inferences about the impact of police work and its implications for social organization. Much can be learned about behavior in a social matrix without knowing how it is experienced. The consequences of behavior, moreover, are indifferent to their mental origins.

Secondly, the strategy pursued in this analysis is not sensitive, except in the broadest terms, to the temporal dimension of police–citizen transactions. Thus, simply because the complainant's preference is treated prior to other variables does not mean that it is temporally prior to other aspects of police–citizen interaction. Like the other variables treated in this investigation, the complainant's preference is prior in time only to the final police response.

Relational Distance

Like any other kind of behavior, criminal behavior is located within networks of social organization. One aspect of that social organization consists in the relationship existing between the criminal offender and the complainant prior to a criminal event. They may be related by blood, marriage, friendship, neighborhood, membership in the same community, or whatever. In other words, the adversarial relation that is created by a crime may itself be viewed as it is structured within a wider social frame. The findings in this section permit the conclusion that the probability of official recognition of a crime varies with the relational network in which the crime occurs:[9] The greater the relational distance between citizen adversaries, the greater is the likelihood of official recognition.

Citizen adversaries may be classified according to three levels of relational distance: *(a)* fellow family members; *(b)* friends, neighbors, or acquaintances; and *(c)* strangers. Since the complainant's first speculation generally is that a stranger committed the offense in question, the vast majority of the cases fall into the "stranger" category, though some of these probably would be reclassified into one of the other relational categories if the criminal offender were detected.

Table 3–1 shows that when a complainant expresses a preference for official action the police comply most readily when the adversaries appear to be strangers to one another. They are less likely to comply by writing an official crime report when the adversaries are friends, neighbors, or acquaintances, and they are least likely to give official recognition to the crime when the complainant and suspect are members of the same family. The small number of cases in the "fellow family members" category prohibits comparison between felony and misdemeanor situations, but in the other relational categories this comparison reveals that the police follow the same pattern in the handling of felonies and misdemeanors. With the relational distance between the adversaries held constant, however, the probability of an official report is higher for felony than for misdemeanor situations. The highest probability of an official response occurs when the crime is a felony and the adversaries are strangers to one another (91%); the lowest calculable probability is that for misdemeanors when the adversaries are related by friendship, neighborhood, or acquaintanceship (43%). On the other hand, it appears that relational distance can override the legal seriousness of crimes in

---

9. Hall (1952:318) suggests that the relational distance between the victim and offender may influence the probability of prosecution. The present investigation, following Hall, seeks to predict social-control responses from variations in relational distance.

A different strategy is to predict community organization from the relationships between adversaries who enter the legal system, under the assumption that legal disputes bespeak a relative absence of informal control in the relational contexts where they arise (see Nader, 1964).

TABLE 3–1

Situational Outcome in Police Encounters with Complainants according to Type of Crime and Relational Tie between Citizen Adversaries:[a]

Complainant Prefers Official Action

	Type of Crime and Relational Tie between Citizen Adversaries								
	Felony			Misdemeanor			All Crimes		
Situational Outcome	Family members	Friends, neighbors, acquaintances	Strangers	Family members	Friends, neighbors, acquaintances	Strangers	Family members	Friends, neighbors, acquaintances	Strangers
Official report	(4)	62	91	(3)	43	74	41	51	84
No official report	(5)	38	9	(5)	57	26	59	49	16
Total percent	—	100	100	—	100	100	100	100	100
Total cases	(9)	(16)	(92)	(8)	(23)	(62)	(17)	(39)	(154)

[a] By percent. Figures in parentheses are used whenever the total number of incidents is statistically too small to justify a generalized assertion of rate and for total number of cases.

conditioning police action, since the police are more likely to give official recognition to a misdemeanor involving strangers as adversaries (74%) than to a felony involving friends, neighbors, or acquaintances (62%). Here again, therefore, the law screens but does not direct the impact of an extralegal element in the production of crime rates.

Another implication of these findings lies beyond an understanding of crime rates as such. Because a follow-up investigation of the crime report by the detective division may result in apprehension of the criminal offender, it is apparent that the probability of an official sanction for the offender lessens as the degree of social intimacy with his or her adversary—usually the victim—increases. When an offender victimizes an intimate the police are most apt to let the event remain a private matter, regardless of the complainant's preference. A more general consequence of this pattern of police behavior is that the criminal law gives priority to the protection of strangers from strangers while it leaves vulnerable intimates to intimates. But then victimizations of strangers by strangers may be comparatively more damaging to social order and hence, from a functional standpoint, require more attention from the forces of control. A victimization between intimates is encapsulated by intimacy itself. Furthermore, as social networks are more intimate, it surely is more likely that informal systems of social control operate. Other forms of legal control also may become available in more intimate relationships. In contrast, there is hardly anyone but the police to oversee relations among strangers. Seemingly the criminal law is most likely to be invoked where it is the only operable social-control system. The same may be said of legal control in general (see Pound, 1942; Schwartz, 1954; Nader and Metzger, 1963). Law melds with other aspects of social organization.

The Complainant's Deference

Evidence accumulates that the fate of suspects sometimes hangs upon the degree of deference or respect they extend to the police in field encounters (Westley, 1953; Piliavin and Briar, 1964; Black, 1968; Black and Reiss, 1970). As a rule, the police are especially likely to sanction suspects who fail to defer to police authority, whether legal grounds exist or not. Situational etiquette may thus weigh heavily upon broader processes of social life (see Goffman, 1956b; 1963). This section offers findings showing that deference toward the police conditions the official recognition of crime complaints as well.

The deference of complainants toward the police can be classified into three categories: *(a)* very deferential or very respectful; *(b)* civil; and *(c)* antagonistic or disrespectful. As might be expected, complainants are not often antagonistic toward police officers; it is the suspect who is more likely to be disrespectful (Black and Reiss, 1967:63–65). In fact, the number of cases of police encounters with antagonistic complainants is too few for separate analysis of felony and misdemeanor situations. When felonies and misdemeanors are combined into one statistical base, however, it becomes clear that by a large margin the probability of an official crime report is lowest when the complainant is antagonistic in the face-to-face encounter (see Table 3−2). Less than one-third of the disrespectful complainants who prefer official action see their wishes actualized in a crime report. Because of the small number of cases this finding should be taken as tentative, but the comparison between the very deferential and the civil complainants, which is more firmly grounded, is noteworthy as well: The police are somewhat more likely to comply with very deferential complainants than with those who are merely civil. In sum, then, the less deferential the complainant, the less likely are the police to comply with his or her manifest preference for official action in the form of an official crime report.[10]

Table 3−2 also shows that the complainant's degree of deference conditions crime reporting in both felony and misdemeanor situations. It even seems that the complainant's deference can predict official recognition as well as the legal seriousness of the crime: The probability of a crime report in misdemeanor situations where the complainant is very deferential (85%) is higher than it is in felony situations where he or she is only civil toward the police (80%). Still, when we hold constant the complainant's deference, the legal seriousness of the incident looms to importance. In felony situations where the complainant is very respectful, the police satisfy his or her preference for official action in no less than 100% of the cases.

The findings in this section reveal that the level of citizen respect for the police in field encounters has consequences beyond those known to operate in the

---

10. The findings in this section present a problem of interpretation, since no information about the police officer's behavior toward the citizen is provided apart from whether or not he wrote an official report. Therefore, nothing is known from the tabulation about whether the officer behaved in such a way as to *provoke* the citizen into one or another degree of deference. Nothing is known about the subtle exchange of cues that takes place in any instance of face-to-face interaction. Other studies of the role of deference in police work are subject to the same criticism. Although in this analysis no inquiry is made into the motivational dimensions of the pattern, it should be emphasized that whatever the motivation for the complainant's behavior may have been, it was not the failure of the police to write an official report. The complainant ordinarily did not even know whether or not an official report was written, since the officers ordinarily wrote the report in the police car or at the police station after leaving the encounter with the complainant. During the encounter itself they recorded the relevant facts about the incident in a notebook, whether or not they intended to write an official report. As some officers say, they do this "for show" in order to lead the complainant to believe that they are "doing something." Thus, in the average case, it can be assumed that the complainant's deference was not a consequence of the anticipated outcome. Furthermore, the observers were instructed to record only the level of citizen deference that appeared prior to the situational outcome. A separate item was provided in the observation booklet for recording the citizen's manifest level of satisfaction at the close of the encounter. It therefore remains plausible that the complainant's deference may aid in calculating the probability of an official crime report.

TABLE 3–2

Situational Outcome in Police Encounters with Complainants according to Type of Crime and Complainant's Degree of Deference:[a] Complainant Prefers Official Action

| | Type of Crime and Complainant's Degree of Deference | | | | | | | | |
| | Felony | | | Misdemeanor | | | All Crimes | | |
Situational Outcome	Very deferential	Civil	Antagonistic	Very deferential	Civil	Antagonistic	Very deferential	Civil	Antagonistic
Official report	100	80	(2)	85	65	(1)	91	73	30
No official report	—	20	(1)	15	35	(6)	9	26	70
Total percent	100	100	—	100	100	—	100	99	100
Total cases	(15)	(127)	(3)	(20)	(79)	(7)	(35)	(206)	(10)

[a] By percent. Figures in parentheses are used whenever the total number of incidents is statistically too small to justify a generalized assertion of rate and for total number of cases.

sanctioning of suspects. We see that the fate of citizens who are nominally served as well as those who are controlled by the police rides in part upon their etiquette. Official crime rates and the justice done through police detection of criminal offenders reflect the politeness of victims, or the situational style in which a citizen presents a complaint. That sanctions are sometimes more severe for alleged offenders who are disrespectful toward the police can be understood in many ways as a possible contribution to the social-control function. Perhaps, for example, disrespectful offenders pose a greater threat to society, since they refuse to extend legitimacy to its legal system. Perhaps deterrence is undermined by leniency toward disrespectful suspects. Perhaps not. The point is that rationales are available for understanding this pattern as it relates to social control by the police. But it should be apparent that such rationales do not apply as readily to the tendency of the police to underreport the victimizations of disrespectful complainants. Surely this pattern could have only the remotest connection to deterrence of illegal behavior. Etiquette, it would seem, can belittle the criminal law.

The Complainant's Status

The literature on police work abounds in speculation but provides little observational evidence concerning the relation of social status to police outcomes. The routine policing of blacks differs somewhat from that of whites, and the policing of blue-collar citizens differs quite massively from that of white-collar citizens. Nevertheless, there is a dearth of evidence that these differences arise from discriminatory behavior by the police. It appears that more consequential in determining these outcomes are aggregative differences between the races and classes in the kinds of incidents the police handle along with situational factors such as those the present analysis examines (see, e.g., Skolnick, 1966; Black, 1968; Black and Reiss, 1970). In any event, the research literature remains far too scanty to permit confident generalization on these questions (but see "Postscript: 1980" at the end of Chapter 4 for a further assessment).

Studies in the discretionary aspects of police work focus almost solely upon police encounters with suspects. In contrast, the present sample provides an opportunity to investigate the relation between a complainant's race and social-class status and the probability that the police will give official recognition to his or her complaint. The tabulation limits the cases to those where complainants express a preference for official action and are civil toward the police. This section concludes that the race of complainants does not independently relate to the production of official crime rates, but there is some evidence that the police give preferential treatment to white-collar complainants.

For all crimes and social-class statuses taken together, the difference between blacks and whites in the probability of an official crime report is slight and negligible (see Table 3–3); it is a bit higher for whites. Table 3–3 also shows that this probability is the same for blue-collar blacks and blue-collar whites in felony situations, though it is comparatively higher for blue-collar blacks in misdemeanor situations. Evidence of racial discrimination thus appears weak and inconsistent. It should nonetheless be noted that if there were consistent evidence of a race differential it is not readily clear to whom a disadvantage could be attributed. Considered from the complainant's standpoint, a higher frequency of police failure to comply with complainants of one race could be viewed as discrimination *against* that race. But police failure to write a crime report also lowers the likelihood that the offender will be subjected to the criminal process. Since we may assume that complainants more commonly are victims of offenses committed by members of their own race than by members of another race (Reiss, 1967), disproportionate failure by the police to comply with complainants could be viewed as discrimination *in favor* of that race, considered from the offender's standpoint. Race differentials in arrest rates for crimes where there is an identifiable victim necessarily pose a similar dilemma of interpretation. In sum, there is always a conflict of legal interests between offenders and victims, and, at the same time, offender–victim relationships tend to be racially homogeneous. The social organization of crime therefore complicates questions of racial discrimination in law enforcement.[11]

Along social-class lines, there is more evidence of discrimination. Table 3–3 shows that in felony situations the police are somewhat more likely to comply with white-collar complainants than with those of blue-collar status. In fact, an official crime report resulted from virtually every encounter between the police and a white-collar felony complainant of either race, whereas the probability of official recognition drops to about three-fourths for blue-collar felony complainants. There does not appear to be a clear social-class differential in misdemeanor situations, however.

Only in felony situations, then, does an inference of discrimination clearly offer itself: The police discriminate against blue-collar complainants. Moreover, when both white-collar and blue-collar complainants report felonious offenses, we should be able to assume that the offenders characteristically are of blue-

---

11. It may seem that in criminal matters the costs are slight for the complainant when the police fail to comply with his or her preference for official action. However, it should be remembered that crimes frequently involve an economic loss for the victim, a loss that can sometimes be recouped if and when the offender is discovered. In other cases, discovery and punishment of the offender may net the victim a sense of revenge or security or a sense that justice has been done—concerns that have received little attention in social science. For that matter, social scientists generally examine questions of discriminatory law enforcement *only* from the offender's standpoint. Ordinary citizens in high-crime-rate areas are probably more interested in questions of discrimination in police allocation of manpower for community protection.

TABLE 3–3

Situational Outcome in Police Encounters with Complainants according to Type of Crime and Complainant's Social-Class Status and Race:[a]
Complainant Prefers Official Action and Is Civil toward Police

Type of Crime and Complainant's Social-Class Status and Race

Situational Outcome	Felony						Misdemeanor						All Crimes and Classes	
	Blue-collar		White-collar		Class Unknown		Blue-collar		White-collar		Class Unknown			
	Black	White	Black	White	Black	White	Black	White	Black	White	Black	White	Black	White
Official report	77	77	(5)	100	(3)	90	69	55	(2)	64	(2)	80	72	76
No official report	23	23	—	—	(5)	10	31	45	—	36	(3)	20	28	24
Total percent	100	100	—	100	—	100	100	100	—	100	—	100	100	100
Total cases	(64)	(22)	(5)	(18)	(8)	(10)	(26)	(22)	(2)	(14)	(5)	(10)	(110)	(96)

[a] By percent. Figures in parentheses are used whenever the total number of incidents is statistically too small to justify a generalized assertion of rate and for total number of cases.

collar status. There is every reason to believe, after all, that white-collar citizens rarely commit the common felonies such as burglary, robbery, and aggravated assault. (A possible exception is auto theft, a crime in which youths from white-collar families occasionally indulge.) Since this study was conducted in predominantly blue-collar residential areas, the assumption of blue-collar offenders should be all the more warranted. It would follow that the police discriminate against blue-collar citizens who feloniously offend white-collar citizens by being comparatively lenient in the investigation of felonies committed by one blue-collar citizen against another. Here then is an instance in which the legal system listens more attentively to the claims of higher-status citizens. The pattern is recorded in the crime rate, underestimating the number of offenses against people of lower status.

Conclusion

The foregoing analysis yields a number of empirical generalizations about the production of crime rates. For the sake for convenience, they may be listed as follows:

1. *The police officially recognize proportionately more legally serious crimes than legally minor crimes.*
2. *The complainant's manifest preference for police action has a significant effect upon official crime reporting.*
3. *The greater the relational distance between the complainant and the suspect, the greater is the likelihood of official recognition of the complaint.*
4. *The more deferential the complainant toward the police, the greater is the likelihood of official recognition of the complaint.*
5. *There is no evidence of racial discrimination in crime reporting.*
6. *There is evidence that the police discriminate in favor of white-collar complainants in the official recognition of legally serious crimes.*

On the surface, these findings have direct methodological relevance for those who would put official statistics to use as empirical data, whether to index actual crime in the population or to index actual police practices. Crime rates, as data, systematically underrepresent much crime and much police work. To learn some of the patterns by which this selection process occurs is to acquire a means of improving the utility of crime rates as data.

It should again be emphasized that these patterns of police behavior have consequences not only for official rates of detection as such; they also result in differential investigation of crimes and hence differential probabilities of arrest, prosecution, and conviction of criminal offenders. In other words, the life chances of criminal violators partly depend upon who their victims are and how their victims present their claims—as complainants—to the police. The role of the complainant in the criminal process is thus appreciable. Surely the complainant has a central place in other kinds of legal and nonlegal social control as well, though there is as yet little research on the topic. Complainants are the consumers of justice. They are the prime movers of every legal system, the human mechanisms by which legal services are routed into situations where there is a felt need for law. Complainants are the most invisible and they may be the most important social force binding law to other aspects of social organization.

The Social Organization
of Arrest*
4

This chapter offers a set of descriptive materials on the social conditions under which police officers make arrests in routine encounters. At this level, it is a modest increment in the expanding literature on the law's empirical face. A considerable body of scholarship on the law in action has concentrated upon the criminal law in general and the world of the police in particular (see generally Skolnick, 1965; Bordua and Reiss, 1967; Schur, 1968; Manning, 1972), but what these studies will yield beyond the mere hoarding of facts is still unclear. Perhaps a degree of planned change in the criminal-justice system will follow, be it in legal doctrine or in legal administration. In any event, evaluation appears to be the purpose, and reform the expected outcome, of much empirical research. The present chapter pursues a different sort of yield from its findings: a contribution to the sociological theory of law.[1] Hence, the analysis is self-consciously inattentive to policy reform or evaluation of the police; it is intentionally bloodless in tone. It examines arrest in order to infer patterns relevant to an understanding of all instances of legal control.

The empirical analysis queries how a number of circumstances affect the

*This chapter is reprinted with minor revision from the *Stanford Law Review* 23 (June, 1971): 1087–1111.

Comments on the essay in its original form were made by David J. Bordua, John Griffiths, Michael E. Libonati, Maureen Mileski, Albert J. Reiss, Jr., and Stanton Wheeler.

The findings presented in this chapter derive from the larger project described in the Preface and in Chapter 3 of the present volume.

1. It should be noted that the approach taken here differs radically from the strategy of Philip Selznick, an influential American sociologist of law who attempts to follow the path of natural law. Instead, the approach in this essay seeks to follow the general direction of positivism, or the conventional philosophy of science. In Lon Fuller's language (1940), Selznick is willing to tolerate a confusion of the *is* and *ought,* while I am not (see Selznick, 1961; 1968; 1969).

probability of arrest. The factors considered are the suspect's race, the legal seriousness of the alleged crime, the evidence available in the field setting, the complainant's preference, the social relationship between the complainant and suspect, the suspect's degree of deference toward the police, and the manner in which the police come to handle an incident, whether in response to a citizen's request or through their own initiative. The inquiry seeks to discover general principles according to which police officers routinely use or withhold their power to arrest, and thus to reveal a part of the social organization of arrest.[2]

The chapter begins with a brief ethnography of routine police work, designed to place arrest within its mundane context. Next the findings on arrest are presented, first for police encounters involving both a complainant and a suspect, and then for encounters with lone suspects. The essay closes with some speculations about the relevance of the empirical findings at the level of a general theory of legal control, the focus shifting from a sociology of the police to a sociology of law.

Routine Police Work

As a subject of study, arrest may easily misrepresent the reality of routine police work. Too often the routine is equated with the exercise of the arrest power, not only by members of the general public but also by lawyers and even many police officers. In fact, however, the daily round of the patrol officer—the subject of this chapter—infrequently involves arrest[3] or even contact with a criminal suspect. The most cursory observation of patrol officers on the job overturns the imagery of people who make their living parceling citizens into jail.

Modern police departments are geared to respond to citizen calls for service. The great majority of incidents the police handle arise when a citizen telephones the police and the dispatcher sends a patrol car to deal with the situation. Officers thereby become implicated in a wide range of human troubles, most not of their own choosing, and many of which have little or nothing to do with criminal-law enforcement. They transport people to the hospital, write reports of auto accidents, and arbitrate and mediate between disputants—neighbors, husbands and wives, landlords and tenants, businesspeople and customers (see Chapter 5 of the

---

2. As used in this chapter, the broad concept of "social organization" refers to the supraindividual principles and mechanisms according to which social events come into being, are maintained and arranged, change, and go out of existence. Put another way, social organization refers to the descriptive grammar of social events.

3. In the present study "arrest" refers only to transportation of a suspect to a police station. It does not include the application of constraint in field settings, and it does not require formal booking of a suspect with a crime (see La Fave, 1965).

present volume). They take missing-person reports, direct traffic, control crowds at fires, write dogbite reports, and identify abandoned autos. They remove safety hazards from the streets, and occasionally scoop up a dead animal. The police disdain this kind of work, but they do it every day. Such incidents rarely result in arrest, and yet they comprise nearly half of the incidents uniformed patrol officers encounter in situations initiated by phone calls from citizens (Black, 1968:51– 57; see also Cumming, Cumming, and Edell, 1965). Patrol officers also spend much of their time with "juvenile trouble," a policy category typically pertaining to distinctively youthful disturbances of adult peace—noisy groups of teenagers on a street corner, ball playing in the street, trespassing or playing in deserted buildings or construction sites, and rock throwing. These situations, too, rarely result in arrest. In fact, some officers view the handling of juvenile trouble merely as work they do in the service of neighborhood grouches. The same may be said of the ticketing of parking violations in answer to citizen complaints. It might be added that all of these chores necessitate much unexciting paperwork.

Somewhat less than half of the encounters arising from a citizen telephone call have to do with a crime—a felony or a misdemeanor other than juvenile trouble. Yet even criminal incidents are so constituted situationally as to preclude arrest in the majority of cases, since in most no suspect is present when the police arrive at the scene. In 77% of the felony situations and in 51% of the misdemeanor situations the only major citizen participant is a complainant (Black, 1970:737). In a handful of other cases the only citizen present is an informant or bystander. When no suspect is available in the field setting, the major official outcome that is possible is a crime report, the basic document from which official crime statistics are constructed and the operational prerequisite of further investigation by the detective division (see Chapter 3 of the present volume for an analysis of these cases). Only that minority of citizen-initiated encounters where a suspect is present when the police arrive is the appropriate base for a study of arrest, then, and in the great majority of these a citizen complainant takes part as well. Hence, any study of routine arrest must consider the complainant's role as well as those of the police officer and the suspect.[4]

Patrol officers occasionally initiate encounters on their own authority as well. This is *proactive* police work, as opposed to the *reactive*, citizen-initiated work that consumes the greater part of the average patrol officer's day.[5] On an evening shift (traditionally 4 P.M. to midnight), a typical workload for a patrol car is

---

4. In fact, all the felon cases the police handled in response to a citizen request by telephone during the three-city study, only 3% involved a police encounter with a lone suspect (Black, 1968: 94).

5. The concepts "reactive" and "proactive" derive from the study of individual action, the former referring to actions originating in the environment, the latter to those originating within the actor (see Murray, 1951). See Chapter 2 of the present volume for an explication of these concepts and their relevance to the study of legal life.

about six radio-dispatched encounters and one proactive encounter. The ratio of reactive to proactive encounters varies enormously by shift, day of week, patrol territory, and number of cars on duty. An extremely busy weekend night could involve as many as 20 dispatches to a single car, for example, and under these rushed conditions the officers might not initiate a single encounter on their own. At another time in another area a patrol car might receive no dispatches at all, while the officers might initiate as many as eight or ten encounters on the street. During the three-city observation study, only 13% of the incidents came to police attention without the assistance of citizens.[6] Still, most officers as well as citizens probably think of proactive policing as the form that epitomizes the police function.

The police-initiated encounter is a bald confrontation between state and citizen. Hardly ever does a citizen complainant take part in a proactive field encounter, and then only if a police officer were to discover an incident of personal victimization or if a complainant were to step forth subsequent to the officer's initial encounter with a suspect. Moreover, the array of incidents the police handle—their operational jurisdiction—is quite different when they have the discretion to select situations for attention compared to what it is when that discretion is lodged in citizens. In reactive police work they are servants of the public, with one consequence being that the social troubles they oversee often have little if anything to do with criminal law. Arrest is usually a situational impossibility. In proactive policing the officer is more a public guardian, and the operational jurisdiction is a police choice; the only limits are in law and in departmental policy. In proactive police work, therefore, arrest is totally a matter of the officer's own making. Yet the reality of proactive police work has an ironic quality about it: The organization of crime in time and space generally deprives officers on free patrol of legally serious arrests. Most felonies occur in off-street settings and must be detected by citizens, but even those that occur in a visible public place usually escape the officers' ken. When the police do have an opportunity to initiate an encounter, the occasion is more likely than not a traffic violation. Traffic violations comprise the majority of proactive encounters, and most of the remainder concern minor "disturbances of the peace."[7] In short, where the police role is most starkly aggressive in form, the substance is drably trivial, and these legally trivial incidents provide practically all of the grist for arrest in proactive police operations.

Perhaps a study of arrest flatters the legal significance of the everyday police

---

6. This proportion is based upon the total sample of 5713 incidents.

7. Much proactive patrol work involves a drunken or disorderly person. Typically, however, arrest occurs in these cases only when the citizen is uncooperative, often after the officer begins the encounter by giving an order such as "Move on," "Take off," or "Take it easy." Arrest is thus an outcome of interaction rather than a simple and direct response to what the officer first observes.

encounter. Still, even though arrest situations are uncommon in routine policing, invocation of the criminal process accounts for more formal legal cases, more court trials and sanctions, more public controversies and conflicts than any other mechanism in the legal system. As a major occasion of legal control, then, arrest cries out for empirical study.[8]

* * *

Before proceeding, it should be noted that although the observers recorded a total of 5713 incidents, the base for the present analysis is only a little more than 5% of that number. This attrition results primarily from the general absence of opportunities for arrest in patrol work previously discussed. Traffic encounters were excluded as well, even though technically any traffic violation presents an opportunity for arrest. Still other cases were eliminated because they entailed factors that could invisibly distort or confuse the analysis. In this category were those initiated by citizens who walked into a police station to ask for help (6% of the total) or who flagged down the police on the street (5%). These encounters involve peculiar situational features warranting separate treatment. For similar reasons encounters with citizens of mixed race or mixed social-class status were also set aside.[9] Finally, the sample here excludes suspects under 18 years of age—viewed as "juveniles" for these purposes—and suspects of white-collar status.[10] The analysis thus pertains only to patterns of arrest in police encounters with adult suspects, predominantly of blue-collar status.

---

8. Earlier observational studies have neglected patterns of arrest in the everyday work of uniformed patrol officers. Emphasis has instead been placed more upon detective work, vice enforcement, the policing of juveniles, and other more marginal aspects of police work (see, e.g., Piliavin and Briar, 1964; Skolnick, 1966; Bittner, 1967b; Black and Reiss, 1970; but see La Fave, 1965). Several observational studies emphasizing other dimensions of police work also are directly relevant (see Reiss and Black, 1967; Tiffany et al., 1967; Yale Law Journal Editors, 1967a). There have been a number of studies based upon official arrest statistics as well (see Goldman, 1963; Terry, 1967; Wilson, 1968; Green, 1970). For a more speculative discussion, see Goldstein (1960).

9. Hence, encounters involving a complainant and suspect of different races are excluded. Those where a police officer and one or more citizens were of different races, however, are included, though they are not given separate attention in the analysis.

10. Because field observers sometimes had difficulty in judging the age or social class of a citizen, they were told to use a "don't know" category whenever they felt the danger of misclassification. Two broad categories of social class, blue-collar and white-collar, were employed. Since the precincts sampled were predominantly lower- and working-class in composition, the observers labelled the vast majority of the citizen participants as blue-collar in status. In fact, not enough white-collar cases were available for separate analysis. The small number of adults of ambiguous social class were combined with the blue-collar cases into a sample of "predominantly blue-collar" citizens. The observers probably were reasonably accurate in classifying the suspects because the police frequently interviewed such people about their age and occupation.

Complainant and Suspect

The police encounter involving both a suspect and a complainant is a micro-cosm of a total legal system. In it are personified the state, the alleged threat to social order, and the citizenry. Complainants are to police encounters what interest groups are to legislatures or plaintiffs to civil lawsuits. Their presence makes a dramatic difference in police encounters, particularly if they assume the role of situational lobbyists. This section will show, among other things, that the fate of suspects rests nearly as much with complainants as it does with the police officers themselves.

Of the 176 encounters involving both a complainant and a suspect, a little over one-third were alleged to be felonies; the remainder were misdemeanors of one or another variety. Not surprisingly the police make arrests more often in felony than in misdemeanor situations, but the difference is not as wide as might be expected: An arrest occurs in 58% of the felony encounters and in 44% of the misdemeanor encounters. The police thus release roughly one-half of the persons they suspect of crimes. This strikingly low arrest rate requires explanation.[11]

EVIDENCE

Factors other than the evidence available to an officer in the field affect the probability of arrest, for even exceptionally clear situational evidence of criminal liability does not guarantee what the outcome of an encounter will be. One of two major forms of evidence ordinarily is present when the police confront a suspect in the presence of a complainant: Either the police arrive at the setting in time to witness the offense itself, or a citizen—usually the complainant—gives testimony against the suspect. Only rarely is some other kind of evidence available, such as a physical clue on the premises or on the suspect's person. On the other hand, in only three of the complainant–suspect encounters was situational evidence entirely absent. In these few cases the police acted upon what they knew from the original complaint as it was relayed to them by radio dispatch and upon what they heard about the crime from the complainant, but they had no other information apparent in the field situation linking the suspect to the alleged crime.

In a great majority of felony situations the best evidence available to the police is citizen testimony, whereas in misdemeanor situations the officers generally

---

11. At this point a word should be said about the explanatory strategy to be followed in this analysis. The approach is radically behavioral or, more specifically, supramotivational, in that it seeks out supraindividual conditions with which the probability of arrest varies. Implicit in this strategy is a conception of arrest as a social event rather than an individual event. Accordingly, the mental processes of the police and the citizens whose outward behavior our observers recorded are not important to this strategy. The sole aim is to delineate aspects of the social context of arrest as a variety of legal intervention.

witness the offense themselves. These evidentiary circumstances are roughly equivalent as far as the American law of arrest is concerned, since the requirements for a misdemeanor arrest without a formal warrant are more stringent than are those for a felony arrest: In most jurisdictions the police generally must observe the offense or acquire a sworn complaint before they may arrest a misdemeanor suspect in the field, whereas in felony situations they need only have "probable cause" or "reasonable grounds" to believe the suspect is guilty. Thus, though the evidence usually is stronger in misdemeanor than in felony situations, the law in effect compensates the police by giving them more power of arrest in the felony situations, thereby undermining the advantage felons in the aggregate would otherwise enjoy.

Table 4–1 indicates that the police do not use all of the legal power they possess, however. They arrest only slightly over one-half of the felony suspects against whom testimonial evidence is present in the field encounter, although "probable cause" can be assumed to have been satisfied in nearly every such incident. Furthermore, during the observation study the police released two of the six felony suspects they observed in seemingly felonious activity. These two cases

TABLE 4–1

Arrest Rates in Citizen-Initiated Encounters according to Type of Crime and Major Situational Evidence[a]

Crime	Evidence	Total Number of Incidents	Arrest Rate
Felony	Police witness[b]	6	(4)
	Citizen testimony	45	56
	Other evidence	1	(0)
	No evidence	0	(0)
Misdemeanor	Police witness[b]	52	65
	Citizen testimony	39	31
	Other evidence	0	(0)
	No evidence	3	(0)
All crimes[c]	Police witness[b]	58	66
	Citizen testimony	84	44
	Other evidence	1	(0)
	No evidence	3	(0)

[a] By percent. Figures in parentheses are used whenever the total number of incidents is statistically too small to justify a generalized assertion of arrest rate.

[b] This category also includes all cases in which observation of the alleged offense by the police was supplemented by other types of evidence.

[c] This excludes 30 cases for which the observer did not ascertain the character of the evidence. Thus the total is 146 cases.

are noteworthy even though based upon a sample several times smaller than the other samples. In misdemeanor situations, the arrest rate is about two-thirds when the police observe the offense, while it drops to about one-third when the only evidence comes from a citizen's testimony. An evidentiary legal perspective alone, therefore, cannot account for the differentials in arrest practices. On the other hand, evidence is not irrelevant to these differentials. In none of the three cases where no evidence was available did the police make an arrest, and where the legal standing of the police was at best precarious—misdemeanor situations with nothing beyond citizen testimonial evidence—the arrest rate was relatively low.

THE COMPLAINANT'S PREFERENCE

While complainants frequently are present when the police decide not to invoke the law against suspects who are highly vulnerable to arrest, the complainants do not necessarily resent police leniency. In fact, in 24% of the misdemeanor situations and in 21% of the felony situations the complainant expresses to the police a preference for clemency toward the suspect.[12] The complainant manifests a preference for an arrest in 34% of the misdemeanors and in 48% of the felonies. In the remainder of encounters the complainant's preference is unclear; frequently his or her outward behavior is passive, especially in misdemeanor situations.

The findings in Table 4–2 indicate that arrest practices, in both felony and misdemeanor situations, sharply reflect the complainants' preferences, whether they be compassionate or vindictive. In felony situations where a citizen's testimony links a suspect to the crime, arrest results in about three-fourths of the cases in which the complainant specifies a preference for that outcome. When the complainant prefers no arrest, the police go against his or her wishes in only about one-tenth of the cases. Passive or inexpressive complainants see the police arrest suspects in a little under two-thirds of the situations where the police have testimonial evidence. Thus, when the complainant leaves the decision to arrest wholly in police hands, the police are by no means reluctant to arrest the felony suspect. They become noticeably reluctant only when a complainant exerts pressure on the suspect's behalf.

The findings for misdemeanor situations likewise show a high rate of police compliance with the complainant's preference and also demonstrate the relevance of situational evidence to the suspect's fate. Encounters where the complainant outwardly prefers arrest and where the police observe the offense itself

---

12. In such cases a complainant's preference is clear from his or her response to a question posed by the police. When the police did not solicit the complainant's opinion, the observer classified the complainant's preference according to the audible or visible clues available to him. Some complainants made explicit demands upon the police; others appeared more confused and made no attempt to influence the outcome.

TABLE 4-2
*Arrest Rates in Citizen-Initiated Encounters according to Type of Crime,
Major Situational Evidence, and Complainant's Preference*[a]

Evidence	Complainant's Preference	Total Number of Incidents	Arrest Rate
	FELONY		
Police witness	Arrest	2	(1)
	Unclear	4	(3)
	No arrest	0	(0)
Citizen testimony	Arrest	23	74
	Unclear	11	64
	No arrest	11	9
All felonies[b]	Arrest	25	72
	Unclear	15	67
	No arrest	11	9
	MISDEMEANOR		
Police witness	Arrest	21	95
	Unclear	23	52
	No arrest	11	18
Citizen testimony	Arrest	10	70
	Unclear	15	27
	No arrest	11	9
All misdemeanors[c]	Arrest	31	87
	Unclear	38	42
	No arrest	22	14

[a] By percent. Figures in parentheses are used whenever the total number of incidents is statistically too small to justify a generalized assertion of arrest rate.
[b] Excludes one case of "other evidence" and seven cases in which the observer did not ascertain the evidence.
[c] Excludes three cases of "no evidence" and 23 cases in which the type of evidence was not ascertained.

have an extremely high probability of arrest—95%—a proportion somewhat higher than that for felony situations involving testimonial evidence alone (74%). When the major situational evidence is citizen testimony against a misdemeanor suspect, the proportion drops to 70%. On the other hand, even when the police observe the offense, the arrest rate drops to less than one-fifth in those encounters where the complainant outwardly prefers leniency for his or her adversary. Plainly the complainant's preference is a more powerful situational factor than evidence, though the two operate jointly. As might be expected, evidence is particularly consequential only when the complainant expresses no clear preference for police action: In those cases the suspect is almost twice as likely to be arrested when the police observe the offense as when the major evidence is the complainant's or another citizen's testimony. As noted above, however, the complainant does make his or her preference clear in the majority of encounters.

RELATIONAL DISTANCE

When the police enter into an encounter involving both a complainant and a suspect they find themselves not only in a legal conflict but also in a conflict between people with a social relationship—one between family members, acquaintances, neighbors, friends, business associates, or strangers. The findings in Table 4–3 suggest that arrest practices vary with the relational nature of complainant–suspect conflicts. The probability of arrest is highest when the

TABLE 4–3

Arrest Rates in Citizen-Initiated Encounters according to Type of Crime, Relational Tie between Complainant and Suspect, and Complainant's Preference[a]

Relational Tie	Complainant's Preference	Total Number of Incidents	Arrest Rate
	FELONY		
Family members	Arrest	20	55
	Unclear	8	(6)
	No arrest	10	0
	Total	38	45
Friends, neighbors, acquaintances	Arrest	5	(4)
	Unclear	8	(6)
	No arrest	0	(0)
	Total	13	77
Strangers	Arrest	3	(3)
	Unclear	2	(2)
	No arrest	3	(2)
	Total	8	(7)
	MISDEMEANOR		
Family members	Arrest	15	80
	Unclear	13	38
	No arrest	8	(0)
	Total	36	47
Friends, neighbors, acquaintances	Arrest	11	64
	Unclear	15	40
	No arrest	20	5
	Total	46	30
Strangers	Arrest	15	87
	Unclear	15	47
	No arrest	5	(0)
	Total	35	57

[a] By percent. Figures in parentheses are used whenever the total number of incidents is statistically too small to justify a generalized assertion of arrest rate.

citizen adversaries have the most distant social relation to one another, that is, when they are strangers. The felony cases especially reveal that arrest becomes more probable as the relational distance increases. Forty-five percent of the suspects are arrested in matters involving family members, 77% in those involving friends, neighbors, or acquaintances, and seven out of eight, or 88%, in stranger relationships.[13] In the misdemeanor cases the pattern is not so consistent. Although the likelihood of arrest is still highest in conflicts between strangers, the lowest likelihood is in situations involving friends, neighbors, or acquaintances. Table 4–3 also shows the effect of the complainants' preference within the several relational settings, but the number of cases in each category is too small for meaningful comparisons.

RACE, RESPECT, AND THE COMPLAINANT

Table 4–4 demonstrates that the police arrest blacks at a higher rate than whites. But no evidence is available here to support the view that the police discriminate against blacks. Rather, the race differential seems to be a function of the relatively higher rate at which black suspects display disrespect toward the police. When the arrest rate for respectful black suspects is compared to that for respectful whites, no difference in the probability of arrest is apparent (see Table 4–5). Before examining this last finding in detail, however, the importance of citizen respect in itself should be established.

Considering felony and misdemeanor situations together, the arrest rate for very deferential suspects is 40% of 10 cases. For civil suspects it is effectively

TABLE 4–4

Arrest Rates in Citizen-Initiated Encounters according to Type of Crime and Race of Suspect[a]

Crime	Race	Total Number of Incidents	Arrest Rate
Felony	Black	48	60
	White	11	45
Misdemeanor	Black	75	47
	White	42	38
All crimes	Black	123	52
	White	53	39

[a] By percent.

---

13. Little confidence can be placed in findings based upon fewer than 10 cases. Nevertheless, such findings are occasionally mentioned when they are strikingly consistent with patterns seen in the larger samples. In no instances, however, do broader generalizations rest upon these inadequate statistical bases.

TABLE 4–5

Arrest Rates in Citizen-Initiated Encounters according to Complainant's Preference, Suspect's Race, and Degree of Deference[a]

Race	Suspect's Deference	Total Number of Incidents	Arrest Rate
COMPLAINANT PREFERS ARREST			
Black	Very deferential	2	(2)
	Civil	19	68
	Antagonistic	12	83
White	Very deferential	1	(1)
	Civil	15	(67)
	Antagonistic	4	(2)
Both races[b]	Very deferential	3	(3)
	Civil	34	68
	Antagonistic	16	75
COMPLAINANT'S PREFERENCE IS UNCLEAR			
Black	Very deferential	2	(0)
	Civil	18	33
	Antagonistic	15	93
White	Very deferential	1	(1)
	Civil	7	(2)
	Antagonistic	3	(1)
Both races[c]	Very deferential	3	(1)
	Civil	25	32
	Antagonistic	18	83
COMPLAINANT PREFERS NO ARREST			
Black	Very deferential	3	(0)
	Civil	13	23
	Antagonistic	4	(1)
White	Very deferential	1	(0)
	Civil	6	(1)
	Antagonistic	1	(0)
Both races[d]	Very deferential	4	(0)
	Civil	19	21
	Antagonistic	5	(1)

[a] By percent. Figures in parentheses are used whenever the total number of incidents is statistically too small to justify a generalized assertion of arrest rate.

[b] Excludes 16 cases for which the suspect's degree of deference was not ascertained.

[c] Excludes 15 cases for which the suspect's degree of deference was not ascertained.

[d] Excludes 18 cases for which the suspect's degree of deference was not ascertained.

the same at 42% of 71 cases, but it is 70% of 37 cases for antagonistic or disrespectful suspects.[14] Suspects who refuse to defer to police authority thus take a gamble with their freedom. This pattern persists in felony and misdemeanor situations when they are examined separately, but the small samples that result from dividing the data by type of crime prevent any more refined comparison than between civil and disrespectful levels of deference. The police made an arrest in 40% of the 25 felony encounters in which the suspect was civil, as compared to 69% of the 16 felony encounters in which he or she was disrespectful. In misdemeanor situations the corresponding proportions are 43% of 46 cases and 71% of 21 cases. Moreover, in the aggregate of cases the police are more likely to arrest a misdemeanor suspect who is disrespectful toward them than a felony suspect who is civil. In this sense the police enforce their authority more severely than they enforce the law.

The complainant's preference can erode the impact of the suspect's degree of respect somewhat, but, as Table 4–5 shows, when the complainant's preference is held constant there is some evidence that the pattern remains. When the complainant expresses a preference for arrest, the police appear to comply more readily if the suspect is disrespectful rather than civil toward them (though only a small number of cases is involved). Table 4–5 also reveals that when the complainant desires an arrest and the suspect is civil, the probability of arrest for black and white suspects is almost exactly equal. But black suspects are disrespectful toward the police more often than are whites, and this operates to increase disproportionately their overall arrest rate. In addition, it should be noted that when the complainant's preference is unclear the degree of deference of the suspect is especially consequential. The police arrest civil suspects in 32% of these cases, while they arrest disrespectful suspects in 83%. This difference is wider and more significant than where the complainant expresses a preference for arrest (68% and 75%, with only 16 cases involved in the disrespectful category). Especially when complainants are passive, then, it can be seen that suspects carry their fate in their own hands. Moreover, under these circumstances blacks more than whites tend to be disrespectful toward the police, a pattern that again operates to their disadvantage.

The small sample of cases rules out a complete analysis of the encounters in which the complainant favors clemency for his or her adversary. The cases are only

---

14. The observers classified a suspect's degree of deference on the basis of whatever clues they could cull from his or her behavior. They undoubtedly made classificatory errors from time to time since some suspects, particularly some disrespectful suspects, are extremely subtle in their communicative demeanor. Some, for example, were exceedingly deferential as a way of ridiculing the police. In the great majority of cases, however, the classifications accurately describe the outward behavior to which the police were relating. Of course, the suspects' *feelings* were not necessarily reflected in their behavior.

adequate for establishing that a civil suspect is less likely to be arrested under these conditions than when the complainant prefers arrest or expresses no preference. Although statistically negligible, it is also noteworthy that four of the five disrespectful suspects were released by the police under these conditions, indicating that complainants may have voices sufficiently persuasive to save disrespectful suspects from arrest.

Encounters without Complainants

Police encounters with lone suspects comprise a minority of the cases, but they nevertheless carry special significance in a description of police work. When there is no complainant available to deflect the outcome, the encounter is all between the state and the accused. This kind of situation often arises when citizens call the police but refuse to identify themselves or when they identify themselves but fail to materialize when the police arrive; in these cases the police handle incidents, usually in public places, as the servants of unknown masters. Only rarely do the police themselves detect and act upon crime situations with no prompting at all from a concerned citizen.

This section treats separately the citizen-initiated and the police-initiated encounters. With no complainant participating, however, the analysis contains fewer variables. Absent are the complainant's preference and the relational distance between the complainant and suspect. Because the police so seldom encounter felony suspects without the help of a complaining witness, the legal seriousness of the lone suspect's offense is likewise invariable: Nearly all police-initiated encounters involve misdemeanors. Finally, the situational evidence in the vast majority of these cases is a police officer's claim of having witnessed an offense, and the size of the sample is too small to allow separate analysis of those resting upon other kinds of evidence or those apparently based only upon diffuse suspicion. The analysis therefore is confined to the effect on arrest rates of the suspect's race, the suspect's degree of respect for the police, and the type of police mobilization—that is, whether a citizen or the police initiated the encounter.

RACE, RESPECT, AND THE LONE SUSPECT

In 67 situations the police witnessed a misdemeanor after being called to the scene by a citizen's telephone request. They arrested a suspect in 49% of these cases. In another 45 situations the police witnessed a misdemeanor and entered into an encounter with a suspect wholly upon their own initiative. In these latter cases the arrest rate was somewhat higher—62%. Hence, the police seem a bit more severe when they act completely upon their own authority than when they respond to citizens' calls. When a citizen calls the police but avoids the field situation, then, to a degree the officers match the citizen's seeming indifference with their own.

Table 4–6 shows the arrest rates for blacks and whites in citizen- and police-initiated encounters where no complainant participated. Under both types of mobilization the police arrested blacks at a higher rate, though in police-initiated encounters the difference is statistically negligible, given the sample size.

Table 4–7 shows, however, that as in encounters involving complainants, the race difference disappears when the suspect's level of respect for the police is held constant. In citizen-initiated encounters, black suspects disproportionately show disrespect for the police, and the police reply with a high arrest rate—83%. They arrest only 36% of the civil black suspects, a rate comparable to that for civil white suspects (29%, a difference of just one case of the 14 in the sample). Considering both races together in citizen-initiated encounters, disrespectful conduct toward the police clearly is highly determinative for a suspect whose illegal behavior is witnessed by the police. A display of respect for the officers, on the other hand, can overcome the suspect's evidentiary jeopardy. In the encounters initiated by the police, arrest rates for civil blacks and civil whites are again nearly the same, but no significant difference emerges between the vulnerability of civil suspects and that of suspects who are disrespectful toward the police. Hence, neither race nor the suspect's degree of respect predicts arrest rates in police-initiated encounters with misdemeanor suspects. The similarity of arrest rates for disrespectful and civil suspects is the major difference between police-

TABLE 4–6

Arrest Rates in Police Encounters with Suspects in Police-Witnessed Misdemeanor Situations without Complainant Participation according to Type of Mobilization and Suspect's Race[a]

Type of Mobilization	Race	Total Number of Incidents	Arrest Rate
Citizen-initiated	Black	43	58
	White	24	33
	Total	67	49
Police-initiated	Black	28	64
	White	17	59
	Total	45	62

[a] By percent.

TABLE 4-7
Arrest Rates in Police Encounters with Suspects in Police-Witnessed Misdemeanor Situations without Complainant Participation according to Type of Mobilization, Suspect's Race, and Degree of Deference[a]

Race	Suspect's Deference	Total Number of Incidents	Arrest Rate
	CITIZEN-INITIATED ENCOUNTERS		
Black	Very deferential	5	(0)
	Civil	14	36
	Antagonistic	18	83
White	Very deferential	3	(1)
	Civil	14	29
	Antagonistic	5	(3)
Both races[b]	Very deferential	8	(1)
	Civil	28	32
	Antagonistic	23	78
	POLICE-INITIATED ENCOUNTERS		
Black	Very deferential	2	(1)
	Civil	13	69
	Antagonistic	10	70
White	Very deferential	1	(0)
	Civil	10	70
	Antagonistic	6	(3)
Both races[c]	Very deferential	3	(1)
	Civil	23	70
	Antagonistic	16	62

[a] By percent. Figures in parentheses are used whenever the total number of incidents is statistically too small to justify making a generalized assertion of arrest rate.
[b] Excludes eight cases for which the suspect's degree of deference was not ascertained.
[c] Excludes three cases for which the suspect's degree of deference was not ascertained.

initiated and citizen-initiated encounters. In fact, it is the most glaring anomaly in the findings presented in this analysis, though it might well disappear if the sample of police-initiated encounters were larger.

Generalizations

The major findings of this study may be restated as empirical generalizations in order to provide a manageable profile of police behavior in routine situations where arrest is a possibility. But arrest patterns may also suggest broader principles according to which legal policy is defined, legal resources mobilized, and dispositions made.[15] Hence, when it seems appropriate, inferences are drawn from these findings to more abstract propositions at the level of a sociological theory of law.

MOBILIZATION

Most arrest situations arise through citizen rather than police initiative. In this sense, the criminal process is invoked in a manner not unlike that of private-law systems that are mobilized through a reactive process, depending upon the enterprise of citizen claimants in pursuit of their own interests (see Chapter 2 of the present volume). In criminal law as in other areas of public law, although the state has the formal authority to bring legal actions on its own initiative, the average case is the product of a citizen complaint.

One implication of this pattern is that most criminal cases pass through a moral filter in the citizen population before the state assumes its enforcement role. A major portion of the responsibility for criminal-law enforcement is thus kept out of police hands. Much like courts in the realm of private law, then, the police operate as moral servants of the citizenry. A further implication of this pattern is that the deterrence function of the criminal process to an important degree depends upon citizen willingness to mobilize the criminal law, just as the deterrence function of private law depends so much upon citizen plaintiffs.[16] Sanctions cannot deter illegal behavior if the law lies dormant because of an inefficient mobilization process.[17] In this sense, all legal systems rely to a great extent upon private citizens.

COMPLAINANTS

Arrest practices sharply reflect the preferences of citizen complainants, particularly when the desire is for leniency. The police are thus an instrument of the complainant in two ways: Generally they handle what the complainant wants them to handle, and they handle the matter in the way the complainant prescribes.

Often students of the police comment that a community has the kind of police it

---

15. These three functional foci of legal control—prescription, mobilization, and disposition—correspond roughly to the legislative, executive, and judicial dimensions of government, though they are useful in the analysis of subsystems of legal control as well as total systems. For instance, the police can be regarded as the major mobilization subsystem of the criminal-justice system. Yet the police subsystem itself can be approached as a total system involving prescription, mobilization, and disposition subsystems (compare Laswell, 1956:2).

16. The contemporary literature on deterrence is devoted primarily to the capacity of criminal sanctions to discourage crime (see, e.g., Andenaes, 1966; but see Jhering, 1877).

17. Roscoe Pound concludes that the contingent nature of legal mobilization is one of the major obstacles to the effectiveness of law as a social engineering device (1917; see also Bohannan, 1965; Jones, 1969:21–26).

wants, as if the community outlines the police function by a de facto legislative process of some kind (see, e.g., Slater, 1970:49). But that view is overly vague, if not altogether mistaken. In fact, the police serve an atomized mass of complainants far more than they serve an organized community. The greater part of the police work load involves case-by-case, isolated contacts between individual officers and individual complainants. In this sense the police serve a phantom master who dwells throughout the population, who is everywhere but nowhere at once. Because of this, the police are at once an easy and yet an elusive target for criticism. Their work evades planned change, but as shifts occur in the desires of the atomized citizenry who call and direct them, changes ripple into their actual behavior, wittingly or not.

Police compliance with complainants gives police work a radically democratic character. The result is not, however, uniform standards of justice, since the moral standards of complainants vary to some extent across the population. Indeed, by complying with complainants the police in effect perpetuate the moral diversity that they encounter in the citizen mass.[18] In this respect again, a public-law system is similar to systems of private law (see Pashukanis, 1927). Both are organized, visibly and invisibly, to give priority to the demands of their dispersed citizens. Whoever may prescribe the law and however the law is applied, then, many sovereigns call law to action.[19] Public-law systems are peculiar in that their formal organization allows them to initiate and pursue cases without complainants as sponsors, but the reality of public-law systems such as the police belies their appearance. Moreover, citizens continually undermine uniformity in public- as well as private-law enforcement. It may even be that democratic organization inevitably jeopardizes uniformity in the application of law.[20]

---

18. This generalization does not apply to proactive police operations such as vice control or street harassment, which seldom involve a citizen complainant. Street harassment refers here to selective and abrasive attention directed at people who are, at best, marginally liable to arrest—for example, a police command to "move on" to a group of teenagers. Proactive policing of this kind sometimes involves an attack upon particular moral subcultures (see, e.g., Clébert, 1963:87–119; Hagan, 1966; M. Brown, 1969).

19. This has been true historically as well. Legal systems usually have made the citizen complainant the sine qua non of legal mobilization, except under circumstances posing a direct threat to political order. A dramatic example was the legal process in Republican Rome, where even extreme forms of personal violence required the initiative of a complainant before government sanctions could be imposed (see generally Lintott, 1968).

A theory of legal control should treat as problematic the capacity and willingness of governments to initiate cases and sanction violators in the absence of an aggrieved citizen demanding justice (see generally Ranulf, 1938).

20. The norm of universalism reflected in systems of public law in advanced societies is a norm of impersonalism: The police are expected to enforce the law impersonally. But by giving complainants a strong role in the determination of outcomes, the police personalize the criminal law. This pattern

LENIENCY

The police are lenient in their routine arrest practices; they use their arrest power far less often than the written law would seemingly allow. Legal leniency, however, is hardly peculiar to the police. Especially in the private-law sector (see, e.g., Macaulay, 1963), and also in other areas of public law (see, e.g., Mileski, 1971b), the official process for redress of grievances is invoked far less often than illegality is detected. Citizens and public officials display a reluctance to wield legal power in immediate response to illegality, and a sociology of law must treat as problematic the fact that legal cases arise at all.

EVIDENCE

Evidence is an important factor in arrest. The stronger the evidence in the field situation, the more likely is an arrest. Thus, when the police themselves witness a criminal offense they are more likely to arrest the suspect than when they only hear about an offense from a third party. But rarely do they confront persons as suspects without some evidence; still more rarely are arrests unsupported by evidence of any kind.

The importance of situational evidence hardly constitutes a major advance in knowledge: Evidence has a role in every legal process. Instead, it is the definition of evidence, not whether evidence is required, that differs across legal systems. It should also be emphasized that even when the evidence against a suspect is very strong, the police frequently take action short of arrest. Evidence would thus seem to be a necessary but not a sufficient basis for predicting invocation of the law.

SERIOUSNESS

The probability of arrest is higher in legally serious crime situations than in those of a relatively minor nature. This finding is not unexpected either, but it has theoretical significance. It means that the police levy arrest as a sanction to correspond with the defined seriousness of the criminal event in much the same fashion as legislators and judges allocate punishments. The legal conception of arrest contrasts sharply with this practice, holding that arrest follows upon detection of any criminal act, without regard to levels of legal seriousness. In this sense arrest represents legislation and adjudication by police officers. Arrest practices should therefore contribute disproportionately to the deterrence of serious crime, for the perpetrator of a serious crime whose act is detected risks a

---

allows fellow family members and friends to mobilize the police to handle their disputes with little danger that the police will impose standards foreign to their relationships. At the level of disputes between strangers, however, the same pattern of police compliance with complainants can, given moral diversity, result in a form of discriminatory enforcement. A law-enforcement process that takes no account of the degree of intimacy between a complainant and suspect may upset the peculiar balance of close social relationships (see Kawashima, 1963).

greater likelihood of arrest as well as more severe punishment. This also means that the higher risk of arrest may help to offset the lower probability of detection for some of the more serious crimes (see Black, 1970:735).

INTIMACY

The greater the relational distance between a complainant and a suspect, the greater is the likelihood of arrest. When a complainant demands the arrest of a suspect, the police are most apt to comply if the adversaries are strangers. Arrest is less likely if they are friends, neighbors, or acquaintances, and it is least likely if they are family members. Police officers also write crime reports according to the same differential (Black, 1970:740). Relational distance appears to be a major factor in the probability of litigation in contract disputes (Macaulay, 1963: 56) and in other private-law contexts as well.[21] It would seem, indeed, that in all legal affairs relational distance affects the probability of litigation. If so, this means that law has comparatively little to do with the maintenance of order between and among intimates.

Yet the findings on relational distance in arrest practices may merely reflect the fact that legal control is more likely to operate when sublegal control is unavailable (see, e.g., Pound, 1942:18–25; Schwartz, 1954; van der Sprenkel, 1962; Nader and Metzger, 1963; Nader, 1964; Cohen, 1966; Peattie, 1968:54–62). The greater the relational distance, the less is the likelihood that sublegal mechanisms of social control will operate, and so the more likely is law to be brought to bear. This seems a useful principle for understanding the increasing salience of legal control in social evolution as well.[22] Over time the drift of history delivers proportionately more and more strangers who need law to hold them together and apart. Law seems to bespeak an absence of community, and law grows ever more prominent as the dissolution of community proceeds (see Tönnies, 1887:202).

DISRESPECT

The probability of arrest increases when a suspect is disrespectful toward the police. The same pattern appears in youth-officer behavior (Piliavin and Briar, 1964:210), patrol officer encounters with juveniles (Black and Reiss, 1970:74–

---

21. For example, in Japan disputes that arise across rather than within communities are more likely to result in litigation (Kawashima, 1963:45). In American Chinatowns, disputes that arise between Chinese and non-Chinese are more likely to result in litigation than disputes between Chinese (Grace, 1970). The same is true of disputes between Gypsies and non-Gypsies as compared to disputes between Gypsies (Clébert, 1963:90). Likewise, in the United States in the first half of the nineteenth century, crimes committed between Indians generally were left to the tribes (Prucha, 1962:188–212). In medieval England the same pattern obtained in the legal condition of the Jews: Ordinary English rules applied to legal dealings between Jews and the King and between Jews and Christians, but disputes between Jew and Jew were heard in Jewish tribunals and decided under Jewish law (Pollock and Maitland, 1898:Volume 1, 468–475).

22. It is at this level that Pound posits his thesis concerning the priority of sublegal control (1942:33; see also Selznick, 1963; Fuller, 1969).

75), and in the use of illegal violence by the police (Westley, 1953; Chevigny, 1969:51–83; Reiss, 1968a:18). Even disrespectful complainants receive a penalty of sorts from the police, since their complaints are less likely to receive official recognition (Black 1970:742–744).

In form, disrespect in a police encounter is much the same as "contempt" in a courtroom hearing. It is a rebellion against the processing system. Unlike judges, however, the police have no special weapons in their legal arsenal for dealing with citizens who refuse to defer to their authority at a verbal or otherwise symbolic level. Perhaps as the legal system further differentiates, a crime of "contempt of police" will emerge. From a radically behavioral standpoint, this crime has already emerged; the question is whether it will ever be formalized in the written law.

All legal systems defend their own authority with energy and dispatch. To question or assault the legitimacy of a legal process is to invite legal invocation, a sanction, or a more serious sanction—whatever is problematic in a given confrontation. Law seems to lash out at every revolt against its own integrity. Accordingly, it might be useful to consider disrespect toward a police officer to be a minor form of civil disorder, or revolution the highest form of disrespect.

DISCRIMINATION

No evidence exists in this analysis to show that the police discriminate on the basis of race. The police arrest blacks at a comparatively high rate, but the difference between the races appears to result primarily from the greater rate at which blacks show disrespect for the police. The difference thus depends upon the citizens, not the police.[23] This finding is supported by the findings of several other studies based upon direct observation of the police (see generally La Fave, 1965; Skolnick, 1966:83–88; Tiffany, McIntyre, and Rotenberg, 1967; *Yale Law Journal* Editors, 1967a:1645).[24] These results should be taken as a caveat that in general improper or illegal behavior toward blacks does not in itself constitute evidence of discrimination toward blacks. A finding of discrimination

---

23. It should also be recognized that "discrimination" can be defined to include any de facto unequal treatment, regardless of its causes (see Mayhew, 1968:59–60). The evidence in this analysis indicates only that blacks are treated differently not because they are blacks, but because they manifest other behavioral patterns, such as disrespect for the police, more frequently than whites. However, the question of why blacks disproportionately show disrespect for the police cannot be addressed with the observational data. We can only speculate, for example, that in anticipation of harsh treatment blacks may behave disrespectfully toward the police, thereby setting in motion a pattern that confirms their expectations.

Despite the finding of nondiscrimination in this study, the police officers observed did reveal considerable prejudice in their attitudes toward blacks (see generally Black and Reiss, 1967:132–139; see also Deutscher, 1966).

24. These studies either report a lack of evidence of discrimination or fail altogether to mention race as an analytically important variable (but see "Postscript: 1980" at the end of the present chapter).

requires a comparative analysis of behavior toward each race with other variables such as level of respect held constant. No study of citizen opinions or perceptions (e.g., Werthman and Piliavin, 1967) or of official statistics (e.g., Goldman, 1963:45; Wilson, 1968: 113; Green, 1970:481) can hold these variables constant.

In closing this section it is important to note that the findings on racial discrimination by the police should not remotely suggest that law is oblivious to social rank. On the contrary, broader patterns in the form and substance of legal control seem at any one time to reflect and to perpetuate existing systems of social stratification. That the degradation of arrest is reserved primarily for the kinds of illegality committed by lower-status citizens such as blacks exemplifies this broader tendency of the law in action.

Conclusion

A major commitment of this chapter has been to dislodge the discussion from its grounding in empirical findings and to raise the degree of abstraction to the level of general theory. Statements at this level ignore the boundaries and distinctions that ordinarily contain and constrain generalization about law as a social phenomenon. The various subsystems of law—criminal law, torts, contracts, constitutional law, family law, property law, criminal procedure, and administrative law—are assumed to contain common elements. As if this aim were too faint-hearted, a general theory of legal control also seeks to discover patterns present in several functional dimensions of law: prescription, mobilization, and disposition, or, respectively, the articulation of legal policy, the engagement of legal cases by legal organizations, and the situational resolution of legal disputes. This kind of legal sociology shares with jurisprudence the inclusiveness of its subject matter. Each acts upon a longing for a universal understanding of law. For each, the past shares the relevance of the present, and other legal systems illustrate our own. Unlike jurisprudence, however, sociology of law abjures problems of a normative character; unlike sociology of law, jurisprudence bypasses the ordeal of concrete description.

A closing note should state what this analysis has not done. Arrest might have been examined from a number of other perspectives, each of which has its own vocabulary suited to its own form of discourse. For example, arrest may usefully be conceived as one stage in an elaborate processing system, an assembly line of inputs and outputs. Another perspective might see arrest as a political event. When and how the arrest power is used says much about the nature of a political system and the quality of life within it. Then, too, arrest is part of a job. It is a role performance of a bureaucratic functionary. Police work may be contemplated as it arises from its rich occupational subculture with standards and values that police officers share and enforce among their peers. And every arrest is enveloped by the police bureaucracy, so that the arrest practices of individual officers are under some degree of surveillance from their superiors as well as their peers. Finally, as a last example, a study of arrest might inform and benefit from the study of face-to-face interaction. The police encounter is a small group with its own morphology and dynamics. Hence, what happens in an encounter may have less to do with crime and law than with the demands of situational order, with social etiquette or the pressures of group size or physical space. An arrest may be the only means available to a police officer bent upon restoring order, and yet sometimes it is the surest way to make a situation explode.

Some encouragement may be taken from the development of sociology to the point where a subject such as arrest can occasion so many diverse perspectives. Diversity of this degree, however, imparts an aura of arbitrariness to whatever theoretical framework is chosen. Although the many perspectives applicable to a study of arrest surely mirror the empirical complexity of arrest itself, its theoretical identity remains precarious and uncertain. Here it is sanction and justice; there input, coercion, expectation, job, criterion, or gesture. Any single theoretical view of arrest is inevitably incomplete.

Postscript: 1980

Ten years have passed since Chapters 3 and 4 were first written, and during that period the scholarly literature on the police has expanded considerably. By and large, the new findings that have accumulated appear to be consistent with those reported above (for a pertinent review, see Sherman, 1980a). It now seems clear, however, that one subject was not adequately understood a decade ago: racial discrimination.

In light of assorted empirical evidence and recent theoretical developments, the findings and references in Chapters 3 and 4 no longer appear sufficient to answer the question of whether the police discriminate against blacks. Rather, the evidence that has accumulated over the years has been strikingly inconsistent, indicating a disadvantage for blacks in some cases, and not in others. It has been shown, for example, that the police are more likely to give traffic tickets to blacks (Lundman, 1979:164–166), more likely to arrest blacks under conditions later viewed as inadequate to justify prosecution (Hepburn, 1978), more likely to use penal and coercive tactics when they handle disputes involving blacks (Chapter 5 of the present volume: 134–141), and more likely to shoot and kill blacks (Knoohuizen, Fahey, and Palmer, 1972:19–22; see also Sherman, 1980b:95–96). It might also be noted that when other variables are left aside (such as social class, the suspect's demeanor, and the complainant's preference), blacks in the three-city study described in this volume were more likely to be interrogated, searched, arrested, and—if victims—less likely to have their complaints officially recognized by the police (Black and Reiss, 1967:76, 81; Friedrich, 1977:300–303). It would thus seem that blacks in the aggregate are more likely to be subject to police authority, and less likely to receive their cooperation. Nevertheless, as mentioned earlier, other evidence fails to show differences of this kind (see page 105; see also Lundman, 1974b:130, 133; Lundman, Sykes, and Clark, 1978:82, 84; Pastor, 1978:379).

In view of these inconsistent results, it is also noteworthy that recent developments in the sociological theory of law imply that the relevance of race in police work may be more complex than was understood a decade ago. In particular, it should not be expected that blacks will always be treated the same—whether severely or not—under all conditions. Rather, it appears that the relevance of race (sociologically a matter of ethnicity and socioeconomic standing)—or of any other characteristic relating to a person's social location—depends upon the characteristics of all of the participants in a legal event, including the complainant and the third parties as well as the alleged offender (see generally Black, 1976; Baumgartner and Black, 1981; see also Chapter 1 of the present volume: 3–5). If an alleged offender is a black, then, the relevance of this for police behavior depends upon the race of the complainant and of the police who participate in the encounter. If the complainant is also black while the police are white, for example, theory predicts that an arrest is less likely than in cases where all of the parties are white (see Black, 1976:17). For this reason it should not be surprising that no evidence of discrimination against black suspects was found in the cases involving complainants in Chapter 4, since the race of the suspect and that of the complainant were matched (and in most cases the police were white). Indeed, under those conditions it is surprising that blacks were not treated *less* severely, a pattern that might well emerge if the cases handled by black officers were excluded and if the alleged offenses were matched more closely for purposes of the comparisons. Where a black allegedly offends a white (and the police are white), greater severity toward the black would be expected, however, while less should occur when a white offends a black (see Black, 1976:21–24). Unfortunately, an analysis of cases of the latter kind—with an upward or downward direction in social space—is not presently available. But in the same three-city sample the relevance of the officer's race has been examined, and shows, among other things, that black police are more likely than white police to arrest blacks and to write official crime reports in response to the complaints of blacks (Friedrich, 1977:308–313). In sum, during the years since Chapters 3 and 4 were first written, it has become clear that race is relevant to understanding the behavior of the police. Its relevance is complex, however, and not merely a matter of greater severity toward blacks.

Dispute Settlement
by the Police*
5

The police in modern society perform many functions beyond the detection of
crime and the apprehension of criminals (see, e.g., Cumming, Cumming, and
Edell, 1965; Bittner, 1967a; 1967b; Black, 1968: Chapter 3; Wilson, 1968:
Chapter 2). Some of these functions have little or no relevance to deviant behavior and social control—such as the transportation of sick and injured people to
the hospital or the removal of dead dogs and abandoned automobiles from the
street—but even where an exercise of authority is involved, the role of the police
may depart considerably from law enforcement in a narrow sense. This might be
seen in the handling of an intoxicated or homeless person sleeping in a public
place, a game of dice or cards in an alley, a noisy party, a gang of teenagers
loitering where they are not wanted, or any of a variety of interpersonal conflicts,
whether between a husband and wife, landlord and tenant, or businessman and
customer. Although the police might make an arrest in any of these situations,
more often they dispose of the matter entirely in the setting where it occurs. They
might simply tell someone to "get moving" or to "keep it down," for example,

*The findings presented in this chapter derive from the larger project described in the Preface and
in Chapter 3 of the present volume. Computer time for this analysis was provided by the Department
of Sociology, Yale University, and other support was provided by the Department's Program in
Deviant Behavior, Social Control, and Law, under a grant from the National Institute of Mental
Health.

I thank M. P. Baumgartner for assistance in the preparation and processing of the data, and also for
commenting upon an earlier draft. In February, 1980, a synopsis of the report was presented at the
Center for Criminal Justice, Harvard Law School, and I thank those who attended for their reactions.
In addition, the following people made suggestions for improving the chapter: John Griffiths, Candace
Kruttschnitt, Peter K. Manning, Sally Engle Merry, Harold E. Pepinsky, Lawrence W. Sherman,
and W. Clinton Terry.

or they might use force or the threat of it, or admonish, mediate, or arbitrate, or they might do nothing at all.

Police work of this kind—where arrest is typically used as only one among a number of possible actions—has been called "peacekeeping" or "order maintenance" to distinguish it from "law enforcement" (Banton, 1964:6–7; Bittner, 1967b:700, 714; Wilson, 1968:16–17). It is a major part of the police role in contemporary America and, for that matter, a major part of the legal life of any modern society. Nevertheless, little is known about who calls the police in these situations and why, and who is handled in what way under what conditions (but see, e.g., Banton, 1964: Chapter 3; Cumming *et al.*, 1965; Parnas, 1967; Wilson, 1968: Chapter 2). Addressing these questions and others, the following report examines one variety of peacekeeping by the police: the handling of conflicts between people in ongoing relationships. A study of this kind contributes to knowledge about police work as such, and also to an understanding of law and dispute settlement in general.

It is a curious fact that, apart from what happens in courtrooms, we know substantially more about how people settle disputes in tribal and other simple societies than in modern societies such as the United States (see, e.g., Barton, 1919; Llewellyn and Hoebel, 1941; Gibbs, 1963; Gulliver, 1963; Nader and Metzger, 1963; Gluckman, 1967). The concept of "dispute settlement" is rarely even seen in the works of sociologists, but appears primarily in the literature of anthropology. Perhaps this is because the concept is most appropriate where social control is conciliatory in style, concerned more with compromise and the reestablishment of social harmony than with who is right or wrong, who wins or loses, or—in the penal style—who is guilty and deserving of punishment. (For an overview of styles of social control, see Black, 1976:4–6; also see below, pp. 130–131). The conciliatory style is especially common where people are relatively homogeneous, intimate, and equal—conditions often found in tribal societies but quite unlike many of the situations confronted by the police in a modern society (see Gibbs, 1963; Gluckman, 1967:20–21; Black, 1976:47–48). Accordingly, what is handled by legal agents (and defined by social scientists) as a "dispute" rather than a "crime" may be more a question of who is involved than of the conduct that occurs. Where the police are called upon to handle a conflict between people in an ongoing relationship, then, such as between members of the same family living in the same residence, it may be expected that the process and outcome will to some degree resemble patterns of dispute settlement in the simpler societies described by anthropologists. But there is also an important difference between any matter involving the police—at least in a large city—and a conflict between people in a simple society: the police themselves. Although the parties in a modern setting may be as intimate as fellow tribesmen living in the same village, the police are likely to be complete strangers, and socially distant from the parties in other ways as well, such as culturally and economically. In a tribal village, however, every agent of social control—whether a chief, family head, elder, or whatever—is acquainted with all of the parties involved, and socially similar to them in nearly every respect. For this reason alone, it should not be surprising that dispute settlement by the police—as described in this chapter—differs considerably from the patterns found by anthropologists in tribal and other simple societies.

*   *   *

The chapter begins with a survey of the nature of the cases in the sample, including details about the conflicts themselves and the people who have them. A speculation is also offered concerning conditions under which people call the police about matters of this kind. This is followed by an outline of the patterns by which the police handle disputes in progress, especially the styles of social control they employ and the degree to which they exercise their authority. The discussion then reaches the major problem of the study: how dispute settlement by the police varies with its location and direction in social space, including its relation to race, social class, the social structure of households, age, intimacy, organization, and the legitimacy of the police themselves. A note on how the police handle business disputes is included as well, along with a comment on the relevance of the written law as a way of understanding how the police handle interpersonal conflicts. The concluding section contains a summary of the findings and a few remarks on their theoretical and historical significance.

The Cases

This report is based upon a sample of 550 cases recorded by observers who accompanied uniformed police officers on their daily rounds in four American cities. Most of the cases—527—were gathered in Boston, Chicago, and Washington, D.C., during the summer of 1966. (For details about the three-city study, see Chapter 3 of the present volume, pages 69–70.) The remaining 23 cases derive from the author's own observations of the Detroit police during the years 1964–1965. Whereas the three-city study was carried out in police precincts inhabited predominantly by lower- and working-class people, the Detroit observations were made in a variety of settings, including middle-class neighborhoods on the periphery of the city. Information for the present analysis was obtained from the observation forms used during the three-city study, specifically from the part of the form (called the "capsule description") in which the observer was asked to provide a detailed report of the incident that occurred in his presence (see Appendix B:228), and from the author's discursive field notes prepared after each of 19 rides with Detroit patrol officers.[1]

All of the 550 cases in the sample involved a conflict between two or more people who were related in some way prior to the matter that resulted in a call to the police.[2] However, not all of these conflicts were in progress when the police arrived, and even when they were, not all involved a request for the police to exercise their authority. These features are found together in only a little over one-half of the cases (58%). From the standpoint of the present study, only these are true disputes (a total of 317 cases), since they alone explicitly demand a settlement of some kind by the police who handle them. The other cases nonetheless merit a brief overview before a closer analysis of the true disputes is begun.

---

1. In neither study were the police aware of the purpose of the research, or even that the incidents would be recorded at the end of each day of observation. Rather, they were given to believe that the research was not concerned with the behavior of the police at all, but only with the behavior of citizens—including their requests for service—and with the problems for the police created by citizens. This element of deception was introduced in order to assure that the police would conduct themselves in a natural fashion despite the presence of observers.

Although such deception may be subject to criticism on ethical grounds, it is also possible that it contributed to the quality of the information obtained. This is indicated by the degree to which the officers casually engaged in conduct ordinarily considered improper despite the presence of observers. During the hours after midnight, for example, the officers routinely spent some of their time sleeping in their patrol cars—occasionally missing radio calls—and a number of them drank alcoholic beverages while on night duty, confiscated property for their own enrichment (such as money from dice games or beer from underage drinkers), accepted money, free meals, and other favors from citizens, and carried in their patrol cars weapons that they admitted to observers would be used as false evidence should the need arise. On one occasion, an officer beat himself on the forehead with his nightstick following a minor traffic accident in order to be able to file a claim for an injury sustained in the line of duty. He then offered the nightstick to the observer, explaining that it was "a chance to make some money." It seems unlikely that the police would have so incriminated themselves had they been told that their conduct would be recorded and published. On the other hand, it should be recognized that the mere presence of the observers surely inhibited the officers to some degree.

For additional remarks concerning the methods used in the three-city study, see Reiss (1968b; 1971b). See also Van Maanen (1978) for a general discussion of problems involved in field research on the police.

2. Like most incidents, conflicts of this kind typically come to the attention of the police by means of a citizen's telephone call. During the three-city study, they comprised 12% of the cases that the police handled in response to such calls $(N = 4371)$. They comprised 17% of the cases originating by telephone in which the police had a face-to-face encounter with one or more citizens $(N = 3055)$. These figures should not be taken as precise indicators of the amount of all police work that pertains to interpersonal conflict, however, since the sample was drawn from a limited number of precincts in the cities studied, and, as noted above, these were areas populated mostly by lower- and working-class people. As a consequence, the sampling procedure probably overestimates the number of disputes the police handle (see pages 124–128). It should also be noted that while observations were

This section describes encounters in which only a complainant or an offender is present, as well as encounters in which both are present but neither requests help from the police. Finally, it describes several features of the true disputes.

ENCOUNTERS WITHOUT OFFENDERS

Frequently the police have contact with only one of the parties to a conflict, and most often this is the complainant. Nearly one-third (30%) of the 550 cases in the sample were of this kind. Although this usually means that the alleged offender has left the setting before the arrival of the police, in some cases it is the complainant who has left and who meets the police elsewhere, and in others the police refuse to initiate contact with the alleged offender even though he or she is still at hand and readily available. When only the complainant is present and the parties have an ongoing relationship of some kind (as in all of these cases), the police tend to minimize the importance of the conflict and avoid an exercise of their authority as much as possible. Even when most lawyers would define the matter as a crime, and the apparent offender is available for arrest or other action, the police generally do little or nothing to satisfy the complainant.

The typical case of this kind involves a woman complaining that a man—her present or past husband or boyfriend—has beaten or threatened her. In one case in the sample, for instance, the police arrived to find a black woman and her two boys waiting on the street after fleeing from their apartment. The woman said that her husband was drunk and had just threatened her with a knife, and that she was now afraid to go back inside. The officers—both white, as they were in the vast majority of cases in the sample—told her that they could not do anything,

---

made at all hours of the day, on all days of the week, evenings and weekends were intentionally oversampled. These are times when people tend to be at home, often drinking, and so police work on a Friday or Saturday night in the areas studied entails the handling of a much larger than average number of disputes. A rough estimate might be that one-fourth to one-half of all the cases dealt with by the police at such times involve conflicts between people who know each other. Even this estimate may be conservative: It has been reported that in Atlanta 60% of the calls during the "morning watch" (midnight to 8 AM shift) pertain to family conflict (Anonymous, 1974). The oversampling of evenings and weekends in the present study is thus another reason why the number of disputes handled by the police is probably overestimated here. Nonetheless, another investigator estimates that the frequency with which the police handle family disputes alone "probably exceeds the total number of murders, aggravated batteries, and all other serious crimes [Parnas, 1967:914, note 2]."

It might be added that a large proportion of the calls about interpersonal conflict appear to be made by a limited segment of the population, known by the police as "regulars." For example, the police in Kansas City found in their own survey that one-half of their calls about family matters occurred in households that they had visited at least five times during the previous two years (Anonymous, 1974). Some of these "regulars" call as often as once a week (see Schulz, 1969:67), and the police often mention people who call about once a month. It also has been estimated that as many as one-half of all lower-class urban black families call the police at least once about their domestic problems (Schulz, 1969:72, note 16).

since they had not witnessed the incident.[3] They advised her to take the boys and stay at a friend's house for the night, and on Monday to go downtown and swear out a complaint. They left the woman on the street, and reported the incident as a "family dispute." In another case of this kind, a white woman met the police on the steps of her house and said that her husband, now behind the locked door, had beaten her and chased her with a knife. She wanted them to break in and make an arrest. (The observer noted that the woman was "bruised on the face.") The police replied that they could not break into the house, and that she would "have to get a warrant." They also questioned her about "messing around and making her husband jealous." She eventually "admitted" this, and "changed her mind" about the desirability of an arrest. The case was reported as a "family fight." In another instance, two welfare workers met the police and led them to a black woman who had been beaten so badly that she could not stand up. The observer noted that she had "severe cuts and very swollen hands." The apparent offender, a male acquaintance who lived across the street, was sitting outside her back door. The observer reported, however, that the police "didn't want anything to do with it." They did not question or otherwise approach the man identified as the offender, but simply told the woman to "get a warrant." In still another case, the alleged offender was asleep and they decided not to wake him.

To the police, matters of this kind are not really "crimes." They are defined merely as "family trouble," "domestic disputes," "common-law fights," "lovers' quarrels," or something similar, and the alleged offenders are effectively granted an immunity from the criminal law. It might be added that the police generally believe the complainant in these cases is unlikely to make a formal complaint no matter what they do, and that, if she does, the case is likely to be dismissed in court anyway because of her own failure to appear as the complain-

---

3. It might be noted that the written law of arrest (whether statutory or case law) varies somewhat across American jurisdictions, and is often unclear, but generally seems to require that the police witness a misdemeanor before making an arrest without a warrant from a judge, though in practice the warrant may be granted retroactively if the officer obtains a sworn complaint from a citizen. In cases of a felony, however, they need only have "reasonable grounds" or "reasonable cause" to believe that such a crime has been committed before they may arrest a suspect (see La Fave, 1965: Chapters 11–12). Most lawyers probably would label the incident described here as a felony—an "aggravated assault"—and would also probably view the woman's statement as reasonable grounds for arrest. Certainly nothing in the written law prohibited the police from talking to the alleged offender, or from preparing an official crime report so that the case would be referred to the detective division for further investigation.

The reader should recognize that throughout this report legal interpretations of a similar kind could be brought to bear upon literally all of the cases. Since, however, the purpose of the study is merely to describe and, where possible, explain what the police do, hereafter the incidents generally will not be discussed from a legal—or lawyer's—point of view. Only at the end of this report (on pages 180–186) will a few remarks be offered about the relevance of the written law as a means of understanding dispute settlement by the police.

ing witness. They also anticipate that even if the offender were to be convicted, a jail or prison sentence would be extremely unlikely (see Parnas, 1970). Such beliefs, moreover, are probably supported by the facts (see, e.g., Vera Institute of Justice, 1977).

In cases where the offender is not available for arrest but is known to the complainant—when he is her ex-husband, boyfriend, or whatever—the police rarely write a report officially designating the incident as a crime. This precludes a follow-up investigation by detectives, with the possibility of subsequent action against the alleged offender, and also means that no record of the case will appear in official statistics on "crimes known to the police." If the alleged offender were less intimately related to the complainant, however, many of these incidents would be handled as crimes—not only as cases of "assault" but also sometimes as cases of "burglary," "larceny," and "malicious destruction of property" (see Black, 1970:740–741). In one case a black woman complained that while she was at work, her estranged husband had entered her apartment, wrecked it, loaded all of her clothes into his car, and driven away, presumably headed for his new home several hundred miles away. (A neighbor had observed the entire incident.) The police told her there was nothing they could do since it was a "civil matter." Other people handled in this way included women whose boyfriends had "stolen," respectively, a welfare check, a purse, and an automobile. In some of these cases the police openly display indifference or contempt toward the complainant, even where violence is involved or threatened. In one case, for instance, the police responded quickly to a call of "a man with a gun," but when they arrived and learned that the alleged offender—a black man—was the complainant's ex-boyfriend, they seemingly lost interest. The complainant's father was quite agitated and angry, however, and told the police that if the offender returned they would get a call "to pick up his body," since he himself would "shoot him on sight." One of the officers replied, "No big thing—we'll bring the morgue wagon." In a similar incident involving whites, a separated husband's threat to kill his father-in-law was dismissed by the police as "standard," and the observer added in his report that the police "didn't want to be in the middle of a family quarrel" because it was "near quitting time." In another case, a black woman whose boyfriend had threatened her was driven home from the police station, only to find that the alleged offender was gone. The officers searched her house and waited for the man to return, but one of them also "propositioned" the woman before they left. A somewhat different form of contempt was expressed toward a young white man who complained that he had been threatened by his former roommate: Inferring that he was a homosexual, halfway through the encounter one of the officers "began to speak with a lisp" in order to "mock" the complainant. Finally, the police were "extremely abusive" toward a black woman who said that her common-law husband had beaten her and asked their help in getting her children out of the apartment. They refused to do anything on her behalf, and, before leaving her on the street, one of them "openly criticized her marital status."

Since all complainants in interpersonal disputes do not have experiences such as those above, the degree of intimacy between the parties can only partially explain these patterns. Also relevant is their social status: Those least likely to be helped are people at the bottom of society, poor and mostly black. This is expanded upon below (pages 134– 147).

ENCOUNTERS WITHOUT COMPLAINANTS

In a little less than one-tenth of the cases (8%), the complainant is not present when the police arrive, but they are nonetheless able to surmise what gave rise to the original complaint. Most of these are "noise complaints" by neighbors who prefer to remain anonymous (see also Pepinsky, 1976a:94). Sometimes the complainants give what the police call a "bullshit name"—for example, "Mrs. Jones" or "Mrs. Smith"—and sometimes they refuse to give a name at all when they telephone the police; in either case they are able to lodge a complaint without damaging their relationship with the offending neighbor. It seems likely that if the police were not available to handle these calls, many of the complainants would simply "lump it," tolerating the situation without taking any action at all.[4] Usually the noise problem is someone playing music or having a party, and in these cases the police simply ask the offenders to "keep it down." In the typical case they are immediately assured that there will be no further disturbance, though occasionally the offenders are outwardly resentful of the intrusion. Many officers themselves consider these cases unworthy of their attention, and, perhaps because of this, are willing to absorb a degree of hostility from the people involved. In fact, in several reports observers commented that the police approached noise complaints in an apologetic manner, and tried to shift the blame onto the anonymous complainant (e.g., "We don't want to spoil your party. We're here just because somebody complained, that's all.").

Occasionally the police arrive on the scene to find an interpersonal conflict in progress, but handle the matter only as a simple noise complaint. This is their usual response to what they label "outside calls," or cases initiated by someone

---

4. On "lumping it" as a response to conduct that might otherwise be subject to social control, see Felstiner (1974).

It is largely unknown how much social control would decrease or disappear altogether if the police and other legal agencies were to withdraw from arenas where they are now available. In some cases people would engage in self-help, and in others they might have recourse to paralegal agencies such as the "vigilance committees" of the Old West, but in many instances they would very likely do nothing at all. The last possibility would seem especially likely in matters where people presently insist upon anonymity when they make complaints. In addition to noise complaints such as those noted in the text, this would include many complaints about the conduct of juveniles, the use of narcotics, and the occurrence of other so-called vice (e.g., gambling and prostitution). For a discussion of the possible consequences of "depolicing," see Black and Baumgartner (1981:forthcoming).

not involved in the dispute itself. For example, in one case the police were dispatched to " a woman screaming." Arriving at the address, they heard screams, found the room in the boardinghouse from which they were coming, and knocked on the door. A white man answered and told them that "nothing was wrong." One of the officers asked a woman who was in the room if everything was all right, but she could not speak English. The officer then told the man to "keep the noise down" or he would be arrested for "disturbing the peace." In another case, the police arrived to hear a loud argument between a man and a woman, knocked on the door, and asked what was happening. Here again, the man replied that "nothing" was happening. The officer explained that there had been a complaint about the "noise." The man assured him that they would be quiet, and the police left. (For another example of this kind, see Parnas, 1967:920–921.) These cases further illustrate the passivity of the police in the face of conflicts between people who know each other.

Apart from matters in which an outsider calls the police but does not participate in the encounter, as in many noise complaints, in another 5% of the cases one of the parties involved in an interpersonal conflict calls the police, but when they arrive they are given to understand that their intervention in the conflict itself is not wanted. When this happens, they generally comply. In most of these cases the person who answers the door indicates that they are no longer needed, and they simply leave without further ado.[5] Occasionally citizens are quite aggressive in their refusal of police service, but still the usual practice of the officers is to withdraw without an investigation or other inquiry of any kind. An extreme example was a call that came over the police radio as "a man with a gun." Two patrol cars were dispatched. The first officers to arrive were confronted by a black man with a .38 revolver who said that he and his wife had no need for the police. Talking from behind a tree, one officer asked the man to let his wife out of the house, and assured him that the police would take no action against him if he were to come out as well. But the man would not be convinced, and continued to threaten the police with his gun. At this point one of the officers called police headquarters and was told by a deputy chief to "pull out" since the man "had not committed any real assault." All of the officers left shortly thereafter, and no further action was taken.

Often the police intentionally dally en route to "family trouble" calls, hoping that the conflict will be resolved—at least superficially—by the time they arrive (also noted by Lundman, 1974a:25). Moreover, when a specific request is made, their practice is to do only what is asked, without delving further into a conflict than is demanded in the encounter. Where a victim of violence requests only

---

5. Cases in which people deny that the police were called in the first place are excluded from the sample, though many of these probably involved efforts to conceal interpersonal conflicts that had occurred earlier or that were still smoldering within the dwelling.

transportation to a hospital, for example, they nearly always handle the matter strictly as a medical problem, ignoring its interpersonal and possibly criminal elements entirely, regardless of whether the person responsible is present in the setting, and no matter what the evidence about the event. Thus, there were cases in the sample in which one of the parties admitted what most lawyers would call a "felony," but still the police did not in any way relate to the incident as a crime. In one such case, for instance, the police entered an apartment to find a white man sitting in the kitchen, holding a towel over his chest. He explained that his daughter (age 19) had stabbed him, but so as to avoid giving her a criminal record he wanted the officers to report that he was drunk and had fallen on a knife. His daughter admitted that she had stabbed him, suggesting to the police that this was a response to his sexual advances upon her: "He went too far." Her father denied this accusation, saying that he "didn't lay a hand on her." Without further inquiries, however, the police simply took the man to the hospital and reported the incident as he had requested. In another case, they entered an upstairs apartment and found a black man sitting in a chair, his arms and legs badly cut and bleeding profusely. He said that an unknown assailant had attacked him with a straight razor. The man's common-law wife was also present, and she expressed concern that he might die from loss of blood. One of the officers called an ambulance. As the police waited downstairs with the man, he admitted that his wife had actually done the cutting. She must have overheard the discussion, since, as they were taking the man away, she called out, "If you tell the police—I loves you—but I'll get you, Jeff." An officer turned back to her and replied, "Shut up, you fat bitch." According to the observer, the man was "pretty scared," and did not want to press charges. The police agreed to go along with his wishes, and reported that the offender was unknown. Still another case involved a black man whose former common-law wife had thrown lye in his face. All that he wanted was transportation to the hospital, and the police complied. But when they learned that one of the victim's acquaintances had a car, one officer remarked that the man had "no business" calling the police when other transportation was available. He also told the observer, "These goddamn niggers won't do a goddamn thing for themselves. They'll tie up police on every shitting problem they have." The next call these officers handled was from the very same woman who had thrown the lye, complaining that her former common-law husband had been bothering her and threatening to kill her, but the officer did not reveal that he knew what she had done to the man earlier in the evening. The police also handled a white woman who, after a dispute with her husband, had slashed her arms with a razor. Although the police knew what had happened, they reported the incident as a woman who had cut herself washing the dishes, and explained to the observer that this would allow them to avoid the paperwork required for an attempted suicide.

It should be added that the police commonly display indifference toward the medical as well as the interpersonal and legal aspects of the cases they handle. In fact, after one incident in which they somewhat casually transported a bleeding black woman to the hospital in what the observer described as a dilapidated and uncomfortable vehicle, one of the officers commented, "Of course, these colored don't care, but imagine if you wanted to take someone like your mother or sister to the hospital." Here again it would seem that the social location of the people involved is important to an understanding of how they are handled.

DISPUTES

As previously noted (page 112), in only a little more than one-half of the cases—a total of 317—did the police arrive to find a conflict in progress between people who knew each other, where at least one of the parties wanted them to intervene. For purposes of the present study, these are the true disputes,[6] and they will be the primary concern of the remaining pages of this chapter.

The most frequent problem in this category—as defined by the complainants—is a "disturbance" of some kind. In all, this accounts for almost one-third of the 317 cases (30%), and mostly involves complaints by one neighbor about another's "noise." Also included here are other various and sundry situations that people define as improper, such as a drunken person or someone who is simply said to be "causing a disturbance." Next in frequency, constituting almost one-fifth of the cases (19%), is a complaint by a woman that she has been physically injured or threatened by a man. Typically the complainant says that her husband has "hit" her or has been "beating" her, and provides no further details except, perhaps, that the man has been drinking. Also common (14%) are disputes about property (including money), such as allegations of "stealing," conflicts over the use of an automobile, and disagreements about the disposition of furniture or

---

6. Nader and Todd distinguish between a "grievance," a "conflict," and a "dispute" as follows: A *grievance* is "a circumstance or condition which one person (or group) perceives to be unjust, and the grounds for resentment or complaint [1978:14]." A *conflict* comes into being "if the aggrieved party opts for confrontation—if he throws down the gauntlet—and communicates his resentment or feeling of injustice to the offending party [1978:15]." Finally, a *dispute* "results from escalation of the conflict by making the matter public [1978:15]." In its pure form, then, a grievance is monadic, involving only one person or group, a conflict is dyadic, and a dispute is triadic, since it involves the participation of a third party who is called upon as an agent of settlement (Nader and Todd, 1978:14–15; for a similar conceptualization, see Gulliver, 1979: Chapter 3).

In Nader and Todd's vocabulary, the 317 cases featured here are "disputes," since they involved a confrontation—in progress—between two or more people, into which the police were drawn by a party's request for help. On the other hand, included in the larger sample of 550 cases are incidents in which the alleged offender was not present when the police arrived, and it is likely that in some of these the absent party was not even aware that the police were called. It does not seem that such cases would fit into Nader and Todd's scheme at all.

other possessions after a relationship has ended. A number of physical fights and threats other than those between men and women are reported as well (11%). Somewhat less frequent but nonetheless routine are calls from people who want a nonresident to leave their premises, such as women who want a bothersome man—usually an ex-husband or ex-boyfriend— "thrown out" of their apartments (7%), people who want a fellow resident to leave (6%), disputes about children, such as conflicts arising when someone—usually a man—tries to visit or take custody of a child after a marital separation (4%), requests for escorts, such as when a person—usually a woman—is afraid to enter an ex-lover's apartment to retrieve clothing and other possessions (3%), and cases in which one resident is locked out by another (2%). Finally, some incidents (4%) do not fit neatly into any of these categories, such as cases in which a woman said that her husband had been "cheating on her," a man was upset because he believed that someone else had fathered his children, a tenant complained that water and fecal matter had overflowed into the hallway and that the landlord (also her brother) would not do anything about it, a landlady wanted a tenant's guest removed, a young woman complained that her father had "tried to get in bed" with her, and several others in which people reported that someone was "crazy" and needed to be committed or recommitted to a mental hospital. Before considering other characteristics of these cases, it should be noted that although for these purposes the problems were defined by the complainants, the complainant is not always the one who calls the police in the first place. The complainant appeared to be the caller in 85% of the cases, but the caller seemed to be a third party in 3%, and in the remaining 12% it was entirely unclear who had called, whether a party in the dispute, someone else in the household, a friend, neighbor, or whatever. It should also be understood that the complainant's version of the problem should be taken as that alone, and not necessarily as an objective description of what happened.

The complainant reports violence of some kind in 43% of the disputes brought to the attention of the police. A threat of murder or severe injury is reported in 10% of the disputes, and a severe injury occurs or is attempted in an additional 5%. A weapon is involved in nearly one-fifth of the disputes (17% of 317 cases). Usually this is a knife or similar instrument (43% of the weapons), or a gun (26%), but a substantial number—almost one-third—involve something else as a tool of violence. Perhaps it is worth recording that the sample of 550 cases included, besides ordinary knives and guns, all of the following weapons: scissors, a razor, an ice pick, a meat cleaver, garden clippers, a baby bottle, sugar shaker, lamp, table, drainpipe, broomstick, rod, golf club, shovel, sledgehammer, baseball bat, wrench, brick, rock, firecrackers, sparklers, a lighted cigarette, lye, a shod foot, and teeth. In addition, a German shepherd was commanded to attack one of the people involved in a dispute between neighbors.

The Parties

The purpose of this section is to survey the social characteristics of the people centrally involved in the 317 disputes. The observers' reports provided information about the nature of the relationship between the parties, their sex, age, race, and—for cases pertaining to a single household—their status in the structure of the household itself. The social-class status of the parties (blue-collar or white-collar) was provided as well, but here the variation was negligible: As judged from outward indicators such as dress and style of life, the people involved in these disputes were of blue-collar status in 95% of the cases, of white-collar status in 3%, and of mixed status in the remaining 2% of the cases. The predominance of lower-status people itself invites further analysis, and the discussion returns to this topic in the next section (pages 124–128). First, however, the social context of the complaints is examined more closely.

THE RELATIONSHIPS

Most of the disputes—about two-thirds—arise between people who are, or were, members of the same family (including people describing themselves as "common-laws"). The typical case is a conflict between a husband and wife, comprising 35% of all disputes, while estranged couples account for another 10%. Parent–child conflicts are also frequent (11%), as are matters involving other relatives, such as siblings or in-laws (10%). Aside from family disputes, the most common are those between neighbors (15%). Others involve landlords and tenants (5%), friends or acquaintances (4%), boyfriends and girlfriends (3%), unspecified relationships in which people are said simply to "know" each other (3%), and, lastly, miscellaneous relationships such as that between an employer and his employee or a mother and daughter in conflict with the daughter's boyfriend (4%).

When the police arrive at the scene, a conflict of this kind is generally presented as a complaint by one party against another rather than a cross-complaint where each party claims to be right and presents a grievance. Thus, in 87% of the cases the complaint has but a single direction, by one person against another, while in only 12% is the matter more two-sided. The initial definition of the situation does not necessarily prevail throughout the encounter, however. Whether the police recognize a complaint and agree that the other party is the offender varies across the cases and will be discussed later in this report. Suffice it to say here that, far from having their complaints recognized, some of the complainants even find that by the close of the encounter they have been defined as the offender. Consider now the direction of the complaints presented to the police when they first arrive at the scene.

SEX

A complaint by a woman against a man is by far the most common of the various possibilities, at 56% of the total. A man complains against a woman in only 6% of the cases. Slightly more common are disputes between two men (9%) or two women (8%). Mixed cross-complaints, with a man and a woman complaining against each other, have about the same frequency (7%). Other possibilities, in which one or both sides consist of a mixed group, account for fewer than 5% of the cases each.

It should be noted that, by itself, sex is nothing more than a biological characteristic, and its sociological relevance cannot be taken for granted (see Black, 1979c:153). This depends entirely upon the social conditions that are associated with sex in any given setting, and, in a modern society such as the United States, these vary considerably across the population. Among middle-class whites, for example, women are generally dependent upon men for economic support, whereas among lower-class blacks women tend to be more independent (see pages 124–128). Hence, the fact that the most common dispute handled by the police is one in which a woman complains against a man tells us very little unless we know other facts about the social condition of the people in each case, such as who pays the rent or otherwise provides their support. Only with information of this kind can we understand, sociologically, why the pattern exists or what its implications are. This matter will be discussed in the next section.

AGE

In the vast majority of cases—83%—the parties in dispute are adults (18 years or older). Also, a substantial number—10%—are complaints by adults against juveniles. Each of the other possibilities accounts for 2% or less of the cases. It should especially be noted that juveniles rarely complain against adults (1% of the cases) or against other juveniles (1%).

Since most juveniles in modern society are dependent upon adults for their economic well-being, they tend to be subject to authority exercised by adults, particularly their parents. A number of other adults with whom they have dealings, such as teachers or employers, also have authority over them. Generally, therefore, juveniles have no standing to complain against adults, and adults who are able to exercise their own social control over juveniles do not complain to the police. But when adults have no authority of their own, as in matters involving juveniles on the streets—other people's children—they do not hesitate to call the police. The same applies when their authority over their own children is weak or unstable (see Schulz, 1969:68–70), a situation that may arise when the children are relatively independent economically. Children of lower status would appear to be more independent in this way, since their parents have less to give them, and they may therefore find means to manage on their own.

RACE

The majority of the disputes involve a black complaining against another black (62%), with nearly all of the remainder involving a white against a white (36%). Interracial complaints are extremely uncommon in the sample, then, presumably because interracial relationships were uncommon in American cities at the time of the observations, and also because where ties of this kind did exist, such as employment relationships, blacks tended to be subject to the authority of whites. In only one of the 317 cases did a black complain against a white. In addition, there were two complaints in the opposite direction, and just one interracial cross-complaint occurred. People of other races, such as Asian Americans and Native Americans, were almost entirely absent from the sample.

Like sex or age, race is not in itself a social variable, but may be more or less associated with social conditions of one kind or another. Thus, in modern America, blacks are more likely than whites to be poor, unemployed, undereducated, and of low status in other ways. The structure of family relationships among blacks also differs from that among whites to some degree (see, e.g., Frazier, 1948: Chapter 21; U.S. Department of Labor, 1965; Liebow, 1967: Chapters 3–5). Lower-class black women are relatively independent of men for their economic subsistence, for example, and so male–female relationships among lower-class blacks tend to have a more equal distribution of authority (see Frazier, 1948:344). As will be suggested below, this may explain why lower-class blacks are less able than whites to settle their own family disputes, and so are more likely to turn to the police (see pages 124–128, where further references are also provided).

HOUSEHOLD STATUS

About three-fourths of the disputes pertain to the affairs of a particular household (73%). Most of the remaining cases involve parties who represent different households, as in the typical dispute between neighbors, though occasionally a dispute may occur in a public place or other setting and may be entirely unrelated to a household as such. In any event, among the disputes in or related to a household, the complainant in the vast majority of the cases is a person with economic control over the premises. This generally means that the complainant is the one who pays the rent for an apartment or house, though sometimes he or she pays the mortgage for the property. In either case, this person speaks of the dwelling as "my apartment" or "my house," and is its "owner" for all practical purposes. A household may thus contain a social-class system in miniature, with the breadwinner at the top. The one who owns or pays the rent for a dwelling is also known as the "head of the household," perhaps because it is understood that economic control entails social control, or authority, as well. In the present cases, however, it is apparent that the heads of the households did not have enough authority to be able to get along without the police. It might be noted that the sample included one conflict between a black couple over precisely the question of who "owned" their apartment: The man wanted the woman to leave "his" apartment, but she refused, insisting that it was "hers" as well. In another, a black man wanted the police to remove a woman from "his" apartment, while she argued that because of the work she had put into it—"painting and fixing"— she had a right to remain. In each of these cases it seems reasonable to infer that the man was paying all or most of the rent, since otherwise it is unlikely that he would have presumed the authority to evict the woman.

For present purposes, unless evidence to the contrary was provided, each dispute involving spouses or common-laws was classified as a complaint between fellow heads of household. This undoubtedly misrepresents the domestic status of some of the parties in the sample. (A total of 43% of the 232 household disputes were classified in this way.) In any event, in some cases the relevant information was provided: Almost one-tenth of the household disputes clearly involve a husband and wife living together, one of whom is economically dependent upon the other (8%), and among these virtually every case is a complaint by the head of the household against the dependent spouse.

Apart from married couples, in some cases the head of a household complains against another resident who is dependent upon his or her resources, such as a child or other relative (12% of the household disputes), a former spouse now residing elsewhere (8%), or another nonresident who is present in the dwelling (12%). Occasionally a former spouse complains against the head of the household (3%), as when a former husband wants to retrieve property that he bought for the dwelling that is now controlled by his former wife, and occasionally a resident of the dwelling such as a child complains against the head of the household or another resident (2%). The remaining cases (12%) involve other combinations—for example, a man demanding visiting rights with his child at his former mother-in-law's, a woman wanting her estranged husband to leave her father's house where she was now living, and a woman's lover complaining that her children had stolen tools from his truck while he was in bed with her.

A Note on Who Calls the Police

The typical dispute handled by the police involves a lower-class black woman complaining against a lower-class black man. Even taking into account that the present sample derives primarily from urban areas heavily populated by low-income people, the fact remains that middle-class people are underrepresented in the cases, and the same pattern has been found by other investigators as well (e.g., Cumming *et al.*, 1965:280; Parnas, 1967:915; Westley, 1970:60; Hutchison, 1975:10–11). To understand why this is so, it is necessary to compare the households of middle- and lower-class people. Consider, in particular, middle-class whites in comparison to lower-class blacks.

As noted above (page 122), a middle-class white woman is more likely than a lower-class black woman to live in a condition of dependency in relation to a man. She is more likely to live on the earnings of her husband, in a dwelling financed by him, and to be, in short, a "housewife." Such a woman is not readily able to leave her situation one day and replace it with an equivalent the next. This also applies to a lesser extent among many middle-class women who are employed outside the home, since their earnings are often not adequate to support a household at the level to which they are accustomed. Moreover, to the degree that a woman is economically dependent upon her husband, she is subject to his authority (see Black, 1976:32).[7] In this respect her situation is similar to a child's. Like a child, she may often get what she wants, but ultimately she is not empowered to enforce her will with sanctions comparable to those wielded by the man of the house. If a conflict occurs, her husband generally has the ability to protect his interests, and does not need the police to do this for him. His wife, on the other hand, is unlikely to define his conduct as a matter for the police. Indeed, to him this would surely be a major offense in itself, a challenge to his authority. It is therefore almost inconceivable that a totally dependent woman would ask the police to remove her husband from his own house. If he beats her, she is unlikely to invoke the law, and in some cases may even accept the violence as entirely legitimate, perhaps a punishment that she deserved because of her misbehavior (see, e.g., Gelles, 1972:58–60). Be they husbands or wives, then, middle-class people are unlikely to call the police about their domestic problems.[8]

It should be added that all of this applies not only to middle-class whites but to any people who live in households that are hierarchical in structure. It applies, for example, to many middle-class blacks as well, and to the patriarchal households of many Appalachian whites, Asian Americans, Puerto Rican Americans,

---

7. Frederick Engels long ago pointed to the relationship between "male supremacy" and the control of wealth by men:

> In the great majority of cases today, at least in the possessing classes, the husband is obliged to earn a living and support his family, and that in itself gives him a position of supremacy without any need for special legal titles and privileges. Within the family he is the bourgeois, and the wife represents the proletariat [1884:137].

Perhaps it should be added that in the text above—as elsewhere in this report—the concept of authority refers only to the capacity to exercise social control (Black, 1979c:152), and implies nothing about its subjective meaning to the people involved (compare Weber, 1922:324–328; for a discussion of the legitimacy of social control, see pages 169–172).

8. It should be recognized that in addition to the structure of their households there are other grounds on which it might be expected that middle-class people would be reluctant to call the police about their conflicts with one another. Especially important is the status inferiority of the police in relation to people of the middle class: When they want a third-party to help them settle a dispute, middle-class people seem to prefer someone closer to their own social status (Baumgartner, 1980b; 1981b:forthcoming). They may also want to avoid the penal style of social control—always a possibility when the police are involved—in favor of another style, such as might be provided by a lawyer, psychiatrist, or marriage counselor (see Black, 1976:29).

Mexican Americans, and others, regardless of social class. Speaking of house-holds such as these, one policeman commented to another investigator:

> The man is expected to beat up his woman to settle arguments. He expects to have his own way without back talk or outside interference. Therefore the woman usually does not complain [Parnas, 1967:952].

As one Puerto Rican woman explained to a judge who was considering what to do about her husband's violence toward her, "He is my husband. He is supposed to beat me [Parnas, 1967:952, punctuation edited]." In short, wherever authority of any kind is strong, in households or elsewhere, there will not be many calls to the police (see Black, 1976:107–108).

Now consider lower-class blacks. In their homes, lower-class black women are possibly the most independent women in America, and among the most independent in the modern world (for a review of the literature, see MacDonald and MacDonald, 1978).[9] Whether by employment or as recipients of public welfare, many black women are the sole support of their households (see, e.g., Farley and Hermalin, 1971). In a substantial number of cases, these households include a man who lives there as a dependent. Other such women share expenses with a man but have enough personal income to get along well without him. These arrangements give black women a considerable degree of domestic author-ity (see, e.g., Rainwater, 1970:164–166). In fact, in many of the cases in the sample a black woman called the police because she wanted a man thrown out of her apartment—a request that is difficult to imagine in a middle-class setting. This does not mean, however, that the condition of a lower-class black woman is altogether comparable to that of a middle-class white man who supports his wife. What is different is that a lower-class black man is never so dependent upon a woman as a middle-class white woman is dependent upon a man. In part, this is because a lower-class black man can more readily find alternative means of support, such as casual employment or the help of his relatives or friends (see Liebow, 1967: Chapters 2, 6; Stack, 1974). The level at which he is accustomed to living is easier to achieve as well. In addition, there is some evidence that the rhythm of intimacy between the sexes in his world, with its relatively high rate of change from one partner to another, may make it easier for a black man to find a replacement for any woman upon whom he depends for economic support (see, e.g., Liebow, 1967: Chapters 4–5; Hannerz, 1970; Stack, 1974: Chapter 7).

---

9. Engels also observed that working women among the lower classes are more independent than the wives of the bourgeoisie:

> Now that large-scale industry has taken the wife out of the home onto the labor market and into the factory, and made her often the breadwinner of the family, no basis for any kind of male supremacy is left in the proletarian household, except, perhaps, for something of the brutality toward women that has spread since the introduction of monogamy [1884:135].

For that matter, as a man he is given much of the initiative in this process, whereas a middle-class woman ordinarily will wait until a man takes an interest in her. A black man may also choose simply to live with a woman, whereas the middle-class white woman seems to be more inclined toward marriage—an arrangement that is surely more difficult to find. For all of these reasons, then, a lower-class black woman is unlikely to enjoy the domestic authority of a middle-class white man. Even when she is the breadwinner, the household is only marginally matriarchal. To a large extent it is egalitarian, and not truly the counterpart of the patriarchal households described earlier (compare Parnas, 1967:952). Moreover, any degree of hierarchy in a lower-class black household is likely to be precarious, constantly threatened by the uncertain future of the household itself and by economic insecurities to which the poor are especially subject. Loss of a job by either partner, for example, is generally followed by a loss of authority at home (see Komarovsky, 1940: Chapter 2). As one observer of lower-class blacks remarks:

> When the father finds a job, his wife and children are willing to listen to him and do what he says. When the father loses his job, his wife becomes much stricter in her evaluation of his demeanor within the household. In one case, the woman had her husband ejected from her apartment because he scratched her furniture, was unemployed, and could not pay for its repair [Rainwater, 1966:122].

In any event, often there is a struggle for authority in these relationships, so that conflicts are prone to escalation and difficult to resolve. And, with nowhere else to turn, the woman involved may decide to call the police.[10]

It is where authority is contested or absent that people call the police. They call when they are themselves unable to handle a problem, to decide who is right or wrong or how a compromise might be reached, and when they have no one else to whom they can resort. It is therefore noteworthy that in nearly every case in the sample (98%) it appeared to the observer that no one other than the parties themselves had attempted or would attempt to settle the dispute in the absence of the police. Other family members, neighbors, and friends are not asked to intervene, nor do they volunteer. Aside from a child or two, no one else is even present at the scene of the typical dispute. The parties are individuals on their own, largely alone in the city, or at least alone for purposes of social control. By contrast, when people live in extended families or traditional ethnic enclaves

---

10. The patterns of domestic life among lower-class blacks, including their propensity to call the police, have led many observers to describe the contemporary black family as "disorganized," "unstable," or even "pathological" (see, e.g., Frazier, 1948; U.S. Department of Labor, 1965). Apart from whether or not this is a meaningful vocabulary in which to describe such patterns, it is important to recognize the extent to which they may be understood as an expression of the relative equality between the sexes, a condition less often seen in the more "normal" families of the middle class.

they are likely to be assisted by others in the management of their conflicts, and so are less likely to call the police (see, e.g., Suttles, 1968:101–102; Doo, 1973; Merry, 1979:914–916).

In closing this section, it should be emphasized that it is not the sex of the parties that explains why so many calls to the police involve men and women as adversaries. This has, in itself, little relevance. Where the authority of either party—the man or the woman—is strong, conflicts are generally settled without the police, and the same applies to hierarchical relationships of other kinds, including those of parents and children, employers and employees, and teachers and students. The parties might be male, female, or mixed. Thus, if two men or two women share the same dwelling, the degree to which their relationship is hierarchical will condition how they handle their disputes. In fact, a number of disputes in the sample involved homosexual couples living together in households remarkably similar to those of many lower-class black couples without a formal marriage relationship, or "common-laws." As in the case of common-laws, these are households in which the parties are both more independent—economically and otherwise—than the typical middle-class housewife, and in which authority is more equally distributed. Since a dispute involving a homosexual couple is socially similar to a common-law dispute, then, it is likely to result in a call to the police for the same reasons. The nature of the homosexuals' disputes themselves also resemble those of common-laws, and are even described in much the same language by the police (e.g., "a lovers' spat between queers"). Often the conflict revolves around the living arrangement itself, as when one party wants the other to leave his or her apartment, or when one wants protection while he or she moves clothing and other property from the other's apartment. Only the fact of homosexuality itself distinguishes these disputes from those of common-laws (see Black, 1976:111–113). Other situations with features conducive to calls to the police include relationships between neighbors, especially in neighborhoods with a high turnover of residents—where authority is largely absent—and three-party relationships of all kinds, such as lovers' triangles and those involving a couple and a parent or other relative of one of the parties—where authority is likely to be contested (see Simmel, 1908:135–136, 145–153). In sum, people are more likely to call the police wherever there is a struggle for authority. In this sense, many of the disputes handled by the police are disputes about authority itself.

Modes of Dispute Settlement

This section provides a broad overview of how the police respond to disputes in progress between people who know each other. It describes the specific requests—if any—that people make of them, and it surveys their general reactions, including the styles of social control they employ and the quantity of social control they exercise.

As noted earlier (page 121), when the police arrive at the scene of a dispute, typically they are presented with a complaint by one party against another. In a number of these cases the complainant also makes a request for a specific action that he or she would like the police to take against the party defined as an offender. Although information about these requests was not recorded by the observers in almost one-fourth of the 317 reports (24%), and in a few other cases the police left the scene before such a request could be made (4%), over two-thirds of the complainants in the remaining cases ($N = 229$) made a specific request (71%). Among those who do ask the police to take a particular action ($N = 162$), 36% want them to order or remove an alleged offender from the setting (usually a dwelling), 25% specifically ask them to make an arrest, and 22% want them to order the alleged offender to alter his or her conduct or to take a positive action of some kind (e.g., to unlock a door or to lower the volume of music being played). A few others (6%) want nothing more than a police escort while they are in the presence of another party, such as when they enter an apartment to retrieve their personal belongings. Still a few more cases involve different requests by each party in reference to the other (5%), while the rest involve a miscellany of requests, such as cases in which people wanted the police to order an alleged offender to make restitution, take an alleged offender to a mental hospital, search for a man with a gun in a neighbor's apartment, or assist in getting children away from an estranged spouse who was allegedly mistreating them (5%). Although a substantial number of complainants make no specific demand upon the police, then (29% of those about whom this information was available), most people seem to know what they want the police to do. For their part, the police entirely comply with the requests that are made of them in about one-half of the cases (52%, $N = 162$), and in a few instances they partially comply (2%). Among the cases in which they fail to comply ($N = 74$), they do so most often (80% of the cases) not because they take the side of the alleged offender or because they side with one party in a cross-complaint, but because they remain neutral, siding with no one. We shall see below that neutrality is one element in a larger style of social control often used by the police when they handle disputes of this kind. Before the various responses of the police are examined in detail, however, perhaps a few words should be said about cases that they refuse to handle at all.

In 13 cases in the sample of 317—about one in twenty—the police left the setting immediately after hearing some of the facts about the nature of the dispute. Sometimes declaring that the matter is "not police business," sometimes referring the parties to someone else, and sometimes simply turning and walking away, in these cases they refuse to exercise any social control at all, even though the parties are present and the conflict is still alive to some degree. With so few of these cases in the sample, it is difficult if not impossible to determine how they differ from those the police agree to handle. It seems more than a coincidence, however, that in about one-half of the refusals the matter in question falls within the jurisdiction of another agency. Thus, in one case a landlord had moved a tenant's furniture out onto the street, explaining that the tenant owed him $38 in back rent. As soon as the police realized that no eviction order had been issued, they told the parties to settle the matter in landlord–tenant court, and left. In another instance, a woman sought to have the police remove a foster daughter whom she no longer wanted, but they told her to contact the social worker who was handling the case, and left. Several other times they refused to get involved in matters pertaining to alleged "mental cases," including once when a couple wanted their daughter to be taken to a mental hospital and again when a woman recently released from a mental hospital complained that her husband had hit her. On the other hand, in the remaining cases of refusal the police backed away from matters that did not so easily lend themselves to alternative means of settlement. Usually these involved neighbors making cross-allegations of some kind. In one case, for example, a woman complained that boys in the neighborhood had been shooting their slingshots at her car, but as she spoke to the police another woman "came storming up" and said that the first woman's son had been throwing rocks at her house. The police left immediately without saying anything at all. In another case, a man claimed that two boys in the neighborhood had kicked his door and cracked it, while the boys said that the door had been cracked before. As soon as the police heard these arguments, they left abruptly, saying that it was "not police business." In another neighbor dispute involving a "torrent of abuse" between two women, the observer commented that the police were not able "to control their laughter" and departed from the scene without further ado. Still another case of refusal was a dispute between in-laws over the question of who would wash the dishes. The police said they had "no power in a situation of this type," and left. They gave a similar reason when they "immediately turned on their heels and walked out" after hearing a woman yell "in a shrewlike voice" that her husband— now watching television—had hit her a short time before. In each of these examples it may not seem surprising to the reader that the police refused to exercise social control of any kind, since from a lawyer's perspective their "legal" obligation was, at best, debatable. And yet these are exceptional cases, not in their substance but in the response of the police. In the vast majority of disputes—96%—the police are perfectly willing to intervene to some extent, no matter what the facts may be. In doing so, their range of responses includes variation in both the style and quantity of social control.

STYLES OF SOCIAL CONTROL

Across societies and other social settings, it is possible to observe several styles of social control, each a distinctive way by which people define and respond to deviant behavior. These include the penal, compensatory, therapeutic, and conciliatory styles (Black, 1976:4–6). In the penal style of social control, the deviant is defined as a violator of a prohibition, an offender deserving of condemnation and punishment. In the compensatory style, he or she is understood as someone who has failed to live up to an obligation, and who therefore owes the victim restitution for any damage that was done. According to the therapeutic style, the deviant is someone whose conduct is abnormal and who needs help of some kind, such as treatment by a psychiatrist. Last, in the conciliatory style, deviant behavior is taken as one side of a social conflict in need of settlement, without regard to who is right or wrong. Not only is there variation in the prevalence of these styles from one society or other setting to another, or from one agency of social control to another, but there also may be variation within a particular agency, even from one case to the next. This applies, in fact, to the police: Although in modern societies the police are formally empowered only to enforce a penal system of social control—the criminal law—they frequently handle cases in other styles as well. This is especially striking in the handling of cases such as those in the present study. Indeed, the language of "dispute settlement" is used in this discussion precisely because the police adopt the conciliatory style of social control in so many of the cases, more even than those in which they employ the penal style. The therapeutic and compensatory styles also appear in their pure form from time to time, and the police often use the styles in combination as well.

In the cases that the police agree to handle, their most frequent response involves a combination of the conciliatory and penal styles of social control (45% of 304 cases). Here the police make an effort to find a solution satisfactory to both parties, but at the same time they relate to the conflict partly in terms of who is to blame, such as by noting that one of the parties could be arrested if his or her conduct recurred or simply by admonishing one of them for what allegedly happened. Nearly one-fourth of the cases (24%) are handled in an entirely conciliatory fashion, with a concern for restoring peace in the situation and without defining either party as the only wrong-doer. Almost as many—22%— are handled in an entirely penal fashion, typically with one party being singled out as the offender and the other as the victim. Only 2% are handled entirely in the therapeutic style, with the alleged offender defined as mentally ill, and less than 1% are handled entirely in the compensatory style. (In the sample, just one case was handled in this way, one in which an employee was told to return the clean uniforms he had taken because he had not—as agreed—reimbursed his employer for having them laundered.) Another 2% of the cases are handled only in a preventive fashion, as when, for example, the police agree to escort someone who is moving out of another's dwelling. The rest (4%) involve other combinations of the various possibilities, such as the conciliatory and therapeutic styles, the penal and therapeutic, or even the conciliatory, penal, and therapeutic styles together in a single encounter.

The cases in the sample were also classified according to the major style of social control by which they were handled, so that those involving combinations could be described more simply for purposes of analysis. Considering again the 304 cases actually handled by the police, the dominant style is conciliatory in slightly over one-half (52%), penal in 41%, therapeutic in 2%, and compensatory in just 1%. The remaining cases involve preventive work (3%) or cannot be characterized in terms of a dominant style (1%). For the most part, then, the police alternate between the conciliatory and the penal styles of social control when they handle disputes.

QUANTITY OF SOCIAL CONTROL

Whatever its style may be, the social control exercised by the police also varies in quantity. They may conciliate a dispute to a greater or lesser degree, for example, at one extreme simply listening to the parties for a few moments before leaving, at the other investing an hour or more of their time and energy in order to learn the history and details of the dispute and to find a compromise that will allow the parties to live in harmony long after they have gone. In this sense, then, conciliation may be understood as a quantitative variable. The degree to which the police relate to a case in the penal style varies in quantity as well, ranging for the most part from a mere scolding to an arrest. Occasionally the police severely punish or even kill one of the parties, as when someone resists arrest or otherwise menaces an officer handling a case.

In instances in which the police are conciliatory to some degree, almost one-fourth of the time they do little or nothing beyond listening to one or both of the parties talk about the nature of their problem (22%). At a minimum, this generally serves to pacify the parties for the time being, though it may also have other less obvious consequences.[11] An extreme example of this tactic was described to another investigator by one of the officers he interviewed:

> One police officer I really admired, he'd come into a family beef with a husband and wife throwing and yelling at each other. Then he'd set down on the couch and take his hat off, and he didn't say a word. Sooner or later the couple felt kind of silly. He'd take 45 minutes in each of these situations, but he never had to come back [Muir, 1977:82].

---

11. As one student of mediation remarks:

   By his very presence a quite passive mediator can encourage positive communication and interaction between the parties, stimulating the continuation or the renewal of the exchange of information. Because he is there, the parties are often constrained to observe minimal courtesy to each other, to reduce personal invective and to listen and to respond with some relevance. A party may feel it necessary to explain and justify his case, directly or indirectly, to the mediator because he is there at all or perhaps because he is perceived as a "generalized other" . . . . This has been a quite deliberate strategy on occasion, for example by some American industrial mediators. They attend a meeting between the two parties, but sit and say nothing and seek to show no particular reaction to what is said and done . . . . Deliberate or not, the strategy appears to be effective where deadlock occurs when positive information is not being exchanged and evident possibilities are not being explored because of that [Gulliver, 1977:26–27].

This might be called passive mediation or even protomediation to distinguish it from the more active kind in which a third party serves as a go-between, assuring that each disputant hears the other's side of the conflict and encouraging them to work out a settlement themselves. (For an overview of forms and elements of mediation, see Fuller, 1971; Gulliver, 1977.) The police engage in active mediation in nearly one-half of the cases in which they are conciliatory at all (45%), and in another one-third they go beyond this to arbitration, acting as go-betweens but also making clear how they feel the dispute should be settled (30%). Occasionally the police simply try to calm or reassure one or both parties (1% of the cases), or they suggest conciliation by a third party other than themselves (another 1%). For instance, in one dispute between a brother and sister that arose when the former poured water on the latter's barbeque grill, the police turned to the mother of the house to settle the problem.

Among the 213 cases handled partially or entirely in the penal style, the degree of severity varied considerably. In almost one-fourth of the cases (23%) the police arrest the alleged offender—for all practical purposes the most severe possibility.[12] Next in severity, and occurring at about the same rate as arrest (24%), is the ordering or removal of a person from the setting of the dispute, or situational banishment. (In a few more cases—6%—the police remove a person from the setting by convincing him or her to leave voluntarily.) Next is the threat of arrest, accounting for 19% of the cases. Still another expression of the penal style, scolding or admonishment, is as far as the police apply their authority in 22% of the disputes. The remaining cases (6%) are handled with a variety of penal tactics, such as a ticket for curfew violation given to a juvenile, physical force, or its threat. In one case, for example, an officer pulled a young white man's hair to encourage him to give more details about a stabbing allegedly committed by his brother. Also included in this residual category were several cases in which the police took people to the station but did not formally arrest them. In each of these cases, in fact, the purpose of the trip was to convince a complainant to withdraw his or her complaint. One of these involved a black juvenile who had been cut by an acquaintance in an argument over a card game. Both were taken to the station, where the victim was persuaded to forget the whole affair, but only after the police threatened to arrest him for gambling if he continued to press his complaint.

In sum, the police use a variety of strategies and tactics when they handle disputes between people who know each other. Although most of the time they relate to the conflict primarily in a conciliatory or a penal style, the quantity of each of these varies, with some people receiving a great deal of attention, others little or none. Both the style and quantity of dispute settlement by the police vary

---

12. More severe possibilities include beating, torture, and execution of the alleged offender, but the police use these tactics extremely infrequently in the context of disputes such as those in the present sample.

with its location and direction in social space, with who complains about whom, to whom, and under what circumstances. Most of the following pages are concerned with patterns of this kind.

Dispute Settlement and Social Space

Each social setting may be conceived as a location in social space, with vertical, horizontal, symbolic, corporate, and normative dimensions (see Black, 1976; 1979c). If there is an uneven distribution of wealth among the participants, for example, the setting has a vertical dimension, and each person or group has a higher or lower position in the distribution. Even if the participants are equal among themselves, all of them may be higher or lower in some larger distribution of wealth. The vertical dimension of social space may also be associated with other differences across the participants, such as differences in race, sex, or age. Thus, in modern America, blacks generally have less wealth than whites, women less than men, and children less than adults. This correspondence varies within and across societies, however, so that the vertical location of blacks, women, and children may be different from one setting to another. As noted earlier, for instance, black women in the United States are generally less dependent upon men than are white women, especially white women of the middle or upper classes (see pages 124–128). Nonetheless, the fact remains that within a single society biological characteristics of this kind may serve as crude indicators of social location. The following discussion shows how dispute settlement by the police varies with its location and direction in vertical space—as measured by the race, social class, household status, and age of the parties—and also with the degree of intimacy between the parties, their organization into groups, and the legitimacy of the police themselves.

RACE

Since in modern America so many more blacks than whites are poor, race is a crude measure of wealth. It is also a crude measure of ethnicity: Most black Americans are members of a cultural minority that to some degree has its own way of life. They are more likely than whites to have certain other social characteristics as well, such as a low level of education, unemployment, and a criminal record. It should be remembered, moreover, that most police are white—nearly 90% of those observed during the present study. All of these conditions increase the legal vulnerability of blacks, and they also decrease their capacity to mobilize law against others (see generally Black, 1976). Hence, when they have disputes such as those in the present sample, it might be expected that blacks will receive less help from the police. This is, in fact, what the evidence indicates: Blacks often call upon the police to settle their disputes—they do so proportionately more than whites—but they are less likely to get what they request, and the police expend less time and energy on their problems. At the same time, they are as likely as whites to be punished.

It is relevant to note that blacks and whites call upon the police to handle a comparable array of problems. This can be seen in Table 5–1. Twice as many of the calls from blacks involve women complaining about the violence of men, however, while only half as many pertain to property disputes or noise and other miscellaneous disturbances. These differences by themselves do not demonstrate that black women are beaten or threatened by men more often than white women, that blacks have fewer disputes about property, or that blacks have quieter neighborhoods, since the propensity of each race to report such matters to the police may differ substantially. The actual patterns of conduct could even be the opposite of what the calls might first suggest. In any event, the larger similarity in calls from blacks and whites makes it possible to compare how the police respond to people of each race.

Table 5–2 shows that the major styles in which the police respond to the calls of blacks and whites is quite similar, with about half being handled in a conciliatory style and most of the remainder in a penal style: The behavior of black and white complainants is quite similar as well, with 72% of the blacks and 69% of the whites making a specific request of the police. Even the requests themselves are similar, with, for example, 29% of the blacks and 20% of the whites asking the police to order an alleged offender to leave the setting (usually a dwelling),

TABLE 5–1

Nature of Dispute according to Race of Parties[a]

Nature of Dispute (in order of frequency)	Race of Parties		
	Black	White	Total
Noise or other disturbance	23	41	29
Physical injury of woman by man (or threat)	24	12	20
Dispute about property (including money)	9	23	14
Physical fight or injury (or threat)—other	13	8	11
Resident wants nonresident to leave	8	5	7
Resident wants fellow resident to leave	8	2	5
Dispute about child	5	3	4
Request for escort	3	2	3
Resident locked out by another resident	2	1	2
Other	5	3	5
Total percent	100	100	100
Total cases	(195)	(113)	(308)

[a] By percent.

TABLE 5-2
Major Style of Social Control Exercised by Police according to Race of Parties[a]

| | Race of Parties | | |
Style of Social Control	Black	White	Total
Conciliatory	54	51	53
Penal	39	45	41
Therapeutic	3	2	2
Compensatory	1	1	1
Preventive action only	3	2	3
Other	1	—	*
Total percent	101	101	100
Total cases	(188)	(107)	(295)

[a] By percent.
*Less than .5%.

and 19% of the blacks and 17% of the whites asking them to make an arrest. How the police respond to complainants of each race, however, is not so similar: White complainants are more successful with their requests. Thus, the police comply entirely with the complainant's request in 61% of the disputes involving whites, but in only 47% of those involving blacks. They also take a greater interest in the nature of disputes involving whites, investing more time and energy in their settlement.

When the police are conciliatory in style, they are actively so in almost nine-tenths of the disputes involving whites, but this proportion falls to about two-thirds for blacks (see Table 5-3). In particular, when dealing with whites the police are more likely to act as mediators or arbitrators, striving to resolve the conflict, whereas in the black cases they are more inclined to stand by passively, doing little or nothing of a positive nature. In one case involving whites, for example, a woman explained that a man she "dated" 7 years before had contacted her at the beginning of the year to renew their relationship. At that time he gave her a check for $600, but now that they had broken up again the man wanted his money back. He said it was always meant to be a loan, whereas she claimed that it was a gift that she did not want to accept in the first place. In any event, the man had been making threatening phone calls, demanding an immediate return of the money. The woman told him that she would not be able to get the money until next week, but he was not satisfied. After hearing the entire story—this is only an outline—one of the officers called the man and told him that he should stop making threats, that the woman said she would return the money, and that if she did not do so he should take her to court. Apparently he accepted this resolution, and the complainant also seemed satisfied that the police had settled

TABLE 5-3

Mode of Conciliation by Police according to Race of Parties[a]

Mode of Conciliation	Race of Parties		
	Black	White	Total
Passive: little or no positive action	29	11	23
Mediation	37	59	45
Arbitration	31	29	30
Emotional support	1	1	1
Refer to nonpolice agency	2	—	1
Total percent	100	100	100
Total cases	(139)	(74)	(213)

[a] By percent.

the matter as well as they could. In another case involving whites, the police arrived to find a couple arguing on the sidewalk. They had been living together until 3 weeks earlier when they fought and the man left. Now he had returned and had "stolen" money from her, kicking in a glass door and cutting his foot in the process. The observer noted that the police "entered the debate." One stated that "it was obvious that they could not get along," and suggested that one of them leave. The woman agreed to do so, without getting her money back. (After the incident one of the officers remarked to the observer that 3 weeks before "the situation was reversed," with the woman "stealing" the man's money and he being the one to leave.)

Later, it will be seen that under the right conditions the police will engage in even more conciliation than is shown in these examples. In cases involving blacks, however, they are less likely to intervene in this way. On a number of occasions the police frankly expressed their lack of concern for the problems of blacks, including incidents in which someone's physical well-being was apparently in danger. In one case, for instance, a black woman complained that her husband had struck her, and he in turn complained that she had threatened him with a knife. The police told the couple to settle their problem in court, and promptly left, abandoning them to their own devices. One officer then commented to the observer, "If we stayed around them a little longer I think we would have been in the fight." The other added, "Maybe them two big niggers will kill themselves before they get to court and save time for everyone." Another case involved a black man whom the police had taken to the hospital earlier that evening after his wife cut him severely with a pair of scissors. It is unclear in the observer's report what was requested of the police at that time, but the case had been handled entirely as a medical problem, without an arrest or crime report. Later, after getting "stitched up," the man returned to the apartment, and his wife, fearing revenge, called the police. According to the observer, the officers "found the whole matter routine." They suggested that the woman wait and see what her husband would do, and told her that she should take the matter to a civil court. As they were leaving, one of the officers nonchalantly remarked, "We'll be back. She'll kill him." In still another case, a black woman said that her common-law husband had assaulted her, and she wanted him arrested. The police said they could not make an arrest since it was a misdemeanor that did not occur in their presence. They advised the woman to get a warrant, and left her with the alleged offender. Back in the patrol car, one of the officers dismissed the complaint as follows: "She's probably on him because he's been playing around with other women. I doubt if he actually assaulted her." In his report, the observer generalized that in matters involving common-laws, "even serious assaults," the police "like to avoid getting involved in mediating," and that they "usually advise warrants and leave as soon as possible." As one officer said, "I don't fuss with these domestics [family disputes] any more than necessary, especially these common-law set-ups." This might be taken to apply to disputes involving lower-class blacks in particular, since in modern America the concept of "common-law marriage" is most associated with that group, and many blacks themselves speak of their relationships in the same way. In short, then, although the police are basically conciliatory in style in as many disputes involving blacks as whites, blacks receive, case by case, less active help of this kind.

In regard to the penal style, the conduct of the police toward blacks is not entirely identical to that toward whites, but it is similar. Thus, as Table 5–4 shows, blacks are slightly more likely to be arrested, while whites are a bit more likely to be ordered to leave the setting of a dispute. Blacks are also more likely to be threatened with arrest, while whites are more likely to be scolded or admonished.

TABLE 5–4

Penal Action by Police according to Race of Parties[a]

Penal Action (in order of severity)	Race of Parties		
	Black	White	Total
Arrest	25	21	23
Order or remove from setting	21	29	24
Threaten arrest	24	12	19
Scold or admonish	18	26	22
Ask or advise to leave setting	8	2	6
Other	4	9	6
Total percent	100	99	100
Total cases	(125)	(82)	(207)

[a] By percent.

The police make an arrest or threaten to do so in almost one-half of the cases in which they are penal toward blacks, but in only one-third of the cases involving whites. It might therefore be inferred that the police are more legalistic and coercive toward blacks, even though an order to leave a setting—more frequent for whites—has legalistic and coercive overtones as well. Moreover, this interpretation is consistent with other features of police conduct toward the two races. In particular, the police seem to vacillate between indifference and hostility toward blacks, reluctant to become involved in their affairs but heavy-handed when they do so. Typically they are aloof if not openly contemptuous, and during the observation period most of the officers expressed much dislike of blacks and their way of life (see Black and Reiss, 1967:132–137). For example, one officer said of a black woman who had asked for help in retrieving her clothes from her former lover's apartment, "She'll be living with another bum tomorrow and call us to bail her out." In another case, the officer spoke of the complainant who called as a "nigger bitch." And an officer remarked after still another encounter, "See how these shines [blacks] live? Like pigs. They're a bunch of drunks. See her friend? Just a boy for tonight."

By contrast, the police seem more likely to identify with the white people they meet. In one instance, the observer noted that the officer "obviously sympathized" with a white woman who bemoaned the fact that she was "trapped in a Negro neighborhood" and "could not afford to move." They also relate to whites in a more personal style, with more camaraderie, whereas blacks are more likely to be treated distantly, as objects rather than people (see Black and Reiss, 1967:56–60). An observer noted how uncomfortable and embarrassed he himself felt merely to be present during one encounter in which the police "did not so much as acknowledge [the] presence" of several black children who stood watching them.

Although in many cases involving blacks the police do little beyond knocking at the door, when they choose to exercise authority it appears that it is more likely to be coercive in character than in comparable cases involving whites. In one case, for instance, the police were called by a black woman whose estranged common-law husband had broken into her apartment in order to repossess furniture that he claimed was his. The woman insisted that the property was jointly owned, not his alone. The officers advised the man to bring a lawsuit against the woman, but he did not seem to take the suggestion seriously, and proceeded to carry a television set toward the door. The woman shoved him, and he fell to the floor, at which time the police intervened and placed him under arrest for being "drunk and disorderly." The observer reported that the officers used "quite a bit of force" to handcuff him and move him to the patrol car, and that he struggled against them, striking his head on the cement landing of the stairs in the process. In the car, the officers called the man "nigger," and one added, "worse than that, you're just a common alley nigger." In another case, a black woman wanted a man "thrown out" of her apartment, but he insisted that he lived there and would not leave. One of the officers "had already drawn his blackjack in anticipation of a struggle," and when the man still refused to leave they took hold of him and told him he was under arrest. The observer described in detail the manner in which the man was taken into custody: "They pinned his arms and grabbed the back of his belt and started to manhandle him out the door. Somehow the man ended up on the floor, and so he was thereupon dragged down two flights of stairs. A commotion started at the foot of the stairway, and one of the officers hit the man with the blackjack."

In each of these examples the arrest and injury of a person might have been avoided if the police had made a greater effort to work out a solution with the people involved. Moreover, black policemen might well have handled these cases in a different manner. Thus, in another case (not included in the sample of disputes) two black officers were dispatched to pick up a black man who had been arrested by a white officer on foot patrol, and they were openly unhappy with how the man had been handled. After they heard the details of what had happened—largely a display of disrespect by the black man—they remarked to the observer that if they had handled the situation there surely would not have been an arrest. Consistent with this, another investigator found that "Negro officers were less reticent, more flexible, and hence more effective than white officers in handling Negro disputes [Parnas, 1967:949]." It should be added, however, that there is also evidence that black officers show more concern than white officers about black victims, a pattern that may result in a higher likelihood of arrest when black officers handle blacks who victimize other blacks (see Banton, 1964:173–174; Friedrich, 1977:308–313).

Though in some cases white officers may be especially coercive toward blacks, this does not mean that they hold blacks to a higher standard of conduct in their dealings with other blacks. On the contrary, they appear to be relatively unconcerned about how blacks treat each other, and less likely to invoke the law when a black complains against a black than when a white complains against a white (see Black, 1976:17).[13] In one case, a white woman complained that a man

13. There is also evidence that white citizens themselves hold each other to higher standards of conduct. Thus, they seem more likely to mobilize the police concerning matters that lower-class blacks presumably ignore or handle themselves, such as "noisiness," juveniles defined as "rowdy" or "disorderly," and intoxicated persons. In fact, lower-class blacks are relatively unlikely to call the police unless violence occurs or is threatened (which may be precipitated by what seem to an outsider to be trivial matters), whereas whites routinely call when physical danger is not involved in any way. It appears, then, that for many lower-class blacks an absence of violence is "public order" enough, while many whites demand what they view as quiet and seemliness as well (see page 135). At the same time, whites may be less likely than lower-class blacks to call the police about violence that occurs within their families (see pages 124–128). In any event, all generalizations about the conditions under which people call the police must be understood as highly speculative until a great deal more information is available about how each group behaves and handles its grievances in everyday life.

(apparently her estranged husband) had broken into her apartment and threatened her children. She directed the police to a nearby tavern where the man was drinking. Doing what the woman asked, the police walked into the tavern and immediately placed the man under arrest for "disorderly conduct." It is difficult to imagine the same response to a complaint by a black woman under the same circumstances. Instead, it is more likely that the complainant would have been told that there was nothing the police could do. White policemen are less likely to make a judgment of any kind when a black complains about another black. Thus, when a black woman complains of a beating or threat by a man, the dominant style of the police is penal in only 29% of the cases $(N=44)$, whereas in a small number of cases involving whites this proportion is 43% $(N=14)$. The use of coercion against a black seems to become more likely primarily when a police officer rather than another black citizen is the offended party, including cases in which a black person is hostile or uncooperative toward an officer (see pages 169–172). Otherwise the police behave with relative indifference toward blacks, offenders as well as complainants.

It might be added that this indifference toward blacks has been found in several other studies of the police. After noting how the police handled the cutting of a black man by his wife as nothing more than a medical problem, for example, one investigator commented as follows:

> If the family were white, the police would take the offense more seriously. A stabbing by a white woman of her husband suggests a potential homicide to police, while a similar Negro cutting can be written off as a "North Westville battery" [Skolnick, 1966:172].

Another investigator makes a similar comment about the handling of violence in a black area:

> What might appear to be an aggravated assault to an officer assigned elsewhere would, to the officer in this precinct, be looked upon merely as a family disturbance [La Fave, 1965:112].

And still another generalized about what he saw while observing the police:

> An officer who came across a Negro woman who had been badly beaten by her lover showed none of the feelings of indignation and sympathy he might have revealed had she been white. There were some exceptions, of course . . . , but generally speaking the white policeman saw beatings and stabbings as customs of the Negro sections, like shooting craps [Banton, 1964:173].

But then, as will be seen in the next section, the present study indicates that disputes involving lower-class people of any kind, white or black, receive relatively little attention from the police.

SOCIAL CLASS

Although nearly all of the cases in the sample involved people of lower or working class (classified as "blue-collar" by the observers), a few cases—3% of the total—involved people described by the observers as members of the middle class ("white-collar").[14] With such a small number (11 cases in all), a detailed comparison with the rest of the sample could be misleading. Nevertheless, these few cases are so different from the rest that they merit further discussion; in fact, they suggest rather dramatically that the social class of the parties is a major predictor of how the police handle disputes. In particular, it seems that middle-class people are less likely to be handled in a penal style and more likely to be handled in a therapeutic or conciliatory style. The police also seem to give middle-class people a measure of special attention, to handle their problems with more time, care, and delicacy.

One illustrative case occurred in what the observer described as an "upper middle-class" white neighborhood, known by the police as "the oasis" because it is surrounded by areas inhabited by low-income blacks. The incident involved an elderly white woman who said that the teenagers who lived next door to her had been throwing refuse into her yard. The police explained to the observer that the woman was a regular caller about matters of this kind, and that "nearly all of her complaints about neighbors are obviously imaginary, but she sees the police as her only friends." They also noted that she had "a peculiar conception of property," since she scattered broken glass in the street to discourage people from parking their cars in front of her house and threw gravel inside cars that were parked there. The teenagers described the woman as "crazy," and it would appear that the police were in complete agreement. Nevertheless, the observer reported that the officer who talked with her was "understanding" and "patient," and, at her request, left his name and phone number for her to call if the "problem" recurred. He promised to keep her yard under surveillance, consoled her, and was generally reassuring and supportive. He also acted as a go-between to the teenagers, and warned them—apparently "for show"—not to bother the woman in the future. Afterward, the officers commented that the supposed offenders were actually "good kids." It is clear that this woman received considerably more attention than the typical complainant of lower social standing, perhaps more than any lower- or working-class complainant in the entire sample, including some who had been physically injured and others who complained that their lives were in danger. Had she been poor and black, the woman might very well have been reprimanded for bothering the police and also, perhaps, for her conduct in general. But the police excused everything she did as an expression of her "craziness."

---

14. Recall also that 2% of the cases involve disputes between people of unequal status (see page 121).

The attribution of "mental illness" seems to be a common response of the police to people who, if lower in status, might be subject to punishments, threats, or admonishments. They also seem more willing to accept claims of "mental illness" made by citizens of higher status. Thus, in one case a black minister called the police because his son had been drinking and wanted to take the family car (though he had no driver's license), had been fighting with the minister's son-in-law, and had run out into the street in front of traffic. It was unclear what he wanted the police to do, but he told them that his "boy" had just served 2 years in the penitentiary, and that this was "too long" and had made him "mentally sick." The police advised the man—whom they always addressed as "Reverend So-and-so"—to take his son to a psychiatrist, and one of the officers suggested to the young man that he go for a walk around the park in order to relax. At no time did the police use coercive tactics of any kind. In another case, a black woman complained that her husband, a preacher, had "gone crazy," threatening her and destroying some of their household belongings. The preacher, locked in an adjoining room, shouted at his wife to get the police out of his home, and they left shortly afterward without saying anything at all to the preacher himself. The police may also use a therapeutic style without specifically employing the concept of "mental illness." In one such case, for example, a white landlord called the police, very upset because his wife had been "taking" money and jewelry from the bedroom of one of their tenants. In relating the details to the police, he alternated between crying and raging about his wife's behavior. What might have been treated as a "theft" under other conditions was in this case treated as a tragedy or burden for the alleged offender's husband. The observer mentioned that the police stayed with the man "longer than was officially necessary" and that "during this time [one of the officers] was exceedingly friendly and provided a great deal of emotional support." The officer handling the incident "went out of his way to avoid any official action in this situation in an attempt to help the citizens solve their problems." The possibility of an arrest was never mentioned, and the woman was not treated as an offender or criticized in any way. She was simply a "problem," and her husband deserved sympathy.

It might be added that if the police so much as suggest that a middle-class person has behaved illegally and is subject to their coercive authority, they are likely to meet with indignation and possibly even a threat of a lawsuit. Thus, in one case in which a young white woman complained that her father was violating a court order to stay away from her house, an officer rhetorically asked the man what he was doing in her kitchen. The man replied, "What does it look like I'm doing here? I'm sitting here drinking a cup of tea. I don't know anything about a court order. If there is one, then let's see it. If you want to take me in, then you go right ahead, and I'll sue you for false arrest." The observer noted that the officer's "voice weakened," and he assured the man that arrest was not being contemplated: "We're not here to make any arrests, sir. We were called because your daughter said she was afraid because you're here." The officers then went upstairs and talked with the daughter about the situation, but nothing more was said to the man, and he was still glowering in the kitchen when they left. Now compare the response of the police to a lower-class black man's assertion of his rights (after he had allegedly tried to throw his wife out of the house and she had called them for help). The man did not want the police to enter, and told them, "This is my house—you can't come in." One of the officers replied, "The hell we can't," and pushed into the house. The man was also told to "shut his goddamn mouth," at which time he became more cooperative and made no further complaints.

It appears that people of white-collar status view themselves as different from what were once called the "criminal classes," and so do the police, whereas both take for granted the appropriateness of the penal style for lower- and working-class people. At the same time, the police seem less willing to define lower-status people as "mentally ill," or in any other way to apply the therapeutic style to their problems. Thus, in one case a lower-class black woman called the police (from an unspecified public place) to complain that her husband was "insane," and that he had threatened to kill her. To this the officer replied that her husband actually was "only drunk," and that if they did not go home immediately both of them would be arrested for "drunkenness." Afterward, the observer recorded that, in his opinion, the man probably was "insane or at least dangerous." It should also be recognized, however, that lower-status people themselves are surely less likely than middle-class people to define one another as "mentally ill" in the first place (see Black, 1976:29).

Although in many cases involving poor blacks the police simply stood by passively, taking little or no action at all, this did not occur in a single case involving people of middle-class status. These cases provide a comparison with the larger sample, making it possible to appreciate the range and diversity of responses of which the police are capable. A case involving a middle-class Jewish family nicely illustrates the extremes to which the police will go under the right conditions: In this instance, the call over the radio directed the officers to "meet the sergeant," and one of them immediately said, "This is it again." He then explained that this call apparently was another stage in a dispute they had handled earlier in the evening, at which time a young woman (18 years old) had called the police because her parents were keeping her baby at their house and would not give it back. This was the most recent episode in a series of often conflictful events going back to the hospitalization of the daughter as "mentally ill" several years before, her relationship with a fellow whom her father described as "just a no-good bum," her pregnancy and subsequent marriage to the young man (also Jewish and from what an officer called a "real good" and a "real wealthy" family), the breakup of the marriage, and the girl's ultimate return with the baby to her parents' large house in a prosperous neighborhood. Now the parents had "kicked her out" of their house and she was planning to move in with a friend, but they refused to let her take the baby, arguing that she would not give it proper care. On their first visit to the home this evening, the officers had told the daughter that her parents would have to keep the baby until she was "settled" and had enough money to pay for its food. She thereupon went to the police station and complained, saying that she had a right to her own baby. The sergeant was then dispatched to meet with the whole group.

 Upon the sergeant's arrival, the father made an apologetic plea for help of a sort rarely seen among people of lower status: "First I want to tell you how sorry we are that you had to come out here, but, honestly, we are in a mess—I never thought it could happen in our family—but God knows we are in a mess, and we just don't know where to turn." The sergeant explained that the police technically had no authority to handle the matter: "I want you to realize that this is not really police business. I can't make any final decisions on this, and when I say something it is strictly off the record. The law says this is not a matter for the police, but I understand the situation you are in, and we'll do what we can." The father seemed to understand the legal character of the dispute: "Oh sure, we're fully aware that this is a civil-law case, but something has got to be done tonight." And the sergeant assured him: "I realize that. We'll see what we can do."

The father continued: "The girl just doesn't know what she is doing. We don't know what's come over her. If she took that baby out of here tonight, God forbid, it could die—the condition she is in. And her husband's not going to care. To give you some idea of what kind of boy he is, he didn't even go to his own son's circumcision. I don't know if you realize what that means." The mother added, "And our daughter, she doesn't seem to care about her own child either. When she was here with the baby, who had to change the diapers, and who had to feed the poor little thing? I did. My daughter doesn't lift a finger for her own baby." The daughter also presented a case to the sergeant: "My parents hit me with a telephone and threw me out. I'll show you the bump on my head where the phone hit me. I'll go, fine, I'll go, but I know I have a right to my own baby." The sergeant replied, "You have a right to your baby, yes, but only if you can take care of the baby." And she in turn said, "I can take care of it, and I've got a place to live, and money. Now I want my baby." And so it went, on and on. The sergeant seemed to be reluctant to take a firm stand: "Now like I said before, the police can't make decisions in a situation like this. It is something for the courts to decide. We can't do anything unless a law has been broken. So far, there haven't been any crimes committed here that I can see." At this, the father became more aggressive: "We realize that, sergeant, believe me. But if that girl takes the baby out of here, then there *will* be trouble. If that bum husband of hers comes around here, I swear to God I'll kill him." And the sergeant repeated, "Well, anything I tell you isn't because it's what the law says." He then called the Women's Division for an opinion on the matter (the parents had also called there earlier in the evening). Each party in turn took the telephone and explained the entire affair to a woman officer at headquarters, and the sergeant talked to her when everyone was finished. Finally, he hung up and announced to the father, "You will keep the baby until your daughter gets a court order for you to give it back to her. So, for tonight anyway, you keep it, but if she gets that court order you have to give the baby to her." The daughter said that she was contacting her lawyer and would soon be back for the baby, and she left. The police assured the parents that they would keep their house under surveillance for the rest of the night, made some small talk, accepted the parents' thanks, and left. Back in the patrol car, one of the officers commented that the young woman was "kookie." The entire incident had consumed a good part of the evening, about 2 hours of police time from beginning to end. If the case had involved lower-class blacks, it is doubtful that the police would have spent as much as 10 minutes on it, and much less would they have dispatched a sergeant or other ranking officer to a dispute of this kind.

As noted earlier (page 117), the police intentionally drive slowly en route to many disputes, hoping that the matter will be resolved by the time they arrive. But it should now be added that this practice occurs primarily when the call comes from a lower- or working-class neighborhood. In such cases, moreover, many police are eager to find excuses to leave the scene of the dispute as soon as possible. They may leave if no one answers the first knock at the door, for example, or if the first person to answer denies that the police were called. In response to a reported dispute in a middle-class neighborhood, by contrast, it is not unusual for more than a single patrol car to be dispatched (as in the case of the Jewish family described above), and in other ways too the police may treat the case as a matter of considerable importance. Thus, in one instance two patrol cars responded to a call indicating a domestic dispute in a middle-class neighborhood. No one seemed to be home (or willing to answer the door), but the observer commented that the officer "must have knocked for close to 5 minutes—longer than I've ever seen officers wait before." He also generalized that "a bigger production was made of the family trouble run [dispatch] than I've seen in lower socioeconomic areas."

One of the officers who handled the dispute involving the Jewish family mentioned that in a certain respect the case was typical: "Most of the time we don't have any trouble with the Jews at all, but when they have trouble, brother, they really go all out." Since it seems unlikely that Jewish disputes are significantly different from those of other people, it may be more accurate to say that it is the police who "go all out," not the Jews. But this would be true only in cases involving wealthier Jews such as those in the incident described above, not poor Jews. Whether Jews or Gentiles, black or white, people of the middle or upper class receive more help from the police when they ask for it. The police are willing to go to great lengths to satisfy these people, particularly if they can do so in a therapeutic or conciliatory style, without coercion. For reasons suggested earlier, however (see page 125), generally such people do not call upon the police to settle their disputes. They call the police readily enough about those of lower status, but not about each other.

HOUSEHOLD STATUS

The vast majority of the disputes in this study occur within single households, and, among these, the vast majority involve complaints brought to the police by household heads (defined for these purposes as those who pay the mortgage or rent for a dwelling—see pages 123–124). Many involve a complainant and an alleged offender who are presumed to be joint heads of a household, but a considerable number pertain to a complaint by a head of a household against someone else, such as dependent spouse, child, other relative, or a former spouse or lover. In no case could it be determined that a dependent spouse had complained against the head of the household, though some incidents of this kind were probably misclassified (as occurring between joint heads) because spouses were considered to be joint heads of households in the absence of information to the contrary. In any event, it is possible to compare how the police handle complaints between people who appear to be equals in the household with complaints in a downward direction, that is, those in which a superior complains against an inferior.

It can be seen in Table 5–5 that the style of the police is far more conciliatory in cases between equals than in those involving a downward complaint: Whereas nearly three-fourths of the disputes between equals are handled primarily in the conciliatory style, this is true of fewer than half of the complaints brought by a head of a household against someone else. Instead, inferiors in the household are more likely to be handled in a penal style, whether by arrest or threat of arrest, removal from the dwelling, or a scolding. This pattern prevails despite the fact that disputes between equals are more likely to involve violence: While 60% of them entail some degree of violence, this applies to somewhat fewer than half of the downward complaints. There is violence in only 22% of the complaints by the head of a household against a dependent other than a spouse, for example, in 25% of those against a nonresident, in 32% of those against a former spouse or lover, and in 42% of those against a dependent spouse—and yet these downward complaints are the ones in which the police are most likely to be penal in their social control (see Table 5–5). It would seem, then, that it is not the greater violence of household inferiors that increases their vulnerability to punishment. Moreover, a difference in intimacy is not an adequate explanation either: Holding constant the intimacy of marriage, it can be observed that spouses who are equals are handled in the penal style in only about one-fourth of the cases, but one-half of the dependent spouses are handled in this way (Table 5–5). It therefore seems that

TABLE 5-5

Major Style of Social Control Exercised by Police according to Household Status of Parties[a]

Household Status of Parties

Style of Social Control	Head of household against:					Former spouse or lover against head of household	Other	Total
	another head	dependent spouse or lover	other dependent	former spouse or lover	other nonresident			
Conciliatory	71	44	32	33	29	(4)	50	53
Penal	23	50	56	67	68	(1)	44	40
Therapeutic	2	—	12	—	4	—	3	3
Compensatory	—	—	—	—	—	—	—	—
Preventive action only	4	6	—	—	—	(3)	—	3
Other	—	—	—	—	—	—	3	*
Total percent	100	100	100	100	101	—	100	99
Total cases	(97)	(18)	(25)	(18)	(28)	(8)	(32)	(226)

[a]By percent. Figures in parentheses are used whenever the total number of incidents is statistically too small to justify a generalized assertion of rate and for total number of cases.
*Less than .5%.

household status itself predicts and explains how the police respond to disputes. In this sense, a household is a microcosm of society, where those at the bottom of the social-class system are more likely to be punished.

The advantage enjoyed by a household head has two dimensions. As a complainant, he or she is better able to mobilize the police against someone else in or about the household, and as an alleged offender, he or she enjoys a relative immunity from punishment. Accordingly, the head of a household is nearly always successful in defining a party of lower status as an offender, and he or she is also likely to receive compliance with any specific request made of the police (see Table 5–6). Conversely, if someone complains about the head of a household —itself an unusual event—the police are far less likely to endorse the complaint or to comply with any requests made by the complainant, and may even overturn the definition of the situation entirely and treat the complainant as the offender. In effect, then, the police generally act as agents of the household elite. Perhaps a few examples will show this more clearly.

In one case, a black woman who was "quite agitated" said that her common-law husband was "no good," was "busting up her place," and had "beat on her," and that she wanted the police to arrest him. Although they did not make an arrest, they told the man that he would have to leave "her place," which he did. After the encounter was over, one of the officers remarked to the observer that they had taken the woman's side only because the apartment was hers: "He probably didn't really do anything—she's just angry about all the money he spent—but she has a right to order him to go." In another case quite similar to this that was handled by the same officers, the police refused to order a common-law husband to leave, explaining that "as he helped pay the rent" they "couldn't force him to leave until she got a warrant for his arrest." The man volunteered to leave anyway, saying he wanted to "cool off." This seemed to please the officers, and one of them later commented, "It was nice of him to leave voluntarily, as he had a right to stay there, being common-law and helping to pay the rent." In another incident, the police refused to take sides in a dispute between a white couple over a third party's right to be in their house. One of the officers explained that they "could do nothing because both of their names were on the deed," and so both had "a right to say what went on." In still another case, a black woman wanted her husband removed from the house or arrested because he was "beating on her." She was supported by her son, but her husband denied the charge, saying that he had "done nothing but yell at her for getting drunk again." The police refused to take action against the man, and later said to the observer, "What the fuck did she expect us to do, kick a man out of his own house on the say-so of a drunk?"

The above examples are somewhat unusual in that the police involved explicitly mentioned economic control of a dwelling as a major factor in deciding how to handle the disputes. In most cases they do not give reasons, but simply favor the

TABLE 5–6

Degree of Police Compliance with Complainant according to Household Status of Parties[a]

Household Status of Parties

Degree of Police Compliance	Head of household against:					Former spouse or lover against head of household	Other	Total
	another head	dependent spouse or lover	other dependent	former spouse or lover	other nonresident			
Total compliance	43	53	58	82	72	(5)	19	51
Partial compliance	2	7	—	9	—	—	6	3
Noncompliance	48	33	42	9	22	(2)	25	35
Opposition	4	—	—	—	6	(1)	25	6
Other	4	7	—	—	—	—	25	4
Total percent	101	100	100	100	100	—	100	99
Total cases	(56)	(15)	(12)	(11)	(18)	(8)	(16)	(136)

[a]By percent. Figures in parentheses are used whenever the total number of incidents is statistically too small to justify a general assertion of rate and for total number of cases.

head of the household. In one instance, a black woman said that her husband, whom she had "left" 3 days before, had beaten her when she tried to retrieve their child. Her dress was torn in two places, and her sandal was broken. Her husband, standing on his front porch, denied that he had beaten her, and the officer took his side, saying that he "knew how the husband felt." The woman was told that all she could do was "get a warrant," and so, the observer noted, "she turned and walked away in disgust." In another case, a black man went to his former wife's house to remove a table that she claimed was a gift, and hers to keep. The police sided with the woman, saying that the man would have to prove his ownership in court and, meanwhile, "as a stranger with no right to presence in her house," would have to leave.

Several other cases show how a person's status in the household can make the difference between arrest and freedom. In one, a young black man complained that his father and a friend of his father's were "drunk" and had abused and threatened him even though he did "all of the work around the house." The police "talked the father into going to bed," but they arrested his friend for "vagrancy." In a somewhat unusual case, the police arrested a white man for "drunkenness" because a woman, described as "almost hysterical," said that he had broken into her apartment and tried to rape her. The alleged offender said that she was lying and that "she's always invited the boys in so's she could get screwed, but when she's had enough she'd holler for the police." According to the observer, "The police didn't believe her story, but took him in to calm her down." Afterward, the police explained that she was a "regular" who routinely made such complaints, often against the man they handled on this visit, and that they "take it as a joke" and "go over there just to have a little fun." Nevertheless, in her apartment they did what she wanted them to do. Another case also dramatizes how far the police will go to comply with the head of the household: A black woman had locked her son out of her apartment because her "lover" did not want the young man to be present while he was visiting overnight. The police arrived to find the woman berating her son as he sat quietly on the stairs outside her door. (It is not clear who had called the police.) One of the officers suggested that the son "spend the night in the park," but he replied that he was "afraid" to stay in the park, had nowhere else to go, and would prefer to go to jail for the night. To accommodate him (and his mother), the police arrested him for "disorderly conduct." In still another incident, a black woman complained that her common-law husband had locked her out of "her" apartment, but he said that it was "his" apartment. The man was able to convince the police that it was his alone, and they arrested the complainant for "drunkenness" when she refused to leave the setting. The observer added in his report that there was no evidence that the woman had been drinking.

The police behave according to the same principle—supporting the head of the household—in other contexts as well. Thus, in dealing with homosexuals, the police generally side with the partner who is the head of the household. In one case, for instance, a white complainant told the police that she wanted them to remove a drunken woman from her apartment. The officers found the woman in a semiconscious condition in the kitchen, threw water on her, took her to the patrol car, and then drove her to the edge of the precinct where they dropped her off on the street. She was dressed in a masculine fashion, had short-cropped hair, and explained to the police that she was "off men." One of the officers remarked afterward that the women were "lesbians," and that the complainant had probably gotten "ticked off" after having sexual relations. In another incident, a white woman complained that a "lesbian" was in her apartment and had asked her to be "her girl." She said that she wanted nothing to do with this, and requested that the police remove the "lesbian." They agreed to do so, and convinced the second woman to leave by threatening her with arrest for "disorderly conduct."

In general, then, the direction of a complaint in the social structure of a household predicts and explains how the police will respond. Whether male or female, the person who owns the house or pays the rent will usually prevail, and the penal style of social control is likely to be applied to his or her opponent. But if the parties share the economic burden of the household, and so appear to be equals, the police are likely to be conciliatory and to refuse to take sides in the dispute. In this way, dispute settlement by the police serves the interests of the household elite.

AGE

As noted earlier, the great majority of disputes that the police are called upon to handle involve conflicts between adults. Occasionally a complaint will be made by an adult against a juvenile, but hardly ever do the police encounter a complaint by one juvenile against another or by a juvenile against an adult (see page 122). Since nearly all juveniles are economically dependent upon adults, these patterns again portray the role of the police under conditions of inequality. The following discussion partially overlaps with that of the last section (on household status), since adult–juvenile conflicts often occur in a domestic setting, but the social inferiority of juveniles is so extreme in modern society that their experiences with the police deserve special comment.

The great majority of police encounters with juveniles occur in public places and are in other ways quite unlike the cases in the present analysis (see, e.g., Piliavin and Briar, 1964; Werthman and Piliavin, 1967; Black and Reiss, 1970). Nonetheless, the fate of juveniles involved in disputes is much the same as it is in the more routine encounters: Juveniles lose nearly all of their conflicts with adults, and in most cases are treated in a penal and moralistic fashion. Moreover, on those rare occasions when a juvenile complains about an adult, he or she is likely to be chastised for even attempting to bring law to bear against an older person.

When an adult complains against another adult, the style of the police is primarily conciliatory in over one-half of the cases, whereas less than one-third of the complaints by an adult against a juvenile are handled in this way. Instead, as Table 5–7 shows, a juvenile is most likely to be handled in the penal style. Beyond this, the penal actions taken by the police are somewhat different in cases involving a juvenile as the alleged offender (see Table 5–8). While a bit less likely than an adult to be arrested and considerably less likely to be threatened with arrest, he or she is correspondingly more likely to be scolded or admonished. It is in this sense that the police are comparatively moralistic toward juveniles, while treating adults—if they handle them in the penal style at all—in a more legalistic fashion. The police give very few lectures to adults about how they should behave. They are unlikely to invoke standards of right and wrong at all, even when making an arrest or threatening to do so. If they exercise their authority, then, they usually do so in an impersonal and bureaucratic manner, without explicit reference to their own values. This does not apply to juveniles, however. In these cases the police readily give lectures and exhortations about the proper way for a young person to behave, particularly toward his or her elders. Typically the elders in question are parents.

In one case, for example, a worried white woman called the police because her 15-year-old son had left the house in the afternoon, saying that he would be back in "a little while," and hours later he had yet to return. While the police were in the house, the boy arrived and explained that he had been on a bicycle trip with a friend. His mother raised her voice and said, "Do you know how much worry you

TABLE 5–7

Major Style of Social Control Exercised by Police according to Age of Parties[a]

Style of Social Control	Age of Parties		
	Adult against juvenile[b]	Adult against adult	Total
Conciliatory	31	54	52
Penal	62	39	41
Therapeutic	7	2	3
Compensatory	—	1	1
Preventive action only	—	3	3
Other	—	*	*
Total percent	100	99	100
Total cases	(29)	(253)	(282)

[a] By percent.
[b] Under 18 years old.
*Less than .5 percent.

TABLE 5–8
Penal Action by Police according to Age of Parties[a]

Penal Action (in order of severity)	Adult against juvenile[b]	Adult against adult	Total
Arrest	17	24	23
Order or remove from setting: citizen complies	29	25	25
Threaten arrest	4	22	20
Scold or admonish	46	18	22
Ask or advise to leave setting	—	7	7
Other	4	4	4
Total percent	100	100	101
Total cases	(24)	(174)	(198)

(Column header group: Age of Parties)

[a] By percent.
[b] Under 18 years old.

put us to? How could you do a thing like this?" The boy "snarled" at her in a loud voice, "Oh, get off my back. Why do you have to make such a big thing out of it?" At this, one of the officers got up from his chair and said, "Just a minute, buddy. You tell me where you learned to act like that to your mother. Don't you know how to behave when your mother talks to you?" The boy replied, "Well, she doesn't have to get so excited about nothin', does she?" This prompted the officer to continue: "Listen here, your mother can say what she pleases, how she wants to, to her son. You know that? My mother never would have allowed me to act the way you do. She would've smacked me in the face. One thing you better get straight—you only have one mother in your life, and you better remember that. You better start respecting her right now. At least you're going to show respect when *I'm* here. You got that?" The boy said, "Yes, sir," and immediately everything quieted down. The woman thanked the police warmly. Afterward, one of the officers remarked that "the trouble" was that "there's no man in the house."

In another case involving a white family, a woman called to complain that her teenaged daughter was staying out too late—violating the city's curfew law—and creating other unspecified "problems" as well. The daughter was sitting outside in a car with her boyfriend when the police arrived, and both were asked to come into the mother's apartment. According to the observer, the officers "tried very hard to convince the girl that she was hurting herself and her poor working mother's well-being by such recurring trouble." The girl was "openly nasty" to the police and told them, "Too bad. I don't like curfews." Before leaving, the police gave her a ticket for curfew violation and warned her that future violations could mean that she would be sent away to an institution.

Another case illustrates what seems to be the typical response of the police to a juvenile who complains about the conduct of a parent: A 16-year-old black girl called the police to complain that she had been struck by her father. The observer inferred that she had "talked back" to her father, he had "hit" her, and now "her pride was hurt." The police "found the girl in the wrong," and proceeded to "belittle" her and to try to "shame" her, admonishing her to "grow up" and to "get rid of her smart attitude." They also "made her apologize" to her father. The observer added that, in the end, the girl's "pride was further hurt" because the police had "degraded" her. In a similar case, a black girl tearfully complained that her mother had "whipped" her, and the officer—with a show of disgust—grumbled, "Whip her again," and walked out the door.

In sum, the police readily use their authority against a juvenile who is criticized by a parent, but when the situation is reversed—with a juvenile complaining against an adult—they show no sympathy at all, and usually treat the complaint itself as an offense. Patterns of this kind should be expected wherever one person or group is far below another in social status, as is true of slaves and women in many societies (see Black, 1976:18–19, 28). In modern America, however, hardly anyone is lower than juveniles.

INTIMACY

Intimacy may be understood as the relational distance between people, known by the degree to which they participate in one another's lives (see Black, 1976:40–41). Although all of the parties in the present sample knew one another before their conflicts arose, the closeness of their relationships varied considerably. Their intimacy ranged from that between people who were married—formally or informally—and living together, to that between estranged couples, relatives living in separate dwellings, friends, landlords and tenants, neighbors, and mere acquaintances. The following discussion examines how dispute settlement by the police varies with this feature of its social location.

Table 5–9 shows that the police are more conciliatory in cases where the parties are relatively intimate. Thus, the dominant style of the police is conciliatory in nearly three-fourths of the cases involving a married couple, but in only a little more than one-third of those involving an estranged couple. An estranged couple is more likely to be handled in either the penal or the preventive style, the latter usually being seen in cases in which the woman wants protection while she retrieves possessions from a dwelling in which a man—possibly uncooperative or violent—is present. Table 5–9 also shows that the penal style occurs most often in cases where the parties are relatively distant family members, where they are friends or acquaintances, or where their relationship is unclear (e.g., where they are said simply to "know each other"). In addition, six of the eight disputes between noncohabiting boyfriends and girlfriends were handled in the penal style. In general, it can be inferred from Table 5–9 that the police are more conciliatory when the parties live in the same dwelling. This is most evident in a

TABLE 5-9

Major Style of Social Control Exercised by Police according to Relationship between Parties[a]

Style of Social Control	Relationship between Parties										
	Married or common-law couple	Estranged couple	Boyfriend-girlfriend	Parent-child	Other relatives	Friends or acquaintances	Neighbors	Landlord/landlady-tenant	Unspecified	Other	Total
Conciliatory	70	39	(2)	45	35	36	55	47	40	33	52
Penal	26	45	(6)	49	62	57	43	40	60	42	41
Therapeutic	2	—	—	6	3	—	2	7	—	8	2
Compensatory	—	—	—	—	—	—	—	—	—	8	1
Preventive action only	2	16	—	—	—	7	—	7	—	—	3
Other	—	—	—	—	—	—	—	—	—	8	1
Total percent	100	100	—	100	100	100	100	101	100	99	100
Total cases	(108)	(31)	(8)	(33)	(29)	(14)	(44)	(15)	(10)	(12)	(304)

[a]By percent. Figures in parentheses are used whenever the total number of incidents is statistically too small to justify a generalized assertion of rate and for total number of cases.

comparison of the disputes between people such as married couples—who obviously live together—and, say, those between estranged couples or friends. (The frequency of conciliation in neighbor disputes is higher than would be expected on this basis alone, and requires an additional explanation—see below, pages 164–168).

Even when the police adopt a penal style in disputes between intimates, there is evidence that they are less legalistic and coercive than in other cases (see Table 5–10). Although they are as likely to make an arrest, they are less likely to threaten to do so when the parties are married than when their relationship is more distant. Thus, when arrest and threats of arrest together are compared to other penal tactics, it can be seen that these more legalistic and coercive actions occur at a lower rate when the parties are married (38%) than when they are estranged (65%) or are merely friends (66%). If they are penal at all in a dispute between a married couple, the police are more inclined simply to tell one party to leave for a while, until the situation "cools down."

It might be thought that the reason the police are more conciliatory—and less legalistic and coercive—toward people in close relationships is that conflicts between these people are less "criminal" in nature. It might be imagined, for instance, that conflicts between intimates are less violent than conflicts between those who are more distant, such as estranged couples or friends, and that this explains the difference in their treatment. But such is not the case, as Table 5–11 shows. Disputes between the most intimate people—married couples—are especially likely to involve violence or the threat of violence. At the same time, the least violent disputes are those between people who are the most distant in the sample—friends and estranged couples (with violence rates of 14% and 29%, respectively, compared to 60% for married couples). Hence, the police are generally more conciliatory and less coercive in the disputes that are the most violent. Even when a married woman specifically complains about violence by her husband, the dominant style of the police is conciliatory in 72% of the cases $(N = 46)$. This is so despite the fact that many of these women do not want conciliation from the police, but rather want them to relate to the alleged offender in a penal style, though without the use of coercive tactics. In the typical wife-beating case, the woman seems to want the police to define her husband as a wrongdoer, to admonish him and to warn him that further action will be taken if he repeats his misbehavior in the future. In other words, she wants them to establish that her husband has violated the moral boundaries of their relationship. But the typical response of the police is to do little or nothing of this kind. As Table 5–12 shows, only about one-third of the complainants who ask the police to take a particular action against a spouse get what they want. By contrast, nearly two-thirds of those who are estranged from the alleged offender are successful in their requests, and of the eight complainants who were merely friends of the alleged offender, seven were successful in this way.

TABLE 5–10

Penal Action by Police according to Relationship between Parties[a]

Relationship between Parties

Penal Action (in order of severity)	Married or common-law couple	Estranged couple	Boyfriend–girlfriend	Parent–child	Other relatives	Friends or acquaintances	Neighbors	Landlord/landlady–tenant	Unspecified	Other	Total
Arrest	26	20	(2)	25	29	33	11	(1)	(2)	(2)	23
Order or remove from setting	31	15	—	17	24	—	31	(4)	(3)	(1)	24
Threaten arrest	12	45	(5)	4	24	33	8	(1)	(2)	(3)	19
Scold or admonish	16	10	—	33	19	—	47	—	(1)	(3)	22
Ask or adivse to leave setting	7	10	(1)	8	—	17	—	(1)	(1)	—	6
Other	7	—	—	13	5	17	3	—	—	—	6
Total percent	99	100	—	100	101	100	100	—	—	—	100
Total cases	(68)	(20)	(8)	(24)	(21)	(12)	(36)	(7)	(8)	(9)	(213)

[a]By percent. Figures in parentheses are used whenever the total number of incidents is statistically too small to justify a generalized assertion of rate and for total number of cases.

158

TALBE 5–11

Presence of Violence according to Relationship between Parties[a]

Relationship between Parties

Presence of Violence	Married or common-law couple	Estranged couple	Boyfriend–girlfriend	Parent–child	Other relatives	Friends or acquaintances	Neighbors	Landlord/landlady–tenant	Unspecified	Other	Total
Violence present	60	29	(4)	29	37	14	37	31	40	75	44
No violence present	40	71	(4)	71	60	86	63	69	60	25	56
Other	—	—	—	—	3	—	—	—	—	—	*
Total percent	100	100	—	100	100	100	100	100	100	100	100
Total cases	(108)	(31)	(8)	(34)	(30)	(14)	(49)	(16)	(10)	(12)	(312)

[a] Figures in parentheses are used whenever the total number of incidents is statistically too small to justify a generalized assertion of rate and for total number of cases.

*Less than .5 percent.

159

TABLE 5–12

Degree of Police Compliance with Complainant according to Relationship between Parties[a]

Degree of Police Compliance	Relationship between Parties										
	Married or common-law couple	Estranged couple	Boyfriend–girlfriend	Parent–child	Other relatives	Friends or acquaintances	Neighbors	Landlord/landlady–tenant	Unspecified	Other	Total
Total compliance	37	64	(6)	36	57	(7)	61	(3)	(3)	(4)	52
Partial compliance	3	5	–	–	–	–	–	–	–	(1)	2
Noncompliance	49	18	(1)	36	43	(1)	28	(1)	(1)	–	34
Opposition	5	5	–	29	–	–	6	–	–	–	6
Other	6	9	–	–	–	–	6	(1)	(1)	(1)	6
Total percent	100	101	–	101	100	–	101	–	–	–	100
Total cases	(63)	(22)	(7)	(14)	(14)	(8)	(18)	(5)	(5)	(6)	(162)

[a]By percent. Figures in parentheses are used whenever the total number of incidents is statistically too small to justify a generalized statement of rate and for total number of cases.

In nearly every case in which a complainant is unsuccessful in a specific request made of the police, this is because the police refuse to be as penal as they are asked to be. Often they even refuse to show any sympathy for the complainant at all. In one case, for instance, a black woman told the police that her husband had beaten her because supper was not ready when he came home from work. As she talked with the police, her husband continued "yelling and swearing at her, and said that he would beat her again when the police left." The observer did not indicate whether the woman made a specific request, but undoubtedly she wanted the police to take some kind of action toward her husband. Instead, one of the officers said, "Lady, we can't do anything. Try and settle this yourselves, or go somewhere else and take out a complaint in the morning." It is unclear how the woman reacted emotionally, but she packed a few possessions and left for her mother's house. The police reported the incident as "family disturbance—argument all settled." Recall too that the police generally refuse to take action in cases where a woman complains about a man who is not present—but is readily available—when the police are told about the incident (see pages 113–116). The same pattern occurs when the complainant is a man and the alleged offender—and intimate— is a woman. In one such case, for example, a black man met the police on the sidewalk and said that his wife had "slashed" him with a butcher knife. He was bleeding from the wound, and wanted to press charges. One of the officers nevertheless "talked [him] into not signing a complaint." In dealing with the alleged offender, they did not admonish or otherwise judge her for attacking her husband, but simply took him to the hospital and reported the incident as a "domestic disturbance." The observer added the speculation that the police did not want a "full case" to "blossom" in this instance because it was close to the end of the shift and they did not want to be late getting home from work. In another case, the police arrived to find a white man lying on the floor, "covered with blood." He had been hit on the head with a baby bottle by his daughter-in-law, who admitted that she had done this because he "had come home intoxicated and had bothered her." She also mentioned that he had "called her vile names." Since the man was only semiconscious, it could not be ascertained what he wanted the police to do, but they decided not to charge his daughter-in-law with "assault" on the ground that "this was a family argument."

On the other hand, and despite all of the foregoing, it must be added that it is not entirely unknown for the police to decide to invoke the law even when the parties are intimately related and do not want the case to be handled as a crime. In one case, for example, a black woman who had stabbed her common-law husband was arrested for "aggravated assault," though the victim wanted nothing more than to be taken to the hospital. Soon after arriving at the scene, one of the officers declared to the other, "That bitch has to be locked up. That's the third time she's stabbed him in 2 months. Let's bullshit [talk] him into signing a complaint." But it must be noted that this case was handled entirely by black officers, even to the extent that the observer—who was white—was kept at a distance from the parties: "This observer was told by the sergeant not to go in [to the emergency room] because it was his experience that as soon as a white man was viewed by a Negro offender, and even sometimes a victim, there would be no cooperation at all." The observer did manage to overhear the following exchange, however: "Mama, did you cut your man?" "No, I didn't cut my man, I love him. Some other bitch did that." The black officers thus related to the parties in their own language and style, and, as blacks, seem to have been more concerned than many white officers would have been about the ultimate fate of the victim (see page 140). In any event, cases of this kind—in which more authority is exercised than the complainant wants—are rare.

In this context, it is relevant to note that a number of officers remarked about the importance of not "getting caught in the middle" of family disputes, that is, of not acting in such a way that the parties put their conflict aside and join forces against the police. Although this is not a frequent occurrence, it did happen on several occasions during the observation study, and it is instructive in its own right. Such incidents indicate what quantity and style of social control complainants define as just and proper when the alleged offender is an intimate. From this standpoint, it appears that a complainant is most likely to turn against the police when they move to make an unwanted arrest. In one case, for instance, a black woman called the police because her husband refused to leave the house as she demanded. Both were brandishing knives when the police arrived. When they asked the woman if she wanted her husband "locked up," however, the observer reported that "she quit yelling at him and said 'no' and for us to 'get out' which we did (rapidly)." As they left, one of the officers commented, "That's the only way to be. If they don't want to sign a complaint, get out." In another case, a black woman complained that her "drunken" husband would not let her take their child and leave for the night. The husband said that he would not give the child to his wife because "she didn't come home when she was supposed to." An officer suggested that the husband let his wife take the child, but he "wouldn't listen and became very belligerent." At that point the police "grabbed him" and said they were going to arrest him for "drunkenness." But as soon as they touched him the wife said, "Leave him alone. He just got home from the hospital." The man then agreed that his wife could have the child for the night and that they would "talk things over" in the morning. Back in the patrol car, one of the officers remarked to the observer, "Did you see that? When we threatened to arrest the guy for DK [drunkenness] the wife sided with her husband. You just can't win on this job." Another investigator has also described this phenomenon:

[A] dangerous situation that arises from the intimacy of the disputants occurs if the police are required to use force to restrain the offender. Under these circumstances, even if the victim called the police in the first instance, she may suddenly come to her intimate's aid by attacking the police officers. One officer told of the following incident: . . . A woman called for police assistance at a tavern where her husband was assaulting her and tearing up the place. When the officers arrived, the husband had to be restrained and was pushed to the floor in the course of the scuffle. At that point, the wife, who had initially called the police, attacked one of the officers with a bar stool [Parnas, 1967:921; see also Westley, 1970:61].

Among intimates, then, the police seem to alternate between taking little or no action at all and, less commonly, exerting a great deal of social control, whereas it would appear that generally the complainant wants something between these extremes. It is the rare encounter in which the police do exactly as they are asked, as in the following instance: A black woman called the police and wanted them simply to tell her husband not to hit her anymore. They responded by asking her "if she wanted her husband arrested," but she said, "No, just tell him not to lay on [beat] me anymore." The officers told her to go to court and get a warrant for his arrest the next time this happened, but before leaving they also "told the offender not to hit the complainant any more." Similarly, in another case, a black woman wanted the police to wake up her husband (who was passed out drunk on the floor) and to "scare him because he had been beating her lately when drunk." They did just as she requested, threatening the man with arrest but taking no further action, even when he became "very belligerent" and said, "Run me in if you want, I don't give a damn."

Sometimes the police pretend that they are going to make an unwanted arrest in order to manipulate the complainant—an intimate of the alleged offender— into accepting a lesser resolution than that initially requested. In one attempted instance of this, for example, the police used the tactic to try to discourage a white woman who had complained that her husband had been "spanking" her. She was Portuguese (or Brazilian) and spoke little English, but seemed to want the police to reprimand her husband for mistreating her. The police said they would arrest him, but, as the observer noted, "No one except the complainant thought the police were serious about locking her husband up, not even the police." Consequently, when the complainant did not object (possibly because she could not understand enough English), the police abandoned their threat and "had to instigate a reconciliation" by admonishing the man not to "spank" his wife. The observer added that the complainant had thus unwittingly "foxed" the police by not objecting to the arrest, since they were planning to use the threat to enable them to leave without doing anything at all: "The threat was used to show the wife how ridiculous her call was. The idea was to threaten to arrest her husband so that she would say 'no' and then the police would go." Still another more coercive tactic designed to encourage the complainant to withdraw a request is to threaten to arrest both of the parties, the complainant as well as the alleged offender (see, e.g., page 144). In one such case, however, this tactic failed completely. A black woman wanted her husband arrested because he had beaten her up, and the police agreed to accommodate her, but only on the condition that the husband be allowed to sign a complaint against her as well. When they suggested this to the man, he was amenable, commenting that his wife had not met her obligation to cook for him. His wife also seemed satisfied with this result, and added that her husband, besides beating her, refused to work and stayed out until 5 A.M. In the end, neither backed down and both were arrested and jailed for "disorderly conduct." Perhaps all of this could have been entirely avoided if the police had taken the woman's side and simply admonished her husband for beating her. Instead, they forced her to choose between arrest for herself or nothing at all.

In sum, when the parties are intimately related, in most cases neither the police nor the complainant wants the alleged offender to be arrested. But the complainant typically wants the police to make a judgment, to declare that the other party has done something that is wrong and that must not be done again. The police, however, tend to be neutral, and to do little or nothing to settle the dispute. When the parties are not so intimate, the police are considerably more willing to take sides. It may therefore be generalized that the willingness of the police to use penal tactics varies directly with the relational distance between the parties in conflict. The same is true of the willingness of the police to comply with the wishes of the complainant, and to the overall quantity of social control they exercise. An alleged offender who is relatively distant from the complainant is thus in a condition similar to that of an alleged offender who is socially inferior. Both are more likely to be defined as wrongdoers by the police and to experience the penal style of social control. On the other hand, intimates, like equals, are more often given a certain immunity from coercive authority, and may even be reconciled by the police with those who claim to be their victims.

ORGANIZATION

Thus far it has not been taken into account that many disputes involve people organized into corporate entities, rather than individuals as such. Yet whether or not a group is a party to a conflict predicts and explains much about how the police respond. In particular, a group is less likely than an individual to be handled with penal tactics, and, in a dispute with an individual, a group is more likely to win (see Black, 1976:92–98). The police also devote more time and energy to any matter brought to their attention by a group.

The kind of conflict most likely to involve groups and to be handled by the police is what officers call "neighbor trouble." This is typically a dispute between households, in which individuals participate as representatives of families. A neighborhood dispute may have a long history, and it often involves charges and countercharges rather than a unilateral complaint by one side against the other. The conflict is likely to have begun as a matter between individuals, into which others from the respective households were drawn, until the issue became which family was right or wrong. Children are frequently the major actors in the earlier stages of such a conflict, and only later, as adults enter, does the affair escalate to the level of a protracted dispute between groups, or a feud. It should be added that families in the same neighborhood in modern America often are well acquainted with each other, and they tend to be equals, similar to each other in wealth and other status, and these factors are also surely relevant to how the police handle their disputes. Organization is a kind of status in its own right, however, and seems to confer advantages of its own (see Black, 1976: Chapter 5).

When the police are called into a dispute between neighbors, their response is likely to be neutral rather than judgmental. A little over one-half of such cases are handled primarily in the conciliatory style. Moreover, this figure would undoubtedly be considerably higher were it not that so many of these cases involve complaints about "noise," which the police nearly always handle by telling the offending party to "turn it down" or "keep it down," a mild version of the penal style. For this reason, of all the cases handled in the penal style, those between neighbors are the least likely to result in an arrest and the most likely to involve only a scolding or admonishment. But when a neighbor dispute pertains to something other than "noise," the style of the police is conciliatory in the vast majority of cases.

In one case, the police were dispatched to "see a woman concerning a larceny." They were met by a lower-class white woman who explained in a Southern accent, "The neighbor's boy done stole my transistor radio, and I want it back." As she told her story, the police made no judgments, but simply replied with remarks such as "Uh-huh," "I see," and "Are you sure of that?" The woman mentioned that her neighbor (who lived in an apartment directly next to hers) had said that her son had taken the radio because the complainant's son had taken *their* radio some time ago. One of the officers then said, "It looks to me like you'd better talk to your son and have *him* straighten this out," but the woman replied that her son was now in the military. At this point the alleged offender's mother joined the encounter in the corridor, and the two women began a hostile exchange of words. An officer immediately stepped in and commanded them to be quiet, then turned to the complainant and said that he would arrest the neighbor's son the next morning if the radio had not been returned; meanwhile, she was to "just be calm and wait." The complainant, however, told the officer that this was impossible: "I'll be honest with you, officer, I'm livin' with a man. And if he comes home tonight and his radio ain't here, he'll beat the daylights out of me!" The officer answered, "Then if I was you, lady, I'd pack my bags and get out of here right now before he comes back." This, according to the observer, "stumped the woman completely," and she "sheepishly agreed to wait until the next morning." It should be noted that at no time did the police directly threaten or criticize the alleged offender's mother, nor did they inquire into the whereabouts of the alleged offender himself. Although a threat of arrest was used to enforce the resolution proposed—introducing coercive overtones—the larger concern of the police appeared to be simply a restoration of peace between the two families involved. The reported "larceny" was never defined as such by either officer. Back in the patrol car, one of them explained why: "That just looks like neighbor trouble."

In many neighbor disputes, the particular incident handled by the police seems only an occasion for the expression of a considerably deeper conflict between the families. In some cases, the larger problem is a clash of lifestyles. Thus, in one instance, a black couple complained that a woman who lived in their building had threatened them with a knife, assaulted one of them (the man), and broken a window on the door—all because they had asked her sister "to move off the steps so people could get by." As they recounted this to the police, however, they also "made other comments about her parentage and her character and its effects on their children and their building." The observer noted that they "ranted and raved about people like [the alleged offender] who are abusing ADC [Aid to Dependent Children] and welfare by living with men, buying the best gin, etc., while others who really need it can't get it, and people who are willing to work have to pay for those who abuse it." They also alleged that she was a prostitute. The police expressed sympathy, and advised them that they might want to contact the landlord (about an eviction of the woman) and her social worker (about her welfare status). They also explained that the couple could make a complaint in court. As the police were about to leave, however, the alleged offender arrived and gave her version of the conflict. She said that she had "civilly asked" one of the complainants why her sister could not sit on the steps with her baby, and that one of the complainants (the woman) had then begun to "yell" at her while the other came "bolting through the door and almost knocked her down, breaking the window, grabbing her clothes, etc." She added that she was "not a prostitute," that she would be "crazy to whore" in her own apartment with her five children present, and that she was out a great deal because she was attending a university four nights a week in a nearby city. The police expressed sympathy with this version of the conflict as well, and also advised the woman how she might make a complaint in court. But at no point did the police invoke their authority or side with either party at the expense of the other. The observer concluded his report as follows: "The police felt that by itself each story was perfectly plausible, and that that's the way it usually is in these disputes, and that it's a civil matter and not for them to settle."

In another case involving neighbors—both white—the observer noted that it "seemed fairly clear that the complainant had been dropping a few hints about the morals" of the alleged offender's sister. A couple of other incidents involving conflict between black and white families contained elements of racial tension, but this was not openly recognized by the police. In one case, in which mutual accusations of harassment were made between a black and a white family, the observer remarked that the dispute had "strong social overtones" and that "many statements showing prejudice were made to us at the [white] complainant's residence." The other such case—in a middle-class neighborhood—constituted the only one-sided complaint by a black against a white in the entire sample of 327 cases, and for this reason alone it is worthy of a detailed description. The encounter began when a black man met the police in his driveway and calmly told them that he could no longer tolerate the behavior of his white neighbors: "I've had just about all I can take of my next door neighbor there. We've been here 2 years, and we haven't had a week go by since we've been here what that we didn't have trouble with them. It's their kids. They've caused about every kind of damage they could over here. Now they've broken the glass on my storm door, and we know they's the ones that did it. I just can't take any more of it." The officers were attentive, and one replied, "Boy, neighbors can really be a pain, can't they? But you know, we don't really have any authority to do anything— now, that is. Right now it's a civil matter. Have you talked to your neighbors about it?" "Oh, sure, talked to them? Brother, I've done everything possible to put an end to this. My wife's at the limit now. She's really hot about this. Every time something happens we tell the woman and she says, 'Oh no, not my kids! They've been here all along.' What can I do? My wife goes over there and those kids bend over and pull up their skirts at her, right in front of the mother, and she don't say a word." The man described the damage done by the children in the past, and the officers were sympathetic and friendly. They even joked with the man, laughingly suggesting that he build a 20-foot fence between the houses. But they repeatedly emphasized that it was a civil matter, and told the man that he could see a detective about the course of action he might pursue in the courts. They also volunteered to talk with the neighbor about the matter. The man "showed a good deal of appreciation" at this, and agreed to go back inside his house while the police went to see her.

It took "some time" for the neighbor to answer the knock at her door. When she finally did so, one of the officers said, "We understand your kids have been causing a lot of trouble for the people next door. What about that?" The woman replied in a foreign accent that she knew nothing about the matter: "No, Mr. Officer, I don't know what you talk about." The officer responded, "Yes, you do. Don't give me that." Then the woman said, "No, I'm sorry. My children do nothing. They in school when he say that happen." This sort of exchange continued for some time, until at last the officer announced, "Now you listen to me, lady. You better do something to straighten this out real fast with your neighbor or you're going to find yourself in court. If we hear any more about this, you're liable to find yourself behind bars before it's over." At this, the police turned abruptly and left. Back in the patrol car, one of the officers remarked, "I know that bitch. I used to get the same thing over where they used to live. What a bitch! She really gives me a big pain." He went on to say that the woman and her husband were Macedonian and very wealthy. Perhaps the officer's past experiences with her explain the heavy-handed manner in which she was handled, but, even with this, the police were not nearly as judgmental as they might have been if a lone individual were the object of the complaining family's allegations. Moreover, neither party was aware of what the other was told, and so no one was defined publicly as the one in the wrong. It might also be noted that the police invested more time and energy in this case of a broken window than is typically seen in cases of violence between lower-class husbands and wives. The complainant was black, but he was middle class, and represented a household.

Other cases in the sample also show how membership in a household, like wealth or intimacy, provides a degree of immunity from the criminal law. In one instance, a white woman called to complain that an apparently drunken man had removed his shoes and was sleeping on her front porch—a situation in which the police are ordinarily very likely to make an arrest. But after they arrived the complainant realized that the drunken man was possibly a neighbor of hers, and, in fact, when he gained consciousness he confirmed that he did live nearby. An officer then walked him home without further ado. Even when neighbors are violent the police are reluctant to use the penal style, often simply suggesting that the parties go home and stay away from each other as much as possible.[15]

The role of groups is especially prominent in disputes between neighbors, but the police encounter corporate actors in other settings as well. Any complaint by a business, school, church, or other organization may be interpreted in this way, for example, and a casual observer can easily see that in these cases the police tend to be particularly attentive. Even a temporary group has an advantage over an individual in dealings with the police. Within a single household, for instance, two or more parties may form a coalition, constituting a group in opposition to an individual, and when this happens the group has an advantage. The police are more likely to comply with complainants, or less likely to use their authority against offenders, when they are organized in this way. The observers' reports also suggest that people who would ordinarily have little vulnerability to arrest, such as heads of households or spouses, lose much of their immunity when they are confronted by a coalition.

In one such case, for instance, the police were met on the front lawn by a young black woman who said that her father was "beating up" her mother. When they entered the apartment, the mother was "crying quite hard" and said that she would sign a complaint against her husband. The husband asked her several

---

15. Mutual or unilateral avoidance is itself a major response to social conflict, and frequently occurs as an alternative to law or other social control (see Fürer-Haimendorf, 1967:22; Felstiner, 1974; Koch, 1974:27–31). The resort to avoidance in an American housing project is discussed by Merry (1979).

times, "For what? It's going to cost us $25, you know." The police arrested the man for "disturbing the peace." Except for the daughter's alliance with her mother, this was precisely the kind of situation in which the police rarely make an arrest. In another case, the police were met by a woman who told them that her husband was "drunk" and had been "causing a disturbance." The landlord of the building was present as well, and he concurred with the woman's claim. The police found the husband "sprawled" on the second floor landing, since she had locked him out of their apartment. The woman wanted them to make an arrest. The police warned her that the man would be sent away for six months if they arrested him, but she "thought that was fine." The husband was then arrested on a charge of "drunkenness." The observer noted that the woman had called the police on a number of other occasions, but that they had always refused to arrest her husband "on the grounds that he was in his own home." This time, however, she had not only locked him out, but "had her landlord on the scene to give support."

If both parties are supported by others, this may create a stalemate, with neither having a clear advantage. Thus, in one case the alleged offender and the complainant both had friends on their side, and the police refused to take action. In this situation, a white man was allegedly "drunk" and had been "publicly threatening his wife," and she and some of her neighbors wanted the police to arrest him. The alleged offender was "yelling incoherently" on the street, but he too was supported by a friend who talked to the officers and "shushed up many of the details" of what the man had done. The friend then "slowly edged the offender away," and the police agreed not to make an arrest, even though in the end the man "began to abuse" his only supporter. The observer noted that "it seemed obvious that all was not over yet" and that the police were engaging in "wishful thinking" when they left and reported the case as "peace restored."

The formation of a coalition gives a degree of organization to either or both parties, then, and the behavior of the police varies accordingly. As is shown in neighbor disputes, the police are reluctant to take sides when groups have conflicts with each other. At the same time, if one party is a group and the other an individual, the group has an advantage. If complained against, a group is less likely than an individual to be handled in the penal style. And if a group wants something from the police, it is more likely to succeed.

LEGITIMACY

People may define and respond to social control as more or less legitimate. In this sense, legitimacy is a quantitative variable, known by the degree to which people cooperate with agents of social control (see Weber, 1922:324–327). At one extreme, they may be highly deferential and submissive, or they may be merely civil, recalcitrant, disrespectful, or even aggressively hostile to the point of open rebellion. In many cases, hostile conduct toward those who exercise social control is itself understandable as social control, a kind of judgment from below, but such conduct is typically treated as an offense by those against whom it is directed. In fact, it appears that the quantity of social control varies in curvilinear relation to its legitimacy, so that, to a point, the less people submit to social control the more of it they experience (see Black, 1971:1108–1109).[16] It also appears, at least in legal life, that people who question the legitimacy of social control are particularly subject to sanctions of a penal nature. Thus, in modern America, "contempt of court" is a crime, and so is every kind of "obstruction of justice."[17]

When the police handle disputes, their legitimacy may be challenged in any of several ways. People may resist their entrance into a private setting, for instance, refuse to answer their inquiries, disregard their commands, insult them, or even physically attack them. While all of the parties are respectful toward the police in the vast majority of the encounters (87%), in a significant minority they are not, and these cases deserve closer examination. As might be expected, it is the alleged offender who is most likely to question the legitimacy of police intervention in a dispute. In 6% of the cases the alleged offender is disrespectful—but not violent—toward the police, and in another 3% this disrespect becomes violent. Occasionally, however, it is the complainant who turns against the police, typically when he or she is unable to convince them to take a particular course of action toward an alleged offender. The complainant is disrespectful in 3% of the cases, and violent in another 1%. In one case, the police were violently attacked by several people representing both sides of a conflict: The officers had responded to what was reported as "a woman screaming." (It later became apparent that they had been called by a neighbor.) As their elevator approached the floor of the reported incident, they heard a woman shouting and crying, "Help! Help! He's going to kill my brother!" But as soon as they stepped from the elevator someone yelled, "Who let the motherfuckin' police in?" A man thereupon "charged" toward a woman in the corridor, and the police attempted to restrain both, holding them by the arms. Another man entered the fray at that point, and "cursed and slugged" one of the officers. A second woman also attacked, striking an officer in the eye. All of the parties were blacks of the lower or working class. In the end, three of the four were arrested, including the "screaming woman," who tried to attack one of the men with a broken lamp. During all of

---

16. There is a point at which social control breaks down entirely when the legitimacy of legal authority is contested, such as when the police and other armed forces retreat or capitulate in the face of a riot or revolution. Perhaps this provides an interpretation of the case reported earlier in which the police backed away when a man threatened them with a gun (page 117).

17. It has been argued that, in evolutionary perspective, legal systems are most punitive and repressive when their legitimacy is most precarious. Hence, it is when law is being imposed upon a population for the first time that it tends to meet the greatest resistance, and it is under these conditions that the penal style is most pronounced and severe (see Spitzer, 1979).

this, the police incurred one broken hand, a kick in the groin, various other blows, and two bites. Even the observer found it necessary to use force in order to protect himself from these citizens.

In any event, no matter who the parties are, and no matter what their relationship with each other may be, if they respond to the intervention of the police as illegitimate they are likely to be handled in a penal fashion, often by arrest. (For the same pattern in other contexts, see, e.g., Piliavin and Briar, 1964; La Fave, 1965:146–147; Black, 1971:1097–1104, 1108–1109.) In fact, a rather substantial proportion of the arrests that occur in the context of disputes may be accounted for in this way. Almost one-fourth of the arrests occur when the alleged offender displays hostility or intransigence toward the police (23%). Another 12% occur after other strategies fail to settle the matter in accordance with the wishes of the police, and 6% occur after violence erupts between the parties involved despite police efforts to prevent it. In all, then, a total of 41% of the arrests may be explained by the failure of a citizen to accord legitimacy to the police.[18] Consider a few more illustrations of this pattern.

One case began as a routine request for a police escort by a white woman who wanted to retrieve her clothing from her husband. She said that he was "drunk," had struck her, and that he had also taken a "swat" at their baby. The police found that he had locked the door, however, and they broke it down. They found the man sleeping (evidently passed out) and awakened him, at which point he "began swinging." The police then became violent, twice kicking the man in the head and "severely" twisting his arm. They arrested him for "drunkenness." (For a similar case, see Parnas, 1967:920.) In another instance, a white man answered the door and denied that anyone in his house had called the police, but his wife stepped forth and said that she had done so. Her husband then promptly closed and locked the door, and the police warned him that if he did not open it they would break it down. When he still refused to let them in, they tore open the screen, unlocked the screen door, and kicked open the main door. They immediately placed the man under arrest for "disorderly conduct," apparently without inquiring into why his wife had called them in the first place. In still another case, the police were called by a black couple after their son came home "loud and boisterous" from his high school graduation. They were annoyed not only by his conduct but also because he had not invited them to the graduation. Despite this, they made it clear that they did not want the police to arrest him. The young man, however, became "very insulting" toward the police—repeatedly saying

---

18. Pepinsky reports impressionistic evidence that a failure to grant legitimacy is a major source of arrests in domestic disputes that involve violence:

> One New York City Police captain who has given training to patrolmen on the handling of domestic disputes confirms that, in the case of alleged family "assaults" at least, patrolmen generally arrest only when they receive abuse, regardless of threat or injury to other citizens [1976a:63].

"fuck you, you white motherfuckers"—and he was arrested for "disorderly conduct." The observer added that the arrest was made in order "to show him respect for the law and his parents."

Even a simple refusal to be quiet when the police arrive may result in an arrest. Thus, in one case a white woman called the police because her husband was causing a "disturbance" in their apartment. The man continued "screaming and yelling" after the police arrived, saying "I want to die, shoot me," because he had come to the conclusion that someone else had fathered his children. He was arrested for "disorderly conduct," and the observer explained that this was because he was "unruly." In another instance, involving an accusation by a black woman that her sister-in-law had "molested" her child, the argument also continued in the presence of the police. The alleged offender "went into a tantrum," and, according to the observer, "her screaming was extremely loud, which forced the police to lock her up, despite regrets about it from her sister-in-law." The charge was "drunkenness," but the observer noted that this "was used as an excuse to take her away."

The police tend to justify such arrests as what they have to do to "restore order," but they may also be understood as how the police respond to a challenge to their authority, explicit or implicit. In fact, mere criticism of the police in a face-to-face encounter is handled as a fairly serious crime. In one case, for example, an arrest for "disorderly conduct" occurred immediately after a black man "claimed that the police had no right to mix in private affairs." This happened in the context of a complaint by his wife that he had "hit and kicked her"—a matter usually treated by the police in a conciliatory rather than a penal style, and as a very minor problem at that.

Since most people readily grant legitimacy to the police, the importance of this variable is usually not evident in the handling of cases. Only occasionally, when individuals refuse to show the police respect or rebel openly against them, does this become visible. It then appears that, to a point, the penal style of social control exercised by the police varies inversely with the legitimacy accorded to their authority.

OTHER VARIABLES

The findings detailed in the preceding sections comprise the major patterns of dispute settlement by the police discovered in the present study. In a small number of cases, however, the response of the police is understandable only by reference to factors that ordinarily are not relevant, including other kinds of social status, social relationships not usually seen among the participants, and even the operation of other kinds of social control not usually present.

Although every kind of social status may be important in the operation of a legal system, typically the police are not aware of all of the social characteristics of the people they encounter. Often, for instance, they do not know whether a person is employed, is a member of an ethnic or other cultural minority, or has a criminal or other record—and yet all of these characteristics might otherwise predict and explain how a case is handled. If an alleged offender has a job or children, for example, this means that he or she is more integrated into social life, and—all else constant—makes such a person less vulnerable to the authority of the police (see Black, 1976:49–53). Thus, in one case a black woman called because her ex-husband was "disorderly and causing a scene" in his effort to see their children. She said that by court order he was allowed to see the children only on Saturdays (this was a Tuesday). She noted that similar conflicts had occurred several times before, and she seemed to want the police to make an arrest. But when the police learned that the alleged offender was a cab driver, they simply warned him that "trouble" could jeopardize his job, and took no further action. In another instance, a black man wanted the police to arrest his wife because she was "mentally unfit to tend their children." She was apparently drunk, and was shouting at all concerned. One of the officers suggested that the man take his wife to a clinic for alcoholics, and added that he would like to arrest the woman for "disorderly conduct" but that this "would mean placing five kids with the Women's Bureau and they wouldn't be happy."

While employment or child rearing may lessen the vulnerability of an alleged offender, other characteristics may entail disadvantages. All else constant, for example, a person known to have a bohemian lifestyle or a criminal record would be more vulnerable to the police (see Black, 1976:69–73, 113–117). In one case (not included in the sample of disputes), a drunken black man was arrested after he was found lying on the grass in a park, nude from his ankles to his chest, and "playing with himself." Before he was charged, however, his record was checked, and the observer explained that "as there was no sex history he was charged with 'drunk and disorderly.' " Presumably a man with a record of "indecent exposure" would have been handled differently. If a dispute arises, a person with a deviant identity is more likely to be the object of a complaint to the police, more likely to be defined by the police as the one in the wrong, and more likely to be treated with severity. On the other hand, if such a person calls the police against someone else, the complaint is less likely to succeed. In one instance of this kind, a black man who had been in bed with a married woman rushed out the back door when the woman's husband came home unexpectedly, only to find that her children had removed the tools from his truck while he was in the house. When the man complained to the police, however, they told him that "this was the price he had to pay for his indiscretion." In another case, a white woman who complained to the police that her husband had struck her was ignored as soon as it was learned that she had recently spent time in a mental hospital (previously noted, page 130). In most cases, though, the police do not know whether or not a person has a record of deviant behavior, and must proceed only on the basis of the facts that are presented to them in the face-to-face encounter itself.

The social relationship between the police and the citizens also helps to account for what happens in their encounters, but its effect is obscured in this study
because it varies so little across the cases. Other than people recognized from
previous calls (such as "regulars"), generally the police were not acquainted
with the citizens they met. While undoubtedly relevant to an understanding of the
patterns found, the sample does not allow a systematic assessment of the strength
of this factor. Two cases involving off-duty police officers are noteworthy,
however, since they illustrate how a close relationship between the police and an
alleged offender can provide him or her with a degree of immunity from the
criminal law. Both of these cases entailed a complaint of assault made by a
policeman's wife. In one instance, the officer had allegedly chased his wife down
the street, threatening her with his service revolver. In the other, the wife said
that her husband had struck her from behind, opening a gash in the back of her
head. In each case the incident was referred to higher-ranking officers who
managed to smooth everything over without official action. In the first, the
observer noted that the accused policeman was "treated very carefully" at the
station. His wife was told that she would be unwise to press charges, since "it
would only hurt the children." In the other case, the officer's wife repeatedly
shouted that her husband's colleagues would "get him off like they always did in
the past"—a prediction that proved to be correct, since she was ultimately
convinced not to press her case. In another encounter (not considered a dispute
for purposes of this study), the police released an apparently intoxicated black
man, allowing him to drive away after they found him slumped over the steer-
ing wheel of his car. The officer who handled the incident had seen his partner
(who also was black) greet the driver in what the observer called "a friendly
manner, as if he knew him," and so he told the man that if he was "O.K."
he could "go on his way." When he returned to the patrol car the officer
remarked to his partner (who had stayed in the car to be near the police radio),
"If you hadn't known him I'd have locked him up. He was obviously drunk," His
partner replied that he actually did not know the man after all—"He wasn't the
person I had in mind." It was then too late to arrest the man, however, for he had
already driven away.

Cultural distance between the police and the parties is also relevant to the
handling of cases. Along with cultural differences between the races (see Rokeach,
Miller, and Snyder, 1977), a degree of cultural distance is found between the
sexes in modern America, with men and women having different lifestyles in
many respects. Since all of the police in this study were men, an essentially
invariable distance existed between the officers and the women involved in the
disputes. The observation reports contain occasional indications that this cultural gap expressed itself in a greater degree of rapport and sympathy between
the officers and the men they encountered than between the officers and the
women. This was especially noticeable in matters involving conflict between

the sexes. Recall, for example, the officer who said "I know how you feel" to the man who had allegedly beaten his estranged wife when she tried to retrieve the children he had taken from her earlier that day (see page 151). In another case, a black woman complained that her estranged husband would not leave her residence, and mentioned that he was also behind in his support payments. But the police were very friendly toward the man. One of the officers told him that he knew his daughter ("a well-behaved girl") who worked at the telephone company, and as the police were leaving the apartment, one of them put a hand on the man's shoulder and said, "Sam, you know women. Sometimes they want you around, sometimes they don't. I think you'd have a better chance of talking to her tomorrow." They ended the encounter by driving the man to his home, all in a spirit of masculine solidarity. In another instance, a black woman wanted the police to remove her husband's cousin from her house because he had said a "dirty word" to her child. They refused to do so, however, telling her that she would have to get a court order, and one of them later dismissed her complaint as follows: "He'd probably been after her pants and she got mad. Happens a lot under the same roof." Finally, a case reported by another investigator provides a further illustration. As the police were leaving the scene of a husband–wife dispute—involving lower-class Southern whites—one of the officers whispered to the husband, "Why don't you go out and buy her a can of snuff—maybe you'll get a little more [sex] tonight." The officer "then gave the man a good-natured slap on the back and he laughed uproariously" (Parnas, 1967:935). Cultural distance between the police and women may also help to explain the casual and conciliatory manner in which they typically handle wife-beating complaints.[19] In any event, it should be recognized that no dimension of the social relationship between the police and the citizens—whether they are complainants or alleged offenders—can be taken for granted. Insofar as those characteristics vary, so does police work.

Yet another variable worthy of brief mention is the parties' ease of access to agents of social control other than the police. As suggested earlier, people who have their own means of dispute settlement are unlikely to call the police in the first place (see pages 124–128). Hence, it is understandable that the disputants in the sample rarely seem to have had family members, neighbors, or other third parties who could or would intervene in their affairs. In the few instances in which the possibility of recourse to such individuals came to the attention of the police, they retreated entirely, leaving the problem to whoever else might be

---

19. It might be noted that during the years since these observations were made, many police departments throughout the United States have begun using women as ordinary patrol officers. Moreover, there are scattered indications that women officers who handle domestic disputes may invest more time and care in them than men, that they may achieve more lasting resolutions, and that in any case they may encounter less violent resistance from alleged offenders in these matters (see Anonymous, 1972).

available to handle it. For example, in one of the cases in which the alleged offender was not present, a white woman said that her estranged husband, a sailor, had found her in the home of friends and had "kicked and hit" her as she held their baby. The police told her that since he was in the Navy she should call the Shore Patrol. More often, however, it is another citizen to whom the police abdicate their authority. Thus, in one case, they were dispatched to handle a "disorderly man," and were met by a black woman who showed them to her living room where the alleged offender was lying "dead drunk" on the floor. The woman "was hollering that she wanted him out." The police might ordinarily have arrested the man, but before they could take action of any kind the complainant's husband—apparently a friend or relative of the alleged offender— arrived and "sympathized" with him. He asked the officers not to make an arrest, and assured them that "he would find a cab and get the man home." The woman continued raging against the man, demanding his arrest, but the police began to ignore her, and one of them commented to her sarcastically, "You're a great help." In the end, they assisted in removing the man from the apartment to the street, and then "left him in the care of" the complainant's husband.

A Note on Business Disputes

During the observation period the police handled a small number of disputes between business people and their customers (six cases). These cases were excluded from the sample used in this study, since they did not involve people in ongoing relationships. They nevertheless provide an opportunity to examine a little known species of police work, closely related to the subject of the larger study, and deserve a few pages of this report.

Before discussing these cases, however, special mention might be made of disputes between landlords and tenants, which were included in the main sample because they generally involve more intimacy between the parties than is found in an everyday business transaction. Although landlord–tenant disputes comprise 5% of the cases in the larger study, only a minority of these pertained specifically to matters of a contractual nature, while the rest involved complaints about such things as "noise" and fights. Moreover, those pertaining to contractual obligations may be complicated by personal elements that transcend the landlord–tenant relationship itself. In one case involving whites, for instance, a landlord told the police that a woman boarding in his house for $25 a month had "gotten drunk" and "tried to kill" him. He wanted the woman removed from the house. The alleged offender said that the landlord was "drunk," and that she had done "no such thing" as he claimed. After further discussion, the police told the landlord that he would have to go to renters' court, and one officer added, "You shouldn't call the police every time a tenant won't sleep with you or cook your meals." Afterward he added, "He's been shacking up with her for 3 years. Now he wants to throw her out." In another instance, a white woman complained to the police that her toilet had backed up and overflowed into the hallway, and that her landlord "refused to do anything." When an officer went upstairs to talk to the landlord, he learned that the parties were brother and sister. Upon hearing this, the officers immediately turned to leave, though the observer remarked that the complainant was "in a state of exhaustion and near hysteria, yelling 'I don't claim him as a brother after all he's done to me!' " As the police were walking out the door, an officer told her, "Lady, this is a civil matter for you to work out," and also mentioned that her brother had said that "the pipes were now alright." In still another case, a roominghouse manager—white and female— asked the police to remove a white man who was sitting on the back steps. The man told them that he lived there ("in room 5"), but the manager insisted that he was lying. The police then went to room 5 and talked to a couple there, who informed them that the alleged offender was the manager's brother as well as a friend of theirs, and that he did stay in the room when the wife—who lived out of town—was not visiting her husband. The manager at first denied that the alleged offender was her brother, but eventually admitted that he was. She was there-upon told by an officer that "a roomer could have as many people as he liked staying in the room and sharing the rent." At this point, the manager telephoned the owner of the boardinghouse and asked the police officer to speak with him. The owner told the officer that the "rules of the house" made it clear to all roomers that "no other persons were to occupy the rooms rented." When he hung up the phone, the officer told the alleged offender that he could not go back into the house after all, and that he would be arrested if he did.

These cases suggest that the police are reluctant to take coercive action in business disputes that involve personal elements. But when these elements are lacking—as in the conclusion of the last case, where the owner of the boarding-house had no ties to the alleged offender—they appear to be willing to intervene with all of their authority. Indeed, they may even go beyond what is generally considered the formal limits of their authority under these conditions. Thus, in another case that turned out to pertain to the occupancy of an apartment, one white woman complained that a second white woman had "twisted" her arm. It developed that the alleged offender had rented a room from the complainant, and had paid her $30 in advance for her first week's occupancy. When she attempted to move into the room, however, she found that the previous occupant had not yet moved out. She then returned to the landlady and demanded a refund of her $30, but was told that she could not have it: "I don't give refunds. A contract is a contract." It was at this point that the prospective tenant became violent and the landlady called the police. After listening to the story, one of the officers told the landlady that she would have to return the $30 to the other woman. She refused, and so the officer threatened to arrest her, saying that it was "plain larceny" for her to keep the money. Although she finally capitulated, she demanded the officer's name and badge number, and threatened to make a complaint about him. He said, "Go ahead, I've gotten letters for less than this," but he also warned her that she had best not make trouble for him: "I'll have the building inspectors down on you." The matter was thus settled in the compensatory style, with the resolution backed by a threat of punishment. As further examples will show, however, this case was highly unusual in one respect. The businessperson lost. The handful of cases collected in this study, along with other evidence (see, e.g., Westley, 1970:71–72), suggest that businesspeople typically are respectful and friendly toward the police, and that the police seem to be very much inclined to side with businesspeople whenever disputes occur.

In one of the six commercial disputes recorded by the observers, the white owner of a shoe store complained that a black man was "causing a disturbance" in his store. It seems that the man's wife had bought a pair of shoes, they had "broken," and he had come to demand a refund. The owner refused, pointing out a sign on the cash register that said no refunds would be made. The customer continued to argue, and at some point the shopkeeper called the police. When the black man saw the police enter the store he shouted, "Look, they sent two white cops!" He also said to the store owner, "You make your money from Negroes, not whites!" The man was using profane language ("cussing"), and one of the officers warned him to "watch his language." After learning about the situation, the police pointed to the sign on the cash register and told the man he would have to leave. He grudgingly agreed to do so, but noted that he would bring the matter to the attention of the Better Business Bureau and the National Association for the Advancement of Colored People. Later, after the encounter, the officers expressed amusement about the incident, and they "joked" about the man's threat to pursue his grievance elsewhere.

In a similar case, a white store owner called the police to complain about a young black man who was "shouting and yelling" that he had not received change for a $20 bill. The store owner claimed that he had returned the bill. The young man's mother was present, and attempted to "quiet him down," but he continued to demand his change. The police—who were white— arrested him for "disorderly conduct," after unsuccessfully trying to convince him that he would not be able to get his way. As he was being processed at the police station, a "crumpled" $20 bill was found in the young man's possession, though it was not determined whether this was the money that had been at issue. In any event, the case illustrates what may happen if a customer refuses to accept a judgment by the police on behalf of a businessperson.

Another case shows how far the police may extend themselves in order to support a businessperson. In this instance, the call came from a white customer who felt that he had been overcharged by a service station. The man—who seemed to have been drinking—told the police that he had left his car at the station for a "tune-up," and that when he returned he had been given a bill that he found exorbitant for the work that was done. He handed the bill to one of the officers and said, "Just look at it!" The officers remained silent. Then the white owner or manager of the service station called out, "He's just a drunk—won't pay his bill." At this point, one of the officers took the trouble to study the invoice, item by item, and commented on the fairness of the prices charged for each piece of work. As he was doing this, the man from the station walked over and said, "He's not getting his car 'til he pays. He was completely sober when he came in, but he went into the bar next door and hung one on [got drunk] while we worked on his car." An officer thereupon said to the customer, "You might as well pay the man. He has a legal right to keep your car 'til you pay." The man asked, "Well, what would you do? Jesus Christ." The officer replied, "I'd pay it. There's nothing wrong with those prices." In the end, the man paid, and also thanked the police for helping him. In another case, the police were called to a "disturbance at a restaurant," and arrived to find a dispute concerning whether a customer had a right to lettuce and tomato on his sandwich. The customer, a black man, had been told by the black waiter that he would have to pay an additional 10¢ for the lettuce and tomato, which he felt should be provided free of charge. The police said that he would have to take his complaint to the "restaurant association," meanwhile paying the 10¢. The customer complied. Another case—though not a business dispute in a narrow sense—also illustrates the willingness of the police to help a businessperson, and to exact a financial settlement if that is desired. A white deaf–mute entered a bar (patronized by whites), planning to distribute cards explaining sign language and then to solicit donations. However, the proprietor told his customers not to give the deaf–mute any money. This so infuriated the man that he went out of the bar and broke one of its windows. A customer brought him back and held him until the police came. The officers told the alleged offender that he would have to pay for the window, and stayed to see that he did so.

It might be added that the police routinely remove patrons of drinking establishments whenever requested to do this by those in charge. Thus, in one case they were asked by the owner of a bar—an Asian American—to remove three black men: "I want these men thrown out of here right away." Without asking why he wanted the men ejected, the police—who were white— simply said, "Let's go, fellas. Out of the bar." The black men shrugged their shoulders and walked out.

In short, it appears that businesspeople generally get what they want from the police. Often what they want is a financial settlement, a kind of social control usually associated with civil rather than criminal law. Nonetheless, the police give them that as well.

The Relevance of the Written Law

Thus far, the disputes the police handle have been presented and analyzed almost entirely without regard to the written law. It was noted earlier that close to one-half of the cases involve violence, and that almost one-fifth involve the use of a weapon (page 120), but little effort has been made to classify them according to the categories that might be used by a lawyer or a judge. Moreover, the actions taken by the police have not been viewed from the standpoint of the rules of legal procedure or formal obligations of any other kind (compare, e.g., Goldstein, 1960; La Fave, 1965). The purpose of this study has been to understand dispute settlement by the police from the perspective of social science rather than law. Nevertheless, how these materials appear in the light of the written law of modern America might be of interest to the reader, if only to provide a legal perspective for its own sake. This also makes it possible to assess the factual value of the police version of their decision making, since officers commonly refer to the written law to explain their actions. It will be seen that however much the written law is used to justify what the police do in handling disputes, it does not seem to correspond closely to how they actually behave.

All of the 317 cases in the sample were classified as to whether or not they presented grounds for legal action of any kind and, if so, whether these grounds were civil or criminal. If criminal, a case was further classified as a "felony" or a "misdemeanor" (the former to designate a crime punishable by more than one year in prison). It is important to emphasize, however, that the proper application of these categories is frequently a matter of opinion, not fact. In addition, it should be noted that unless the factual details of an incident were self-evident to the observer, the classification could only be based upon the complainant's version of what happened. With these qualifications, then, it may be generalized that in about one-fourth of the disputes there are no grounds for legal action of any kind, criminal or civil (26%). Another 9% of the cases have no apparent criminal elements but may be viewed as falling within the province of civil law, such as disputes pertaining to the custody of a child or the division of property after a marital separation. Thus, over one-third of the cases have nothing to do with the criminal law. At the other extreme, almost one-fifth involve felonies (18%), nearly all of which are violent in nature, such as an assault involving a weapon or a threat to kill. Over one-third of the cases may be classified as misdemeanors, divided about equally between violent and nonviolent offenses (respectively 17% and 20%). Finally, the remaining cases could not be assigned to any of these major categories, either because the observers' reports did not include enough details about incidents of criminal violence (6%), or because the disputes did not fit adequately under any of the headings (5%). Of the latter sort, for instance, was the case involving a middle-aged couple who had possession of their daughter's baby and would not give it back (pages 144–146). Another such case involved an elderly black man who wanted a young man and his girlfriend to move out of his apartment. The two were not related to him by either blood or marriage, nor were they paying rent, but they claimed that they had been "taking care" of the man for 6 months, that he was "old and blind" and had "no one to look after him," and therefore they refused to leave. (On learning that they were not related, the police said that they did not "legally live" in the apartment and would have to move out, and stayed until they packed and left with their belongings in a cab.) Cases such as these are subject to so many interpretations that they are better left unclassified in the present analysis.

As noted earlier (page 114, note 3), the meaning of the written law of arrest in American jurisdictions is not entirely clear, but seems to authorize the police to make an arrest without a formal warrant when they have "reasonable grounds" to believe that someone has committed a felony. In the case of a misdemeanor, they usually must witness the offense or have a sworn complaint from a citizen before they can make a "legal" arrest. Since the conditions for a felony arrest are less restrictive, and since a felony is more "serious" in the sense that it is subject to a more severe penalty, it might be expected that the police would be likely to make an arrest when a felony appears to have occurred and the alleged offender is available to them, and it might be expected that a felony arrest would be more likely than a misdemeanor arrest. Indeed, it might be expected that the police would virtually always make an arrest when a felony appears to have occurred and the alleged offender is available to them (as was true of the cases analyzed here). Nevertheless, as Table 5–13 shows, more often than not apparent felons are allowed to remain free, and they are only slightly more vulnerable to arrest than those who have seemingly committed misdemeanors. An arrest is made in a little over one-fourth of the cases involving a violent felony and in nearly one-fifth of those involving a violent misdemeanor. The highest rate of arrest (over 40%) occurs in the cases involving an unspecified degree of violence. Civil matters and nonviolent misdemeanors have the lowest rates (each about one in twenty). Finally, it is noteworthy that an arrest occurs in 17% of the cases that appear to have no grounds for legal action of any kind, criminal or civil. The vast majority of people formally susceptible to arrest are allowed to keep their freedom, then, but a substantial minority of those who do not seem to have committed any illegality at all, criminal or civil, are taken to jail.

The written law also has limited relevance to the style in which the police handle disputes. Their style is primarily conciliatory in a little over one-half of the cases involving a violent felony, a proportion nearly the same as that for cases that have no apparent grounds for legal action of any kind, and only slightly lower than in civil matters (see Table 5–14).Conciliation is less likely in crimes with an unspecified degree of violence, and least likely of all in cases of a

TABLE 5–13

Rate of Arrest according to Legal Status of Complaint[a]

Police Action	Legal Status of Complaint								
	Felony (violent)	Felony (other)	Misdemeanor (violent)	Misdemeanor (other)	Violent crime (degree unknown)	Civil matter	No grounds for legal action	Other	Total
Arrest	27	(2)	17	5	37	4	17	—	16
No arrest	73	(2)	83	95	63	96	83	100	84
Total percent	100	—	100	100	100	100	100	100	100
Total cases	(52)	(4)	(52)	(61)	(19)	(23)	(78)	(10)	(299)

[a] By percent. Figures in parentheses are used whenever the total number of incidents is statistically too small to justify a generalized assertion of rate and for total number of cases.

TABLE 5-14

Major Style of Social Control Exercised by Police according to Legal Status of Complaint[a]

Style of Social Control	Legal Status of Complaint								
	Felony (violent)	Felony (other)	Misdemeanor (violent)	Misdemeanor (other)	Violent crime (degree unknown)	Civil matter	No grounds for legal action	Other	Total
Conciliatory	54	(2)	65	33	47	61	58	40	52
Penal	46	(2)	27	66	47	26	32	40	41
Therapeutic	—	—	—	2	5	4	3	20	2
Compensatory	—	—	2	—	—	4	—	—	1
Preventive action only	—	—	4	—	—	4	6	—	3
Other	—	—	2	—	—	—	1	—	1
Total percent	100	—	100	101	99	99	100	100	100
Total cases	(52)	(4)	(52)	(61)	(19)	(23)	(78)	(10)	(299)

[a]By percent. Figures in parentheses are used whenever the total number of incidents is statistically too small to justify a generalized assertion of rate and for total number of cases.

nonviolent misdemeanor. It is most likely in violent misdemeanors. Hence, the written law does not predict precisely whether an incident will be handled as an offense or merely as an interpersonal conflict.

It should be remembered, in addition, that the behavior of the police generally does not seem to conform closely to the written law in cases where the alleged offender is not immediately available for arrest. (These cases, which were excluded from the main sample of disputes, are discussed earlier on pages 113–116.) When a woman complains that she has been beaten or otherwise injured by a man who is not present, for example, the police almost never define the incident as a crime by writing an official report about it. (This is equally true when the alleged offender is known to be available at a nearby tavern or behind a locked door.) Under these circumstances, a follow-up investigation, and an arrest and prosecution, are generally precluded. Beyond this, such cases are not entered into the crime rate that is published by each city.

Still more evidence bearing upon the relevance of the written law is provided by cases involving weapons. Although disputes involving a gun are more likely to result in an arrest than those involving no weapon at all (36% versus 13%), and although the same is true where makeshift weapons are used (35%), cases involving a knife or similar weapon are not significantly more likely to result in arrest (17%). What is more, although cases involving makeshift weapons are somewhat less likely to be handled in the conciliatory style than those involving no weapon at all (41% versus 52%), those involving a gun or a knife are actually more likely to be handled in this way (64% and 61%, respectively). In other words, in most cases involving a gun or a knife—even with the party wielding the weapon present in the encounter—the police do not invoke the criminal law. As has been shown in a number of illustrations throughout this report, typically in such cases they do not define anyone as an offender of any kind. Recall, for example, the case in which the police preferred not to invoke the law against their off-duty colleague who had chased his wife down the street with a drawn service revolver (page 174), and also the case in which they retreated from a man who pointed a gun at them and refused to let them in his house (page 117). Similarly, the police labeled one of the cases involving a knife threat as a "civil matter," and explained that for this reason it was "not for them to settle" (page 166).

Perhaps a few more cases should be mentioned here. In one of these, a black woman complained that her husband had menaced her with a drawn gun, then left when she threatened to call the police. Just as the officer was leaving the building after talking with the woman, the man returned and proceeded to deny his wife's allegation. The observer noted that he had an "obvious bulge on his hip (possibly a gun), and when he withdrew his hands from his pockets a bullet fell out." Nonetheless, the officer did not search the man, and refused to arrest him on the ground that he "had no gun when encountered." The officer also decided not to search the man's car on the ground that such a search would be "illegal."

In another instance, a black woman complained that "her husband had held a gun to her face." The gun was not immediately visible to the police, however, and the officers said that "as this was a misdemeanor, no search could be made." (Presumably this was an intentional misrepresentation, since surely they knew that the reported offense was a felony according to the written law.) The police left the woman with her husband, telling her to go downtown and swear out a warrant if she wanted him arrested, and they reported the case as a "domestic disturbance." In a third case, the police were dispatched to a "man with a gun" and found two black men—father and son-in-law—fighting and swearing to kill each other. The observer explained the conflict as follows: "The father had a sexual affair with his daughter before her marriage to the husband. Since the marriage, the father has continued to bother his daughter, mostly by phone calls. Such a phone call triggered the fight between them." When the police arrived, they found that the younger man had a knife, but there was no evidence of the gun that one of the disputants reportedly had been wielding. The officers disarmed the son-in-law (remarking that the older man was "not worth it"), told him to see a detective about his father-in-law, and ordered the latter to stay away from his daughter's house. However, they did not inquire about a gun, nor did they explicitly recognize the sexual behavior of the father and daughter as incest. No crime report was filed.

In another case, in which a woman had "come after" her neighbor with an ice pick, the officers told the parties that "they should not expect the police to solve their personal problems." One of the stabbings serves as yet another example: A black man was standing on his front porch "hustling" a woman, and so his wife came downstairs in a jealous rage and stabbed him in the chest with a butcher knife. The man responded by knocking her to the floor, kicking her, and seizing the knife. The wife then called the police and wanted her husband "thrown out" for treating her that way "in public." The police ignored the woman's request, and asked the man if he wanted to press charges, but one of them commented, "Look, if we step in you'll be sorry tomorrow. Now you don't want that." He also said, "You were fooling around, weren't you? You probably deserved it." In the end, the police suggested that the man "take a long walk" until his wife "sobered up and cooled off," and he agreed. The case was reported as a "family fight."

Apart from numerous assaults, the police ignored cases of burglary, malicious destruction of property, larceny, and other matters of a technically criminal nature. In one case of "threatening phone calls," for instance, the complainant (a black woman) gave the police the name and address of the alleged offender, but they reported the incident as "threatening phone calls—caller unknown," thereby assuring that no further action would be taken. Many more examples could be mentioned. It is enough to say, however, that the cases in the sample provide abundant evidence that the police routinely ignore violations of the written law. Moreover, in some cases they lie in order to make this seem reasonable to the people concerned. And when they do invoke the law by making an arrest, they often lie about what happened (see Manning, 1974). Thus, a number of people were arrested for "drunkenness" in private settings, though in each of the cities studied drunkenness is prohibited by the written law only when it occurs in a public place. Some arrested for this crime did not even show any signs of drinking. Still other people were arrested for "disorderly conduct" when they were entirely peaceful by normal standards (e.g., the cases on pages 151 and 164).

In sum, the written law seems to have limited value as a predictor of what the police will do from one case to the next. They nevertheless often make reference to the law, and use it to justify much of their behavior. This is illustrated especially well by one of the cases not included in the sample of disputes. The police stopped to investigate three white teenagers in a parked car. Afterward, the observer asked the officer who handled it whether he had given the driver a ticket. The officer replied, "No, I didn't find anything wrong. Well, I mean, if it would've been somebody else I could've found plenty wrong, but that guy was a pretty good Joe." So it is in dispute settlement and, for that matter, in all police work. Whether the police find that the written law has been violated apparently depends in many cases upon how they choose to exercise their authority, rather than the other way around.[20] And this choice in turn depends upon the social setting in which they find themselves.

Conclusion

When the police handle a dispute between people who know each other, a number of social variables predict and explain what happens. Whether the police define anyone as right or wrong, whether they are penal, therapeutic, compensatory, or conciliatory in their style, whether they use more or less time, energy, or authority—all of this depends upon the location and direction of the dispute in

---

20. It might be argued that the interpretation of the written law by the police functions in much the same way as the invocation of myth:

> Myth . . . can attach itself not only to magic but to any form of social claim. It is used always to account for extraordinary privileges or duties, or great social inequalities, for severe burdens of rank . . . . The function of myth is not to explain but to vouch for, not to satisfy curiosity but to give confidence in power [Malinowski, 1925:84].

social space. The major patterns identified in the present study may be summarized in the following generalizations:

RACE
1. *The police devote more time and energy to the disputes of whites than to those of blacks.*
2. *The police are more coercive toward blacks than toward whites.*

SOCIAL CLASS
3. *The police devote more time and energy to the disputes of middle-class people than to those of lower- and working-class people.*
4. *The police are more conciliatory and therapeutic toward middle-class people, more penal toward lower- and working-class people.*

HOUSEHOLD STATUS
5. *The police favor heads of household when they have disputes in their own dwellings.*
6. *The police are more conciliatory as the parties to a household dispute are more equal, and they are more penal as the parties are less equal.*

AGE
7. *The police favor adults when they have disputes with juveniles.*
8. *The police are more conciliatory toward adults, more penal and moralistic toward juveniles.*

INTIMACY
9. *The police are more likely to comply with complainants as the relational distance between the disputants increases.*
10. *The police are more conciliatory as the parties to a dispute are more intimate, and they are more penal as the parties are more relationally distant.*

ORGANIZATION
11. *The police favor groups when they have disputes with individuals.*
12. *The police are more conciliatory toward groups, more penal toward individuals.*

LEGITIMACY
13. *The police are more penal and coercive as their authority is accorded less legitimacy, but only to a point, when they may withdraw.*

In addition, there is scattered evidence suggesting that dispute settlement by the police varies with other kinds of social status (such as the integration, conventionality, and respectability of the people involved), with the nature of the relationship between the police and the people in a dispute, and with the availability of social control other than the police. Beyond this, there is reason to believe that businesspeople who have disputes with members of the public usually get what they want from the police. The written law, however, does not seem to correspond closely to how the police behave from one case to another. Often they are conciliatory or entirely passive when a lawyer might expect them to make an arrest, and often they are penal and coercive when technically they seem to have no authority to be so.

A striking feature of dispute settlement by the police is that in most cases the officers do little or nothing to help the parties reach a lasting resolution of their conflict. They function primarily as agents of pacification, dealing only with the facts on the surface, rarely inquiring into the underlying causes of the complaints they hear. Their solutions—if any—are situational and temporary, and have little or no bearing on what happens after they leave. In this sense, it can hardly be said that the police settle disputes at all.

It should be apparent that people—especially those of low status—generally do not receive what they want from the police. In fact, many openly express frustration or disgust at the way the police handle (or avoid) their problems. For their part, the police themselves express a great deal of dissatisfaction with this aspect of their responsibilities. Many believe that little is accomplished when they handle disputes, and most would prefer to have nothing to do with them. They complain that these problems are really "not police business" but only "a waste of time." They feel that they have no effective means of dealing with them. As one officer remarked after being sent to a domestic dispute, "This is just one of those cases that cannot be handled." Another policeman commented as follows:

> You talk about a pain in the ass! Something's got to be done about those [domestic disputes] sooner or later. The trouble is that the policeman doesn't have no power to do nothing. There's some guy, probably drunk as hell, who's been beating the shit out of his wife, and he's most likely going to give it to her worse when you leave. All you can do is tell her how to get a warrant the next day. All this time her husband, see, he wants you to get the hell out of his house—he'll tell you his home is his castle and all that. He can stand there and call you every name in the book, tell you to kiss his royal American ass and everything else, and you still can't touch him [author's field notes].

Another officer made a substantially similar remark:

> I hate those goddamn [domestic disputes]. There's not a thing you can do with them. Most of the time I think the woman wants you to give her husband a

punch in the nose for her. You go in there until things get quieted down. They don't amount to anything serious [author's field notes].

And still another policeman said:

All we get when we go in on a family trouble is humiliated–that's all we get out of it. Half the time both parties turn on us and we're used as nothing but scapegoats. Maybe that's the purpose we serve, I don't know [author's field notes].[21]

Several officers also asserted that the police should refuse to handle these matters except in cases involving a deadly weapon. Generally speaking, then, while the police do little to settle the disputes they handle, they would rather do even less.[22] But since their responsibilities are determined largely by the people who call them and not by themselves (see Black, 1973), the handling of disputes remains one of their major activities.

As described here, dispute settlement by the police in modern America contrasts dramatically with the management of conflict in tribal and other simple societies (see, e.g., Barton, 1919; Llewellyn and Hoebel, 1941; Gibbs, 1963; Gulliver, 1963; Gluckman, 1967; for overviews, see MacCormack, 1976; Roberts, 1979). Especially noticeable is the greater degree to which disputes within the villages of simple societies are, so to speak, actually settled. In these settings, conflicts are more likely to be examined in detail and discussed at length by all concerned. Much hostility is sometimes expressed, efforts at deception are com-

---

21. Parnas suggests that something is in fact accomplished when the complainant turns upon the police and they become the target of both parties' hostility: "The complainant's attack on the police at least temporarily directs the disputants' animosity away from each other and toward a common goal and thus in effect reconciles the parties for the time being [1967:921]."

22. Other investigators also report that work of this kind is disliked by the police. Thus, one police official is quoted as follows:

You know, if there is one thing these men hate more than anything else it is to go out on a call for a family quarrel. You ought to see their faces when they hear that call come over the radio [Westley, 1970:61].

During Parnas' study, an officer referred to domestic disputes as "the scum of calls" and added that "nobody thanks you even if you help [1967:921]."

The police also recognize that interpersonal conflicts are among the most dangerous cases they handle. About one-fourth of the officers killed in the line of duty are handling disputes, as are about 40% of those injured (Bard and Zacker, 1976:71; see also Parnas, 1967:919–920). Part of the danger lies in the unpredictability of these cases, an element that many officers dislike in and of itself. As one New York City officer remarked,

When you answer a call for a liquor-store holdup, at least you know what you're getting into. But in a family-dispute call, you never know if someone is going to greet you at the door with a frying pan to smash over your head or a bottle of lye to throw on you [Anonymous, 1974].

mon, there is bargaining and cajoling, and possibly even overtones of violence are present, but in the end a resolution for the foreseeable future is often found.[23] Typically the dominant style of social control is conciliatory or compensatory. In either case, an effort may be made not only to deal with the dispute itself but also to repair any social damage or bad feelings that resulted from the conflict. Sometimes, after a settlement is found, everyone involved may even join in a ritual of solidarity such as a feast or beer party to celebrate the return of peace and to signify that all is forgiven.[24]

Differences between dispute settlement by American police and by third parties in tribal societies cannot be explained by reference to the kinds of cases they handle, since, in substance, the disputes analyzed in the present study largely resemble those described by anthropologists. The same is true of the relationships between the people involved: Usually the parties to disputes handled by the police are quite intimately related to each other, and they are culturally similar as well. Beyond this, electronic communications and the automobile have made the police as readily available to those who wish to mobilize them as any elder or

---

23. Although this characterization is based upon reports of diverse people made by a number of anthropologists (such as those cited above), by no means does it apply to all tribal or other simple societies. As Nader comments, "The notion that people in all primitive societies have access to forums for justice is a romantic one, nothing more" (1978:92; see also Colson, 1974). In fact, some of these societies experience a considerable amount of recurrent bloodshed and treachery, and have little third-party intervention of any kind. (For a cross-cultural survey of dispute settlement, see Schwartz and Miller, 1964.) It should be added that even in societies where lasting resolutions of conflict are frequent, this is likely to be a luxury enjoyed only by limited segments of the population, such as adults, males, and those with particular group affiliations.

24. The conciliatory style of dispute settlement is also well developed in more complex societies where a high degree of cultural homogeneity prevails and where a substantial proportion of social relationships remain comparatively intimate and stable. One example is modern Japan, where a long tradition of mediation is still very strong and expresses itself through new institutions as well as old (see Henderson, 1965). One American observer was surprised at the degree of concern shown by the Japanese police in conciliating disputes:

> The police see masses of ordinary people who have become enmeshed in situations that are tediously complex and meaningful only to the persons immediately involved. The outcomes are of no interest to the community at large; the newspapers will not notice if matters are sorted out or not; superior officers have no way of recording the effort patrolmen expend in trying to be helpful; and the people themselves are incapable by and large of permanently escaping their predicaments. Policemen are responsible for tending these individuals, for showing that they appreciate—even when they are tired, hurried, bored, and preoccupied—the minute ways in which each person is unique. It is, perhaps, the greatest service they render [Bayley, 1976:51–52; see also Kawashima, 1963:55–56].

The Chinese have a tradition much the same as the Japanese that has continued in the People's Republic of China (see, e.g., Cohen, 1966) and, at least until recently, in the Chinatowns of America (see Grace, 1970; Doo, 1973). In short, although tribal and other simple societies may illustrate dispute settlement at its furthest remove from that of the police in modern America, it should not be inferred that it is modernity itself that undermines traditional patterns.

chief in a tribal village is. The question remains, then, why dispute settlement by the police is so different, and so much less satisfying to everyone involved.

In cross-cultural perspective, a peculiar feature of dispute settlement by the police is the social location of the police themselves. Whereas social control in tribal and other simple societies is the responsibility of people who are socially close to the parties in conflict, the police in modern America are in most cases very distant (see above, pages 174–175). Ordinarily those who respond to a call for dispute settlement are strangers, culturally alien, and superior in social status. These conditions are not conducive to conciliation but are associated more with the penal style of social control (see Black, 1976:29–30, 47, 78–79; see also Black and Baumgartner, 1981:forthcoming). What is more, they are radically unlike the conditions that foster a willingness to help in third parties of all kinds (see Black and Baumgartner, 1981). All of this suggests that wherever social distance substantially removes those with the responsibility to settle disputes from the disputants themselves, they will respond with indifference.

* * *

In closing, it might be noted that the demand for dispute settlement in modern America is seemingly growing. To a degree, this may be related to a breakdown of the patriarchal family, in turn a consequence of the increasing economic independence of women (see pages 124–128).[25] Other trends are simultaneously changing the mechanisms available to people for help of this kind. Thus, in the first place, the police and the people are equalizing and homogenizing. Blacks and members of other minorities are increasingly appearing in patrol cars, for example, and so are women. Expressing a redistribution of status and a process of assimilation throughout society, this movement is drawing the police and the people closer together in some respects, even if they remain strangers in others. To an extent, this will encourage patterns of dispute settlement more akin to

---

25. This is occurring not only in modern America but throughout most of the world, wherever social conditions are weakening the authority of men over women. As this happens, women will increasingly call upon third parties of all kinds—and not simply the police—to help them in their conflicts with men (see, e.g., Starr and Pool, 1974:552–553). At the same time, since law varies inversely with other social control (Black, 1976:107–111), they themselves will increasingly become subject to law. More and more women will be the objects of complaints to the police (by their husbands as well as by others), more will be arrested and sent to jail or prison (see Kruttschnitt, 1979: Chapter 7), and more will be the objects of lawsuits. Accordingly, at present, the relative independence of lower-class black women not only explains why they are more likely than white women to call the police about their husbands and lovers (see pages 124–128), but also why they are more likely to be defined as criminals and sent to jail or prison.

those in tribal and other simple societies (see page 175, note 19).[26] At the same time, another movement has begun to create mechanisms of dispute settlement that are entirely independent of the pólice and other legal agencies (see, e.g., Danzig, 1973; Wahrhaftig, 1978). Systems of mediation and arbitration, organized and operated by people socially similar to those in conflict, are appearing in many neighborhoods and communities throughout society, and are expropriating this function of the police.[27] Even as the police draw closer to the people, then, they are being displaced by modes of dispute settlement resembling those of simpler societies. If this continues, dispute settlement by the police—as described here—will not survive, but will only be remembered as a curiosity of the past.

---

26. It should be added that in recent years a number of American police departments have experimented with the creation of special units whose primary responsibility is to handle domestic disputes. Officers in these units are trained in human relations techniques to increase their effectiveness as agents of conciliation (see Liebman and Schwartz, 1973). Changes of this kind may mean that dispute settlement by the police in some cities already differs significantly from the patterns described in the present report.

27. Nils Christie (1977) argues that interpersonal conflict may be understood as a kind of property that modern states have come to monopolize. For a discussion of "depolicing" and other strategies whereby people may be encouraged to handle their own problems, see Black and Baumgartner (1981).

On Self-Help in Modern Society*

With M. P. Baumgartner

6

In a modern society, conflict between people is often defined as crime and is handled by officials of the state such as police, prosecutors, and judges. It is taken for granted that ordinary citizens are unable to solve many of their problems with others, but must turn to law for help.[1] This mode of social control has several distinctive consequences: It dramatizes the deviant character of an offense, for example (see Tannenbaum, 1938:19–21), and it may escalate hostility between the parties involved (see, e.g., Gibbs, 1963). Its patterns of detection and other procedures also affect the nature and distribution of crime itself, making some kinds of conduct in some places more vulnerable to observation and intervention, leaving other kinds in other places relatively immune. Finally, for the offender, law tends to be more stigmatizing and disabling than other social control and so may even render future conformity less likely.[2] If, how-

*This chapter was co-authored with M. P. Baumgartner and will appear in a slightly different version in *Dialectical Anthropology* 5(1981).

It was originally prepared for the Crime Prevention through Environmental Design Program of the National Issues Center, Westinghouse Electric Corporation, Arlington, Virginia, supported by a grant from the National Institute of Law Enforcement and Criminal Justice, Law Enforcement Assistance Administration, United States Department of Justice. The point of view taken here is ours alone, however, and does not necessarily represent the position of the sponsors.

For commenting upon earlier drafts, we thank W. Dale Dannefer, Edward de Grazia, Stanley Diamond, Stephen A. Duennebier, Klaus-Friedrich Koch, Imre R. Kohn, Pat Lauderdale, Peter K. Manning, Frank P. Romo, and Stanton Wheeler.

1. For these purposes, we define law as governmental social control (Black, 1972:1096), in other words, any process by which the state defines or responds to deviant behavior.

2. Social control as a cause of deviant behavior has been a major theme of labeling theory in sociology (for an overview, see Schur, 1971). The conduct so produced has come to be known as "secondary deviation" (Lemert, 1967).

ever, people were to engage in more self-help rather than relying so heavily upon law, that is, if they were to exercise more social control on their own, a different kind of public order would prevail.[3] In the nature of the case, many incidents would effectively be decriminalized, since they would no longer be formally defined and handled as criminal, and beyond this, many patterns of conduct themselves would surely change in response to new risks and opportunities. In this chapter we specify several conditions under which self-help flourishes, and suggest a number of techniques by which it might be stimulated.

Self-help is by no means a new phenomenon. Rather, it is a social practice that has been commonplace in many settings, and which is present to some degree nearly everywhere. It is a quantitative variable, which may be greater in one place and weaker in another. Historically, for instance, the amount of self-help has been highest in the simplest societies, in bands and tribes, and has declined progressively with social evolution and the growth of law (see Hobhouse, 1951: Chapter 3). Within modern societies as well, some groups of people engage in much self-help—even to a point of organized vigilantism—while others are more dependent upon legal control.[4] The same individuals may have recourse to self-help upon some occasions and turn to law upon others.[5] It might also be noted that, like law, self-help has both preventive and remedial aspects, and these vary quantitatively and to some degree independently across social locations. The problem is to isolate the conditions that permit us to predict and explain variation of this kind.

Developments in the theory of law and in the theory of altruism, or helping behavior, provide useful perspectives on this topic. The theory of law is relevant since self-help, like other nonlegal social control, generally varies inversely with law (see Black, 1976:107–111), and what predicts the one may therefore predict the other in a pattern of opposition. The theory of altruism is relevant as well, since the exercise of informal social control by one person on behalf of another, including his or her willingness to intervene in a dispute and to attempt media-

---

3. In this discussion, we use the concept of self-help to refer to any response to deviant behavior in which an offended party takes action on his or her own behalf, with or without the assistance of third parties other than those who are specialized agents of social control.

4. It should be noted that a condition of mutual hostility has often existed between law and self-help, with each system attempting to prohibit or otherwise discourage recourse to the other. For an example of the legal prohibition of self-help, see Pollock and Maitland (1898: Volume 2, 574–578). Human conflict might even be understood as a kind of property that lawyers and the state have come to monopolize in some respects (see Christie, 1977). On the tendency of law to "cannibalize" other forms of social control, see Diamond (1971).

5. In modern America, for example, it would appear that self-help is more likely in matters legally defined as civil—such as consumer complaints against businesspeople (see Best and Andreasen, 1977:710–724; Nader, 1978)—than in criminal matters, where police assistance is readily available to those who choose to make use of it.

tion, is itself a variety of help. Hence, whatever encourages altruism in general may be important in the genesis of self-help as a system of social control. Our approach draws upon these theories, and also upon the body of work known as "crime prevention through environmental design," insofar as that work addresses the phenomenon of social control (see, e.g., Tien, Reppetto, and Hanes, 1976: Chapter 3).[6]

Building on these traditions, we suggest several strategies by which it may be possible to increase the quantity of self-help in modern society. These include an administrative, an architectural, and a technological strategy. The first pertains to the allocation of police, the second to the design of physical space, and the third to the use of electronic and other devices. Each of these allows ready manipulation of variables important to our problem. Hence, for these limited purposes we leave aside strategies that would require large-scale reconstruction of society, such as those affecting the distribution of wealth or the ethnic composition of communities. Our discussion begins with an administrative strategy.

Depolicing

Most people concerned with crime and law enforcement take for granted that more police, with more power, will mean less crime. Increases of this kind are claimed to work preventively against crime through the greater surveillance they entail. They are also asserted to work remedially, by allowing more speedy and certain apprehension of offenders.

While these ideas undoubtedly have some validity, especially in the short term, strengthening the police presence is not a sure means of crime reduction (for a review of evidence, see Wilson, 1974), and it has its own disadvantages as well. Since the relationship between law and self-help is inverse, it follows that the larger and more intrusive a police force is, the weaker self-help will be, a pattern that could in the long term exacerbate the problem of crime. With the growth of law and the police—an evolutionary process involving many variables

6. It might be noted that a movement has recently begun in the United States to establish mediation and arbitration systems operated entirely by ordinary citizens, but thus far the major goal of this effort has been to provide an alternative to criminal justice for people who have conflicts with family members, neighbors, and others in ongoing relationships with them (see, e.g., Danzig, 1973; Lowy, 1973; Anonymous, 1977; Wahrhaftig, 1978). In this movement as elsewhere, however, it has generally been assumed that the social control of strangers cannot be handled by ordinary citizens but must remain the responsibility of the police and other legal officials. We depart from this assumption in the present discussion, and explore the possibilities of social control among strangers in the public places of modern society.

(see Black, 1976)—the citizenry becomes increasingly dependent upon the state to define and maintain order. As this happens, people increasingly cease to take responsibility for their own security and dispute settlement, and hesitate to help others with matters of this kind. Waiting for the police to arrive, they may even stand by passively as an assault or other victimization takes place.[7] Each expansion of police and other legal protection thus results in a new and higher level of need for these very services, leading to their ever-escalating proliferation. A classic analysis of this pattern was made by Peter Kropotkin at the turn of the century:

> The absorption of all social functions by the State necessarily favoured the development of an unbridled, narrow-minded individualism. In proportion as the obligations towards the State grew in numbers the citizens were evidently relieved from their obligations towards each other . . . . In barbarian society, to assist at a fight between two men, arisen from a quarrel, and not to prevent it from taking a fatal issue, meant to be oneself treated as a murderer; but under the theory of the all-protecting State the bystander need not intrude: it is the policeman's business to interfere, or not [1914:227–228].

More recently, Michael Taylor has discussed the same phenomenon:

> Positive altruism and voluntary cooperative behavior *atrophy* in the presence of the state . . . . Thus, . . . the state exacerbates the conditions which are supposed to make it necessary. We might say that the state is like an addictive drug: the more of it we have, the more we 'need' it and the more we come to 'depend' on it [1976:134].

It is partly this dependence that explains why an increase in the number and power of police is usually seen as the solution to problems of public order. Cutting back on the police—or depolicing—is almost never considered as a way to ameliorate these problems.[8]

---

7. In its most extreme form, this pattern has come to be known as the "Kitty Genovese syndrome," in reference to a young woman in New York City whose cries for help were ignored by her neighbors—many watching from their windows—as she was repeatedly assaulted and stabbed. No one even called the police on her behalf—each assumed that someone else would—and she eventually died in the doorway of her apartment house.

8. A notable exception is Richard Sennett, who proposes the creation of "survival communities," densely populated and socially diverse urban areas without centralized planning and social control, where people would be forced to work out their own problems with each other (1970: especially Chapters 6–7). The need for police in a modern city has also been questioned by Roger Wertheimer

If police protection were reduced, however, the volume and intensity of self-help would be expected to rise correspondingly, reversing the trend toward ever greater dependence upon law.[9] This too follows from the inverse relationship between law and self-help. Everywhere, people would undertake more preventive surveillance on their own, would work out more informal settlements of their disputes with the other parties involved, and would lend assistance to those in need of help more readily.[10] There is already experimental evidence to show that people are generally most helpful when the need for their assistance seems most apparent—that is, when alternatives to their participation are most clearly lacking (see Darley and Latané, 1968; Bickman, 1971). The same pattern operates in social institutions. It has been argued, for example, that in societies where blood donorship is entirely voluntary, the need for blood is more likely to be met than in societies where blood is bought and sold so that, in effect, people are hired to perform this service (Titmuss, 1971; compare Arrow, 1972; see also Singer, 1973). In light of this, it would seem that making the police conspicuous by their absence would lead citizens to draw upon their own resources and to assist one another in solving their problems.

Given the currently high level of reliance upon police, it would seem advisable to begin a transition to self-help with small cutbacks and, from there, to proceed gradually. Indeed, in a society in which people have become conditioned to depend upon the government for public order, a sudden and complete removal of

---

(1975). Unusual as the idea of depolicing might first appear, it is important to recognize that most societies in human history—the so-called hunters and gatherers as well as other simpler tribes—have gotten along without police of any kind (see, e.g., Schwartz and Miller, 1964).

It might be added that by depolicing we refer only to a reduction of social control by the police, not to a reduction of other kinds of emergency services that they presently provide, such as assistance to lost, sick, and injured people. We leave aside the question of how these services might best be organized.

9. It should be recognized that, along with self-help, other kinds of nonlegal social control—more organized and specialized kinds—would be very likely to increase with depolicing. It should also be recognized that in some cases—perhaps many—people would do without any social control at all, or "lump it," if the police were not available to them. For example, harassment of prostitutes, homosexuals, gamblers, marijuana smokers, and juveniles probably would decrease enormously. In addition, a modern society provides many opportunities for people simply to avoid those whose conduct they find objectionable or unpredictable, and this might become all the more frequent in the absence of the police. (On "lumping it" and avoidance, see Felstiner, 1974.) These matters deserve further treatment, but lie beyond the concerns of the present essay.

10. While self-help would increase throughout society, this would occur at different rates and reach different levels from one social context to another. Such differences would depend upon a number of other factors in each setting, including the degree to which self-help is already developed and the degree to which other social characteristics conducive to its growth are present. Among the latter are intimacy—treated later in this chapter—and also equality, homogeneity, and other variables.

officials could well precipitate a Hobbesian "war of all against all" (Taylor, 1976:141).[11] There have already been, in fact, a number of cases in which a drastic decrease of police service has resulted in widespread rioting, looting, and assault (see, e.g., Andenaes, 1966:961–962).[12] Nevertheless, extensive disruptions of police service often produce self-help smoothly and quickly. In the wake of disasters such as earthquakes, tornadoes, and floods, for example, routine operations by the police and other authorities frequently break down, while the demand for their services increases sharply. At such times, individuals in the stricken communities typically take command of the situation and willingly lend assistance to one another. Informal social control exercised by the citizens themselves virtually always maintains order; plundering and fighting are rare (for an overview, see Mileti, Drabek, and Haas, 1975: Chapters 4–5).[13] Even a sudden breakdown of police control, then, may give rise to self-help without large-scale disorder, and a program of gradual depolicing should encourage this all the more.[14]

---

11. Taylor argues that the political theory that claims the state is necessary to prevent chaos—a theory espoused by Thomas Hobbes and others—does not necessarily characterize all human behavior in the absence of a state, but more accurately describes "what human behavior would be like immediately after the state has been removed from a society *whose members had for a long time lived under states* [1976:141]." In any event, even such a "war of all against all" would presumably involve self-help to some degree, but it also would involve unprovoked violence and predation on a large scale.

12. These conditions seem more likely to arise when depolicing occurs in the context of community conflict, as when, for instance, the Boston police went on strike in a city strained by underlying ethnic and social-class tensions (see, e.g., Russell, 1975), or, to take an extreme case, when segments of the French population rose up in total revolution (see, e.g., Kinberg, 1935:129–136).

13. The relevance for our topic of the literature on behavior during disasters was suggested by Jan T. Gross.

14. It is important to recognize in this context that recourse to violence occurs only under certain specifiable conditions. Research and analysis to date suggest, for instance, that vengeance and feuding flourish primarily where people who are organized into all-encompassing corporate units—such as extended kin groups—live near others similarly organized, and where there is an absence of cross-cutting ties linking them to each other (see, e.g., Colson, 1953; Hasluck, 1954; Thoden van Velzen and van Wetering, 1960; Peters, 1967). Since modern societies are not structured in this way, it would seem that their potential for large-scale internal violence is greatly reduced. This may help to explain why individuals in contemporary American society routinely settle their disputes nonviolently, without the use of law. For a discussion of the role of violence and its alternatives in dispute settlement in an American suburb, see Baumgartner (1980a; 1981b).

In fact, law itself introduces a large amount of violence into current social relations, a pattern that opponents of self-help generally ignore. Much of this violence is intentional—the use of weapons and threats by the police, involuntary restraint and confinement in prisons, even execution—and is taken to be necessary if a modern society is to function smoothly. Legal agents are also responsible for a considerable amount of violence that is not viewed as legitimate by citizens when it comes to their

Once depolicing has begun, for whatever reason, the self-help that arises tends to feed upon itself. Just as self-help atrophies when law grows, with law continually creating conditions that make itself necessary, so the reverse is true: Self-help engenders more self-help. The more people come to rely upon themselves for dispute settlement and other social control, the more established does their self-reliance become. The more people help each other in any way, the more their mutual aid flourishes (see Taylor, 1976:136–140). This idea has received considerable support from experiments and other research on the phenomenon of altruism. Perhaps most relevant is evidence that people are more likely to behave altruistically if they are presented with "models" of altruism in the behavior of others (e.g., Bryan and Test, 1967; Hornstein, 1970). For example, in one study it was found that people were more likely to help a motorist with a disabled vehicle if they had recently observed a similar situation (staged for the experiment) in which help was being given by another motorist (Bryan and Test, 1967:401–403). It seems reasonable to infer that people are more likely to provide help to victims of crime or related problems when they are aware of others who engage in similar behavior. There is also evidence that people are more likely to behave altruistically if they themselves—or persons close to them—have been recipients of altruism. Thus, for example, many blood donors are people who have been beneficiaries of blood provided by others (Titmuss, 1971:228–229). It seems that the same should apply to beneficiaries of self-help. Moreover, it is likely that if people were more dependent upon self-help they would come to expect this service from each other and would hold in disrepute those not doing their part. This process, a system of social control in its own right, is believed to have occurred in earlier societies that had no law at all (see, e.g., Kropotkin, 1914:131).

In sum, a body of theory and research suggests that depolicing would contribute to the growth of self-help in modern society. Depolicing would in and of itself produce self-help to some degree, and this self-help would in turn produce still more.

---

attention, such as diverse forms of "brutality" by police and prison guards (see, e.g., Westley, 1953; Reiss, 1968a; Chevigny, 1969). Finally, it should be recognized that to an unknown degree these officials—particularly the police—provoke in citizens violence that would not otherwise occur (suggested by Joyce Reilly). This phenomenon is believed to happen during some riots and other collective uprisings (see, e.g., Waskow, 1966), but also seems to happen when the police handle other incidents, in private as well as public places, such as a family dispute in which someone violently reacts to police intervention or a drunken man who responds to the police as a challenge to his self-respect. This means that the police may create some of the violence they are credited with handling (see generally Marx, 1981). In assessing the consequences of depolicing, then, it should be taken into account that all of this violence, governmental and otherwise, would be eliminated.

Physical Design

The design of physical space provides another means for increasing the quantity of self-help. This is an architectural strategy that draws upon a larger body of work on the relationship between human behavior and the physical environment. In particular, it draws upon the well-known principle that social interaction reflects the physical setting in which it occurs (see, e.g., Sommer, 1969). The setting may, for instance, enlarge or limit the range of conduct that is possible and the number of people to which any individual is likely to relate. It may be "sociopetal," bringing people together and fostering contact among them, or it may be "sociofugal," inhibiting or discouraging such contact (see Osmond, 1957:28).[15] Differences of this kind may have implications for both the preventive and the remedial aspects of self-help, especially as these involve actions on behalf of others.

In recent years, in fact, this approach has received considerable attention from city planners and others concerned with the reduction of crime (see, e.g., Tien *et al.*, 1976: Chapter 2). A number of suggestions have pertained to how physical settings might be designed in order to maximize natural surveillance and, to a much lesser extent, create conditions likely to result in mutual aid among citizens. Proposals for increasing surveillance include the diversification of functions in urban areas, which would help ensure the presence of people in all areas at all times (e.g., Jacobs, 1961: Chapter 8), the concentration of flows of pedestrian traffic (e.g., Angel, 1968), and the design of windows, hallways, doorways, courtyards, and other spaces so as to enhance the visibility of social activity (e.g., Wood, 1961: especially 11–12; Newman, 1972: Chapter 4). Proposals for encouraging mutual assistance—including a willingness to take advantage of opportunities for surveillance—have entailed at least implicit recognition that, all else constant, people are most likely to help those with whom they are intimate and least likely to help strangers.[16] In addition, the degree of intimacy between people is positively related to their willingness to help a third party. For

---

15. Humphrey Osmond, who introduced these concepts, defines sociopetality as "that quality which encourages, fosters and even enforces the development of stable interpersonal relationships such as are found in small, face-to-face groups"; he defines sociofugality as "a design which prevents or discourages the formation of stable human relationships [1957:28]." We use the terms somewhat more broadly, referring to the propensity of settings to encourage or retard interaction of any kind, whether stable or not.

16. In other words, helping behavior varies inversely with relational distance, where relational distance refers to the extent to which people participate in one another's lives. (This concept is developed in Black, 1976:40–41.) It might be noted that, generally speaking, patterns of helping behavior are opposite to patterns of social control exerted against a deviant. Thus, people seem to be least likely to exercise many kinds of social control against their intimates, the very people they are most likely to help in every way, including the exercise of social control on their behalf.

example, it was found in one experiment that two friends are more likely than two strangers to help an apparently injured woman (Latané and Rodin, 1969). Any means by which contact among people can be increased will therefore lead to a growth of helping behavior, and one such means is the creation of sociopetal environments. For instance, neighborhoods and dwelling units readily lend themselves to designs that nurture strong ties and hence mutual aid (see Jeffery, 1971:219–220), and most work concerned with the relationship between physical design and social control focuses upon settings of this kind. Thus, it has been suggested that city streets and housing complexes can occasion social cohesion if their design makes people accessible to one another through proximity and natural exposure, while simultaneously setting them apart from the rest of an urban center by actual or symbolic barriers (see, e.g., Tien et al., 1976:78; see also Newman, 1972). It has also been suggested, in another context, that individual dwellings themselves might contribute to social cohesion if they were to contain interior spaces, visible from the street, where inhabitants could make themselves available for casual visits (Alexander, 1967:87–88, 94–96). Yet another architectural means by which personal relationships might be cultivated would involve the construction of parks, playgrounds, lobbies, laundries, and other communal areas that are attractive to people and sociopetal in design (Wood, 1961:12–17; see also Alexander, 1967:88, 96–97).

Beyond the possibilities for self-help inherent in personal relationships of a durable nature, there are others that derive from situational interaction among people in public places. Evidence indicates, in fact, that even very brief encounters between strangers are capable of generating mutual aid. In one experiment, for instance, it was found that people more readily offered assistance to a "victim" staging an epileptic seizure in an adjoining room when they had previously spoken with him than when there had been no prior contact between them at all:

> [Those who had spoken with the victim] reported that they had pictured him in the grip of a fit. Apparently, the ability to visualize the specific, concrete, distressed individual with whom one has had some human contact increases the speed and likelihood of one's helping that person [Darley, 1967, quoted in Hackler, Ho, and Urquhart-Ross, 1974:332, italics omitted and punctuation edited].

Even contact without conversation—including direct eye contact and mere visual exposure—can make helping behavior more likely between those involved (see, respectively, Ellsworth and Langer, 1976; Piliavin, Rodin, and Piliavin, 1969). Accordingly, physical arrangements designed to encourage mutual awareness and interaction in public places would increase the overall incidence of self-help.

One recommendation consistent with this viewpoint is that public places such as subway and railroad stations be designed to concentrate flows of people (see Tien et al., 1976:172–173). Settings designed in this way—if not overcrowded—

would enjoy increased natural surveillance, and would also generate situational intimacy conducive to mutual aid. The same effects might be achieved by decreasing the number of bus stops, park bench sites, and other gathering places. Beyond all of this, the physical structure of each public setting might be made as sociopetal as possible. Corridors might be minimized, for instance, and rooms made round instead of angular (see Osmond, 1957). Seating arrangements, whether in terminals, in lobbies, on buses, or on subway cars, might be designed to foster sociability. In general, then, more self-help would seem likely to occur if public settings were better designed to encourage strangers to form relationships, however ephemeral these might be.

To summarize: Whatever the location, private or public, and whatever the context, personal or not, the design of a physical setting may have profound implications for the quantity of self-help. And, as noted earlier, once self-help begins, it has a tendency to feed upon itself, growing all the more. Now consider still another strategy by which it is possible to stimulate changes of this kind.

Technology

Just as the physical settings inhabited by people may have consequences for their interaction, so may the devices with which they act upon the world. Social thinkers have long recognized that technological resources such as the means of production, warfare, communication, and transportation have implications for human society far beyond the purposes for which they were intended (see, e.g., Cottrell, 1955; Marx, 1956; White, 1962; McLuhan, 1964; Ogburn, 1964). These include implications for the nature of deviant behavior and social conflict of all kinds, and for the strategies by which they are handled, whether preventive or remedial. Technology affects the degree to which a legal system can penetrate a population, for example (see, e.g., Kaplan, 1965), and it also affects the degree to which people can exercise social control on their own. Here we address the relevance of technology, especially electronic communications, for the quantity of self-help. We focus specifically upon its relevance for the capacity of people to help one another.

Modern developments in technology have made possible a pattern of social interaction that is largely independent of the distribution of people in physical space. In part this has resulted from the emergence of rapid transportation, and in part from electronics, with the telephone and similar kinds of communication making people instantly available to one another no matter where they are located throughout the world. To the degree that these devices spread across the population, life in modern society comes to share a characteristic with that of simpler societies, in which fellow villagers are always accessible to one another:

Postliterate man's electronic media contract the world to a village or tribe where everything happens to everyone at the same time: everyone knows about, and therefore participates in, everything that is happening the minute it happens . . . . Just as the Eskimo has been de-tribalized via print, going in the course of a few years from primitive nomad to literate technician, so we, in an equally brief period, are becoming tribalized via electronic channels [Carpenter and McLuhan, 1960:xi– xii; see also McLuhan, 1964].

As a "global village" of this kind emerges, with the social distance between people shortening while physical distances remain the same or even increase, social control changes as well. Already, one consequence has been a great increase in the availability of police—made possible by telephone and radio communications as well as by the automobile—which allows citizens to have police at their homes within seconds. The same technology has allowed the police themselves to coordinate their manpower to a degree never before imaginable. Moreover, new electronic devices are now being developed to further the capacity of citizens to mobilize the police and the capacity of the police to exercise social control (see, e.g., Tien *et al.*, 1976:175–178). But what has not generally been recognized is how these developments have potential impact on the ability of citizens to handle their own problems. Indeed, the need for the police that is now taken for granted may not be so obvious in a society where citizens are available to each other on a moment's notice.

The potential consequences of electronic communications for self-help go far beyond the possibility of citizens performing the same functions as the police, using the same strategies and tactics, a phenomenon illustrated by the radio-equipped vigilantes who have recently been seen in American cities (see R. Brown, 1969:201–207; Marx and Archer, 1971). Electronics is able to extend the reach of people into one another's lives, making more mutual aid available across the population, making it possible, for instance, for individuals to draw upon their intimates for help whenever trouble arises, wherever they may be. Moreover, electronics may create a wider web of communication, extending to anyone with the proper equipment, through which otherwise distant people may be in touch for as long or as little as they wish. This results in a degree of intimacy among all those who participate, and since helping behavior varies directly with intimacy (see page 200), all are in a position to benefit from mutual aid. In fact, a system of this kind is now growing up around the citizens' band radio.

Though it has been available in the United States for at least 20 years, the citizens' band radio, or CB, became popular only during the mid-1960s. First adopted among interstate truck drivers, it has now spread among American motorists from all walks of life. (For a brief history of the CB radio, see Dannefer and Poushinsky, 1979.) The result has been an emergence of constantly fluctuating networks of people who form and end relationships with each other as they meet and pass electronically across the highways of the nation. And as this community has come into being—however fragmentary and temporary it might be—a major consequence has been an extensive system of mutual aid where almost none had existed previously:

> The conversational interaction facilitated by the CB radio transforms relationships so that motorists no longer experience each other as atomized, unrelated strangers. . . . Within this interactional framework, other drivers are not defined vaguely as malevolent strangers but, quite literally, as "good buddies" who can be relied on for information and aid. It is difficult to emphasize sufficiently how radically this new mode of communication changes the experience of highway travel . . . . [The CB] network is anonymous but not impersonal. The interactions that sustain it are fleeting but the network itself is permanent. Membership is wide open and in continual flux, but the shared concerns and the willingness to help each other out appear genuine [Dannefer and Poushinsky, 1979:615–616; see also Kerbo, Marshall, and Holley, 1978].[17]

It might be added that the system of mutual aid arising from the CB radio is highly egalitarian, with help available to all regardless of their social characteristics. This egalitarianism is possible, perhaps, only because most of the social characteristics of the people in the CB network are unknown to their fellows. Nearly all that is known is that each is a member of the electronic community.[18] What is more, self-help of this kind could operate in other settings.

For instance, electronic technology is now being developed for a portable telephone that can be worn on the wrist or carried in a pocket or handbag (see Rockwell International, 1977:13–14), thereby extending to the streets and sidewalks immediate access to family members, friends, and others who might provide assistance. It should also be possible to design a two-way radio of the same size, with the same functions as the larger citizens' band radio, creating an

---

17. In the same paper, Dannefer and Poushinsky comment that the CB radio also makes possible new tactics of victimization, such as calls for help designed to entrap would-be helpers or responses to people in distress undertaken for predatory purposes. Generally, however, practices of this kind have proven to be extremely uncommon.

18. Since differentials in helping behavior, social control, and other social processes are often functions of the characteristics of the people involved, such differentials will correspondingly vary with the amount of information about these characteristics present across cases. (In economics, this factor is known as "signaling." See, e.g., Spence, 1974.) Thus, individuals are able to be systematically selective in help-giving on the basis of, say, social class or ethnicity, only if they have enough information about potential recipients. As a rule, audioelectronic communications transmit less of this information than face-to-face communications. This explains, for instance, the fact that police responses to citizen telephone calls for assistance are less selective than their responses to similar requests in field settings. Nonetheless, it is possible for information about individual characteristics to be transmitted through electronics, and when this occurs, differences in help-giving occur as well (see, e.g., Gaertner and Bickman, 1971).

electronic community in the city among all who happen to tune in, including strangers. What the CB has done for motorists on the highway, devices of this kind could do for pedestrians, fostering a network of concern and putting people within reach of others, able to ask for help or provide it. Still other electronic devices could undoubtedly be invented to make people accessible to each other, further transforming the social life of the city, even tribalizing settings now peopled by strangers. Combined with rapid transportation, these devices would allow citizens to perform services for each other that are ordinarily viewed as the business of the police. Technology thus may contribute to a new kind of civil order, in which people look after their own affairs.[19]

Social Control through Self-Help

Self-help is a mode of social control with a logic and an organization of its own. Not merely a substitute for other modes such as law, it is rather an alternative with distinctive patterns of mobilization, agent recruitment, procedures, outcomes, and other features. Hence, if self-help were to grow to a new prominence in modern society, it would have a number of implications for the normative life of the communities involved.

Perhaps the most significant differences between self-help and law lie in the actual settlements produced by each. In matters of public order, the style of social control[20] found in legal settlements tends toward the penal, with expiation through punishment a standard outcome. It is routine that only one side of any conflict is the object of this sanction, while the other is vindicated and supported. This penal style has a severity rarely seen in other idioms of social control. Another response of law to problems of public order is therapeutic in style, with people processed as "sick" and in need of corrective treatment, coercively applied if necessary. Self-help, by contrast, is more frequently conciliatory. Its settlements are more commonly negotiated between the two or more opposing factions involved in a dispute, both or all of whom make some concessions in pursuit of a resolution (see Gulliver, 1969:67–68). If one of the parties is defined as the greater transgressor, this occurs through mutual agreement, and it is usual

---

19. Gene Youngblood has coined the term "technoanarchy" for a world of this kind (1970: 415–419). In his view, this system is not only possible but even necessary for human survival: "Technology has liberated us from the need of officialdom . . . . Yesterday, man needed officialdom in order to survive. But technology has reversed the process: survival today depends upon the emergence of a natural order [419, 418]."

20. There are at least four basic styles of social control, or strategies by which people define and respond to deviant behavior. These are the penal, therapeutic, compensatory, and conciliatory styles. For an elaboration, see Black (1976:4–5).

for him or her to supply the offended person or group with compensation of some kind, whether in the form of reparation or simply an apology. It might be added that, since it is generally a compromise reached through give and take rather than a decision imposed upon one party who is defined as a loser, a resolution of this kind differs from civil as well as criminal law. Finally, although civil settlements are as a rule less severe than penal settlements, self-help is likely to be less severe than either.

Several characteristics of self-help explain these differences. In the first place, self-help is a radically decentralized mode of social control (see Sennett, 1970: 164). In many cases, this means that the people immediately involved in a dispute participate in its resolution, and no one else. In other instances, one or both parties may draw upon a network of family, friends, or even situational acquaintances or bystanders for assistance, but this remains much different from the formal organization of law with its headquarters, chains of command, and courts. In criminal cases, moreover, it is the state itself—a centralized group par excellence—that brings the complaint. These features are highly consequential in themselves since, all else constant, social control is most penal and most severe where its organization is most centralized, and least where the most decentralization prevails (see Black, 1976:86–91, 98, 101–103). There is even evidence that individuals are less punitive than small groups (see Wolosin, Sherman, and Mynatt, 1975). Accordingly, the relative leniency of self-help, and its conciliatory character, are conditioned by its decentralization as well as the role of individuals in the settlements reached.

Another feature of self-help also explains its patterns to some degree. When parties to a conflict do not invoke legal agents of social control, but draw upon others in solving their problems by self-help, they typically seek the participation of people who are closest to and most like themselves. Those with whom the disputants are intimate and with whom they share tastes and experiences thus come to perform a normative role in their lives. Even situationally, people with whom the parties have had some contact—rather than complete strangers—are most likely to be solicited for a role of this kind. People relatively intimate with the disputants are also more likely to intervene on their own initiative. For that matter, many disputes are settled by the participants alone, and often they themselves have prior ties of some kind. Theory suggests that social control is least severe and most conciliatory precisely when social-control agents are relationally and culturally closest to the parties with whom they are involved (see Black, 1976:40–47, 55–57, 73–80, 82–83). It is therefore understandable that social control through self-help is quite unlike that exercised by police and other legal authorities, who are usually socially unknown and often culturally alien to the people whose problems they handle.

In addition to differences in severity and style, still another difference between self-help and law pertains to the variability in settlements arising from
each. While there is substantial variability in outcomes at every stage of the legal
process, cases handled by self-help vary considerably more.[21] This is a result of
the greater diversity of participation across cases handled by people on their own:
Legal agents are relatively homogeneous in background and other social characteristics, whereas agents of self-help are not. At different times, virtually all
citizens—those of all sexes, ages, ethnicities, occupations, and other categories—
serve as mediators for others and undertake social control on their own behalf.
They emerge from throughout the population, make their contribution to social
order, and fade back again. And since there is more variability in participation,
there is more variability in result.

Yet other differences between law and self-help could be detailed, such as the
lesser emphasis upon issues of procedural fairness in a self-help system, the
greater importance of personal networks and alliances (see Gulliver, 1963:297–
301), its lesser orientation toward rules or principles (see Northrop, 1958:349–351;
Henderson, 1965: Volume 2, 241), and its more immediate resolution of disputes
(Gulliver, 1963:233). Nevertheless, it is impossible at this point to be exhaustive
or definitive about the changes that would accompany any new growth of self-
help. The opportunity for an assessment of this kind depends upon the evolution
of social control.

* * *

We have described several means by which self-help might be encouraged in
modern society, including systematic depolicing, the design of sociopetal environments, and the introduction of new forms of electronic communication. We
have also contrasted law and self-help as systems of social control. In conclusion, it should be noted that our analysis has been concerned solely with the
possibilities of applying theoretical and empirical knowledge in this context, and
not with the desirability of self-help as a social policy. Although self-help could
be a powerful system of public order, there are those who might criticize the
means necessary for its attainment, as well as certain of its characteristics and

---

21. A similar point is made by Philip Gulliver. Contrasting the Arusha of Tanzania, a stateless
people, with groups who have law, Gulliver distinguishes two modes of dispute settlement: a
"judicial process," where a superordinate official hands down decisions in accordance with established norms, and a "political process," where decisions are negotiated between the parties in dispute
without the intervention of an external authority of any kind, and where variability in outcomes is
relatively extensive (1963:297–301).

consequences.[22] Furthermore, a decline of law and growth of self-help would not be equally attractive to all segments of society. Those who enjoy special benefits from law would surely be least receptive to such a development, while others who would gain advantages from self-help would welcome it most. These are matters of value and politics, however, and lie beyond the scope of the present work.

---

22. A world in which people exercise their own social control implies a radically different social order that might be seen as dangerous or unfair in some respects. (Relevant here is our earlier discussion of violence; see page 198, especially note 14.) Self-help might also seem to entail too little privacy. As envisaged here, however, it would intrude upon privacy mostly through exposing people to more day-to-day scrutiny of a casual sort by their associates; any increase in systematic or large-scale observation of citizens by their fellows would be extremely unlikely. Individuals for the most part would continue to lack the incentive and the capability to monitor closely anyone other than members of their own households.

By contrast, modern states routinely engage in the collection and storage of numerous facts about people in their jurisdictions. Government agencies gather data on births, deaths, marriages, divorces, earnings, bankruptcies, inheritances, and other doings, using certificates, registrations, transcripts, licenses, and censuses as tools. These records are readily available to officials empowered by the state to exercise social control. Beyond this, most states to varying degrees surreptitiously uncover additional information about their citizens' habits and conduct through the use of electronic surveillance, networks of informants, and other techniques (see Marx, 1980). All of this intensifies when someone arouses suspicion in government agents such as police officers, even to the point of searches of a citizen's body or property. Hence, any assessment of the impact of self-help upon privacy must also acknowledge the considerable decline in state surveillance that would be involved.

A Note on
the Measurement of Law*

APPENDIX **A**

The sociological theory of law predicts and explains the behavior of law with its location and direction in social space.[1] This theory involves a total and final departure from all discourse that in any way evaluates the legal life of the natural world. It neither approves nor disapproves of law of any kind, but simply passes over in silence all matters of a critical nature. It inquires only into what is observable by anyone, and into what varies with what. It abandons the common sense of law—the discourse of legal practitioners—as well as every other effort to understand law that does not pertain entirely to the facts (see Black, 1972: 1979a).

Law as a Quantitative Variable

Each concept in the sociological theory of law is formulated as a quantitative variable. That is, each can be described in terms of how much or how little exists. There may be more or less inequality in a given setting, for example, more or less intimacy, heterogeneity, organization, or whatever. There also may be more or less law.

---

*M. P. Baumgartner and George Caspar Homans made helpful comments on an earlier draft of this appendix, which is reprinted with minor revision from *Informationsbrief für Rechtssoziologie,* Sonderheft 2 (April, 1979):92 – 106.

1. Although this conception of the theory of law derives from *The Behavior of Law* (Black, 1976), it should be understood that the foundations for an approach of this kind were laid at least as early as the turn of the century. Especially significant was Durkheim's *Division of Labor* (1893), but many other contributions could also be mentioned (e.g., Tönnies, 1887; Weber, 1925; Malinowski, 1926). More recently, a number of works by anthropologists have been influential as well (e.g., Gulliver, 1963; Nader and Metzger, 1963; Nader, 1964; Gluckman, 1967). Nonetheless, the following discussion builds upon the approach as it appears in *The Behavior of Law,* and—without further citation— elaborates specifically upon the conception of law presented in that work.

It is, indeed, a remarkable fact that only now has the concept of law been formulated so that law itself is observable and measurable, so that it can be counted. Before this step was taken, the effort to understand law was metaphysical to some degree, detained at an earlier stage of scientific evolution. Although the conception of law as a quantitative variable is still primitive in its formulation, with its emergence a new stage has been reached, and the study of law will never be the same.

This conception views law as an instance of social control, or conduct that defines and responds to deviant behavior.[2] Moreover, it views law as an appendage of government, which for these purposes means a state of some kind.[3] The quantity of law is thus synonymous with the quantity of governmental social control in a given setting—that is, the degree to which anyone defines or responds to the conduct of anyone else as deviant (whether wrong, negligent, sick, unreasonable, or whatever) within the framework of a state. The more this happens, the more law there is. If a police officer makes an arrest, for example, this is more law than if no such action occurs, since it defines someone's conduct as deviant within a governmental framework. The same applies to a lawsuit or even a complaint to the police by telephone. A conviction in criminal court is more law than a dismissal, since it officially defines someone as a deviant, whereas a dismissal does not. The same applies to a decision on behalf of a plaintiff in a civil proceeding, whereas a finding for a defendant implies that no one is officially defined as a deviant. A longer prison sentence is more law than a shorter sentence, since it indicates that a person so handled is more deviant than one who receives a shorter sentence. When a court of appeals reverses a decision originally made on behalf of a plaintiff, however, this is a decrease of law, since it removes a lower court's definition of the defendant as a deviant. But any decision on behalf of a plaintiff increases the quantity of law, since it always involves a definition of someone's conduct as deviant. Illustrations could be extended for pages, listing every kind of governmental social control that may be brought against a person or group by a citizen, police officer, judge, or other official of any state, past or present.

---

2. For lack of an alternative, the concept of "deviant behavior" is used here in a generic sense, referring broadly to any conduct that meets with a negative reception of any kind, whether penal, compensatory, therapeutic, or conciliatory in style. The concept derives from sociology and may unintentionally connote conduct that is prohibited and subject to punishment, perhaps because sociologists have focused so much upon crime and criminal justice in modern societies. Anthropologists speak more of "disputes," since most of their work has been done in simple societies where the penal style is less developed.

3. It might be added that in this usage law pertains to the conduct of citizens as such, not, for example, to the conduct of an employee, family member, or friend as such. For this reason, everyday supervision of postal workers, tax collectors, or other government employees is not law, since this supervision pertains only to the conduct of employees as such, even if they are government employees.

One implication of this conception deserves special mention: If law is under-stood as the quantity of governmental social control, the so-called rights of citizens—such as a right to criticize a government or a right to privacy—are not themselves instances of law but rather guarantees against law. The more these rights are actually respected, then, the less law there is. Finally, it should be recognized that this conception of law can be applied in any setting at all, even to an entire society. At this level, for instance, a so-called stateless society has—by definition—no law at all,[4] and any given society, community, or social location of any kind may have more or less law than another. This conception of law thus embraces what might at first appear an extremely wide range of different phe-nomena, but it actually provides a way to understand all of these as so many instances of the same thing: governmental social control.

And yet, however revolutionary it may be in some respects, the conception of law as a quantitative variable is only a beginning. It remains to be considered how the quantity of law can be specified with precision—as a numerical value—in any given setting. This is the problem of measurement, and it is a major chal-lenge in the sociology of law.

As it stands, the measurement of law has reached only one stage beyond the mere identification of differences, or nominal measurement. It is a form of ordinal measurement, involving comparisons in which one event is ranked as less or more law than a second event, such as, for example, an arrest versus an informal disposition, a lawsuit versus an out-of-court settlement, or a conviction versus a dismissal. It should be recognized, however, that paired comparisons of this kind can provide the basis for more elaborate scales of an ordinal nature. Thus, for instance, a scale of severity can be constructed for a number of punishments by comparing one to the next until all are ranked into a series from more to less law. It is also possible to rank the stages of a criminal process into a single scale, since the total quantity of law accumulates as a criminal case moves from a call to the police to an investigation, arrest, prosecution, conviction, and sentencing.[5] From this standpoint, then, the so-called funnel effect—whereby fewer and fewer cases reach the later stages of the criminal process—appears as a

---

4. A stateless society has no law of a permanent kind operating on a day-to-day basis, but it may have episodes of law during periods of collective action, such as during a war, migration, or communal hunt. American Plains Indians had "buffalo police" during their buffalo hunts, for example, and "war chiefs" during wars, but they had no law on a full-time basis (see, e.g., MacLeod, 1937; Lowie, 1948).

5. It is important to emphasize that the increase of law across the stages of a criminal process is an effect of the accumulation of law as a case moves across these stages, and does not imply that each successive stage in and of itself constitutes a greater quantity of law than any given stage before it. Nor, for that matter, does it imply that each stage is equal to the next in this respect. It is possible that the actual magnitude of law varies considerably across the stages, and even that an earlier stage such as arrest might involve more law in itself than a later stage such as prosecu-tion or conviction. This is an empirical question that requires more precise measurement than an ordinal scale can provide (see pages 212–216).

212 : THE MANNERS AND CUSTOMS OF THE POLICE

pattern in the distribution of law itself. The same perspective can be applied to the stages of a civil process, a regulatory process, or anywhere else that cases move through stages of governmental social control. A scale might be developed for each style of law as well, whether penal, compensatory, therapeutic, or conciliatory. Just as punishments can be ranked into a scale from less to more law, so might awards for damages, treatments, or modes of dispute settlement. Where law is conciliatory in style, for example, passive mediation might be ranked as less law than active mediation, which in turn might be ranked as less than arbitration. In short, numerous patterns of legal life invite the creation of ordinal scales.

The ultimate challenge, however, is to measure the absolute magnitude of law in each of its manifestations. This is known as interval measurement. Since absolute magnitudes can also be used to compare and rank legal events, an interval scale immediately answers any question that can be addressed with an ordinal scale, and has many advantages in addition. In particular, it would make possible precise computations of the total quantity of law from one setting to another, across different locations and directions in social space. It would allow an assessment of how much law occurs across communities, societies, across history, and how much is directed toward one person rather than another. What is more, measurement of this kind would make it possible to formulate equations specifying exactly how much law increases or decreases with each unit of variation in anything else. This degree of precision may now seem farfetched, but some-day the marvel will surely be how anyone ever attempted a sociology of law without it.

Intervals of Law

In principle, an absolute magnitude—a number—can be assigned to every instance of law. This would indicate the quantity of social control entailed by any event of a legal nature, in other words, the exact degree to which any event defines or responds to conduct as deviant within a governmental framework. To illustrate, it might be that a complaint to the police would be reckoned as 5 units of social control, an arrest might add 20 units for a subtotal of 25, prosecution might add another 5 units for a subtotal of 30, conviction another 20 for a subtotal of 50, and a sentence to prison for one year another 50 for a grand total of 100 units of law. But the question is how these magnitudes can be assigned. Exactly what is an interval of law? When do we know how much governmental social control has occurred? What is a degree of criminality? A degree of negli-gence? What can we count?

FOLK MEASUREMENT

It is well-known that sociologists are rarely able to measure intervals of differ-ence between social variables. Instead, they tend to be satisfied with ordinal scales, and in some cases even persevere with nominal differences alone, as when sex, race, or religion is used as a variable (male and female, black and white, Protestant, Roman Catholic, Jew, etc.). The measurement of absolute magnitudes occurs primarily in contexts in which the intervals are found among the participants in social life itself, that is, wherever people measure their own activities with a uniform standard, such as a calendar, a clock, or a currency of exchange. People in modern society count the money they earn, for example, their years of schooling, and the length of time they have been alive. In turn, sociologists adopt such practices to measure intervals of income, education, age, etc. These scales are ready-made in the folk system, then, *objets trouvés* in the field of measurement.

A few folk practices are available for the measurement of law as well. Thus, for example, people in modern societies and communities keep records known as "crime rates." These records can be used as crude measures of the quantity of criminal law, since they indicate how many events the police recognize as worthy of official attention (see Kitsuse and Cicourel, 1963; Black, 1970). Other public records might also be used in this way. Official arrests and civil lawsuits are recorded, for instance, and these might be used to construct law rates as well. So might criminal convictions and decisions on behalf of plaintiffs in civil cases.[6] But law rates of this kind have a major shortcoming: They generally fail to measure differences in magnitude from one instance of law to another. Apart from rank differences between more and less "serious" crimes (e.g., felonies and misdemeanors), these rates generally do not register the fact that some cases move further in the legal process than others, or that some result in more severe sanctions than others. All "thefts," "murders," and other crimes enter the same rates, no matter how much law actually befalls each case of each kind. The same applies to rates of civil law.

There are, however, a few additional folk practices that can be used to measure the magnitude of law from one case to the next. Thus, many societies employ uniform gradations to scale the severity of their punishments (number of days, months, or years in jail, prison, pillory, or exile; number of lashes with a whip; or the amount of money demanded as a fine). The cost of compensatory damages, or restitution, may also be specified in a uniform system of reckoning (head of livestock, number of shells, copper plates, dollars). Bonds of various kinds—money held on deposit to assure compliance with a summons or other court order—take this form as well. Folk scales such as these are perfectly suitable for incorporation into sociology. This is so despite what may at first appear to be a peculiar shortcoming of their own: a failure to take into account the impact of the practices they measure.

It cannot be denied that the impact of each gradation in a folk scale of law

---

6. Rates of legislation—expanding governmental social control—might be developed from public records too, though the amount of legislation by itself does not necessarily reflect the degree to which people are actually processed as deviant in courts and other legal settings. For a study of the changing content of American criminal law—including changes in the severity of penalties—see the work of Berk, Brackman, and Lesser (1977).

depends upon who is subject to it. In the case of punishment, for instance, the gradations in a folk scale of severity do not necessarily measure the actual intervals of suffering experienced by all of the people who are processed as offenders. Differential suffering is especially apparent where economic sanctions are applied universally, since it is obvious that wealthier people lose proportionately less than people who are not so able to afford a given penalty. This even operates as a kind of immunity for those who can effortlessly pay a particular fine, almost a kind of license. Differential suffering of some degree occurs wherever the consequences of a legal process fall unevenly across a population, including physical punishments, imprisonment, compensatory damages, and bonds. Nevertheless, this differential impact of law does not detract from the value of folk scales for purposes of scientific measurement. Just as it is possible to measure the quantity of heat without regard to its consequences for other phenomena—some liquids freeze and some solids melt sooner than others, for example—so it is possible to measure the quantity of law in its own right, without regard to its consequences.[7]

Even though folk scales provide a satisfactory means by which intervals of law can be measured in some cases, the fact remains that only a few of these scales are available for adoption, and to rely solely upon them would greatly retard the progress of legal sociology. Certainly this has not been the strategy followed in more advanced sciences such as physics and chemistry. It was never self-evident to anyone, for instance, how intervals of heat or electricity could be measured. Folk scales were not available. Scientists therefore had to invent instruments and standards by which numerical magnitudes could be assigned to these phenomena. Gabriel Fahrenheit invented one way to measure heat, for example, and Anders Celsius invented another. Major figures in the measurement of electricity included Alessandro Volta, André Ampère, and James Watt. It should be understood that every kind of measurement in every science is a human creation that is imposed upon the natural world. Each is but one of an infinite number of ways by which reality may be subjected to quantification. Moreover, sociology is now entering a period of development in which the invention of measurement systems presents a major opportunity for those who would make a lasting contribution. As this era proceeds, lifetimes of work will be devoted to the quantification of social life, and many names will be added to those of Fahrenheit, Celsius, and the others.

INDIRECT MEASUREMENT

The invention of measurement devices is necessary in all but those cases in which folk scales are available, ready-made for incorporation into science. Often it is impossible even to observe directly how a phenomenon behaves. When this

---

7. This is not to deny that the differential impact of heat remains an important problem for study; the same applies to the differential impact of law. But the precise impact of a phenomenon cannot be known unless its quantity is known as well.

is the case, an established strategy in science is to measure the phenomenon in question by its relationship to another that can more easily be observed and quantified. The behavior of the latter than provides a measure of the former. Thus, Fahrenheit invented the thermometer in order to measure indirectly intervals of heat with the behavior of mercury in a sealed glass tube. A similar strategy can be used in the measurement of law.

Indirect measurement of law requires an observable and quantifiable phenomenon that varies systematically with the magnitude of law. One such possibility might be the tendency of people to avoid law, that is, to avoid being defined or handled as deviant in a process of governmental social control. If we assume that people avoid law in direct relation to its magnitude, an interval scale for the measurement of law can be based upon observations of this avoidance behavior.[8] People in reality do not generally experience the entire range of legal events, however, and so these observations would have to be made in a contrived manner. (This too is routine in science, as in the case of the thermometer.)

A natural experiment of some kind might be the ideal setting in which to observe how much people avoid law in one or another of its expressions, but this could be difficult to execute. An alternative might be to present subjects with hypothetical situations and to ask them to indicate how much they would avoid each legal event involved. These hypothetical situations might be presented in a face-to-face interview, a questionnaire, or a laboratory experiment. Whatever the setting might be, the subjects would be asked to specify in a quantitative fashion how much they would avoid each of the events on a list that might include experiences such as the following: interrogation by the police, personal search by the police, arrest, prosecution, conviction, a fine of $10, a fine of $50, etc., with other fines up to $50,000 or more, a jail term of ten days, a jail term of thirty days, etc., a prison term of one year, a prison term of two years, etc., a penalty of death by electrocution, by hanging, etc. The list might include events in civil law as well, such as a lawsuit, a finding of negligence, a finding of a breach of contract, an order to pay damages of $10, $50, etc. It could also include therapeutic events such as legal commitment to a mental hospital, and conciliatory events such as mediation in a marital dispute or arbitration in a labor dispute.[9]

---

8. This is not meant to refer specifically to the degree to which law deters people from engaging in illegal conduct, though conformity is one way they might seek to avoid a given legal experience. Rather, the question is simply whether people would choose to experience one legal event more or less than another, and how much. While relevant to this issue, then, the theory of deterrence has a more limited focus.

9. In a different context—a discussion of how "role expectations" might be classified—Dahrendorf suggests that numerical values might be assigned arbitrarily to a range of negative sanctions, legal as well as nonlegal:

If we can succeed in quantifying the weight of sanctions, we shall have a means of ordering, characterizing, and distinguishing all known roles in a given society . . . . All standards are originally arbitrary; there is thus no reason why one should not try to classify sanctions, say,

Since people with different social locations might have different avoidance patterns,[10] this instrument would be administered to subjects whose social characteristics would be known in detail, and who would be as similar as possible. Perhaps they should be statistically typical members of the population, each a sociological version of "the reasonable man" of Anglo-American jurisprudence. In any event, average scores would be calculated from their responses, and these would become the basis for an interval scale of law. A methodology of this kind has already been developed for purposes of psychological research, and has also been applied to the construction of a highly regarded interval scale that measures perceptions of the seriousness of crime (Sellin and Wolfgang, 1964; also see this work for a general discussion of psychological measurement, especially Chapters 15 and 20). But in the case of law it is conduct that we would hope to measure, not perceptions.[11]

From the beginning, it should be realized that any scale for the measurement of law will have, like all measurement devices, its own limitations. It will be more useful for some purposes than others, and may even unavoidably distort reality to some degree. The specific nature of these limitations, and possible adaptations to them, will come into view only as the measurement of law proceeds into its exploratory phase.[12]

* * *

on a scale from 10 (long prison term) to 1 (disapproval by members of reference groups), or 0 (sanctionless role range) [1968:43, 69, note 41].

Dahrendorf also cites approvingly the work of Schumann (1968) on "the theory of techniques of measuring social sanctions."

10. Whether this is actually the case, and to what degree, are empirical questions worthy of investigation in their own right.

11. It might be appropriate to mention briefly a second method by which the quantity of law might be measured indirectly. Since law damages the respectability—or normative status—of anyone against whom it is directed (see, e.g., Garfinkel, 1956), it should be possible to measure the magnitude of a legal event by the extent of this damage. A person convicted of murder loses more of this status than a person charged but acquitted of the same crime, for example, and it should be possible to measure the difference. Since a decline of normative status involves social disadvantages of various kinds, the magnitude of a legal event might be measured by the precise degree of disability incurred by anyone it befalls. How much is the person ostracized, for instance? How much is he or she handicapped in finding employment? The quantity of law might be indirectly observed by its social implications, then, and, in principle, an interval scale could be constructed on the basis of these observations. The possibilities for this approach may be seen in the studies of Schwartz and Skolnick (1962) on the economic consequences of legal sanctions.

12. Advanced sciences have specialties that are devoted to problems of measurement. In physics, for example, thermometry is concerned with the measurement of heat, and the measurement of electricity is known as electrometry. Perhaps it would be appropriate to apply the label of "jurimetrics" to the theory and practice of measurement in the field of legal sociology, even if its original meaning—"the scientific investigation of legal problems" (Loevinger, 1949:483)—was considerably broader.

In closing, it might be noted that the challenge posed by the measurement of law applies, by extrapolation, to every species of social control, whether in a tribe or a community of nations, an organization, a family, among friends or neighbors. Such measurement bears directly on the question of how the behavior of law is related to other kinds of normative life, a major problem in the general theory of social control. At present, little is known about how law compares quantitatively to the varieties of social control that operate without the participation of a state. Although it seems clear that every society has an enormous amount of social control besides law, a precise inventory of each kind is now impossible. Finally, it should be understood that the challenge of measurement in the sociology of law has implications entirely beyond the field itself. Ultimately, the sociological theory of law—or of any other phenomenon—requires a quantitative conception of every dimension of social space. It requires, in effect, the quantification of everything social.[13] Otherwise it can be nothing more than a matter of opinion, indifferent to facts, and immune to evaluation. As this is recognized, sociology will truly enter its era of measurement.

---

13. *The Behavior of Law* contains quantitative conceptions—albeit preliminary—of a number of social phenomena, including culture, intimacy, organization, conventionality, and respectability. It is possible to understand medicine, art, or even an idea as a quantitative variable (see Black, 1979c). In all of these cases, however, the development of interval scales has hardly begun.

Police Observation Form

Reprinted here is the form used by observers in the three-city study to record cases handled by officers in response to dispatches over the police radio.[1] Cases of this kind (known as "runs") originate in telephone calls from citizens, and account for the great majority of incidents handled by patrol officers.

It might be noted, however, that other cases come to the attention of the police when citizens directly hail them on the street, walk into a police station ("walk-ins"), or when officers notice incidents on their own ("on-views").[2] Forms for each of these kinds of mobilization were available to the observers, but their structure and contents largely overlap with the "run" form and so they are not included in this appendix. In addition, the observers were provided with booklets for recording information not related to particular cases (e.g., attitudes expressed by the officers in conversation and characteristics of the patrol territory). All of the forms were completed after each 8-hour observation period, without the knowledge of the officers involved.

---

1. This form also appears in Black (1968: Appendix I) and in McCall (1978: Appendix A). Albert J. Reiss, Jr., who directed the larger project and collaborated with me in the design of the research instruments, kindly gave his permission to have the form reprinted in the present volume. I also take this occasion to thank Donald Dickson, Allan Levett, and Maureen Mileski for their suggestions pertaining to the design of the observation forms.
2. A copy of the on-view form appears in Black (1968: Appendix II).

The University of Michigan
 Center for Research on
 Social Organization

Police Observation Study
1966

RUN FACE-SHEET

R-1 City_____

R-2 Precinct Number_____

R-3 Territory or Beat Number_____

R-4 Date: Day_____ Month_____ Year_____

R-5 Day of Week: [Check] ___1. Sun   ___2. M   ___3. Tu
     ___4. W   ___5. Th   ___6. F   ___7. Sat

R-6 Shift: [Check]   ___1. 12 - 8a.m.   ___2. 8 - 4p.m.
     ___3. 4 - 12 midnight   ___4. Other [Specify hours of the
     overlapping shift:_____]

R-7 Time of Police Activity in This Situation:

                              Time at Start_____

                              Time at Finish_____

     Total Elapsed Time [Hours and/or Minutes]_____

R-8 Run Number_____

R-9 Observer's Name_____

RUN (Mobilization by Departmental Dispatch)

1. Definition of the situation by dispatch: [Check]

Part I--Usually Felonies

___ 01. Assault, aggravated or "serious" (e.g., knifing or
        shooting)

___ 02. Auto theft

___ 03. Burglary--breaking or entering, business place

___ 04. Burglary--breaking or entering, residence

___ 05. Burglary--breaking or entering, unspecified or other
        [Write out: _____]

___ 06. Homicide, criminal

___ 07. Larceny--theft, auto accessory

___ 08. Larceny--theft, bicycle

___ 09. Larceny--theft, from auto (i.e., from inside auto)

___ 10. Larceny--theft, shoplifting

___ 11. Larceny--theft, unspecified or other
        [Write out: _____]

___ 12. Rape, attempt

___ 13. Rape, forcible

___ 14. Robbery--business place

___ 15. Robbery--street (include purse-snatching)

___ 16. Robbery--unspecified or other
        [Write out: _____]

Part II--Other Complaints

___ 17. Abandoned auto

___ 18. Assault, simple or minor (e.g., assault and battery,
        threat, etc.)

___ 19. Burglar alarm ringing

___ 20. Disturbance or dispute, bar-room

___ 21. Disturbance or dispute, domestic ("family trouble")

___ 22. Disturbance or dispute, landlord-tenant

___ 23. Disturbance or dispute, "neighbor trouble"

___ 24. Disturbance or dispute, noisiness or "disturbing the
        peace"

___ 25. Disturbance or dispute, rowdy party

___ 26. Disturbance or dispute, unspecified or other
        [Write out: _____]

___ 27. Drunken person(s)

___ 28. Fight, gang

___ 29. Fight, juvenile or "kids"

___ 30. Fight, unspecified or other
        [Write out: _____]

___ 31. Gambling

___ 32. Juveniles--trouble with teenagers and children (e.g.,
        "trouble with boys")
        [Write out: _____]

___ 33. Liquor law violation, underage drinking

___ 34. Liquor law violation, unspecified or other
        [Write out: _____]

___ 35. Loitering

___ 36. "Peeping Tom"

___ 37. Property, stolen or "suspicious" (e.g., police check
        for suspicion of stolen property, buying and receiv-
        ing, etc.)
        [Write out: _____]

___ 38. Prostitution

___ 39. "Prowler"

___ 40. Sex offense (e.g., indecent exposure)
        [Write out: _____]

___ 41. "Suspect"--a person suspected as offender
        [Write out: _____]

___ 42. "Suspicious person(s)" or "suspicious situation"
        [Write out: _____]

___ 43. Traffic violation, moving (e.g., speeding)
        [Write out: _____]

___ 44. Traffic violation, standing (e.g., parking)
        [Write out: _____]

___ 45. Traffic violation, unspecified or other
        [Write out: _____]

___ 46. Vagrancy

___ 47. Vandalism--malicious destruction of property,
        juvenile

221

1. (Continued)

48. Vandalism--malicious destruction of property, unspecified or other
[Write out: _____]

49. "Wanted person" or possible wanted person
[Write out: _____]

50. Weapon, carrying, possessing, etc.

51. Unspecified or other complaint
[Write out: _____]

Part III--Miscellaneous Incidents and Problems

52. Animal trouble--dogbite

53. Animal trouble, unspecified or other
[Write out: _____]

54. Auto accident, hit and run

55. Auto accident--injuries

56. Auto accident, unspecified or other
[Write out: _____]

57. Fire

58. Injured person (except traffic or dogbite injuries)

59. Information request

60. Information for police

61. Lost person

62. "A man down" (or woman)

63. Missing juvenile

64. Missing person, unspecified or other
[Write out: _____]

65. Police escort request

66. Police surveillance request

67. Sick person (include maternity but not mental cases)

68. Traffic or safety hazard

69. Transportation of mental patient

1. (Continued)

70. Transportation of person(s), other (e.g., juvenile to detention home)
[Write out: _____]

71. Unspecified or other request or incident
[Write out: _____]

2. Write out in the words of the dispatcher, any additional or unusual features of the message that are not captured by a mere specification of the incident. (E.g., "Somebody's got a gun down there" or "the boys are back there again".)

_____

_____

_____

3. Was this an assist of other police officers?

_____ 1. Yes   _____ 2. No

4. Response of officers to mobilization:

_____ 1. Seen as urgent--e.g., use flasher, siren and/or drive fast

_____ 2. Seen as routine--proceed directly or in usual fashion

_____ 3. Seen as unimportant--dally en route to call

_____ 4. Seen as unimportant--give priority to something else, detour
[Specify: _____]

5. Did the officers characterize the situation before they saw it? (E.g., "This guy's a regular. Calls a coupla times a month" or "We're going to have to get in and get out quickly on this one.")

_____ 1. Yes   _____ 2. No

If "yes", specify _____

6. General context of situation:

___ 01. Upper class apartment buildings

___ 02. Upper class houses

___ 03. Middle class apartment buildings

___ 04. Middle class houses

___ 05. Lower class apartment buildings or rooming houses

___ 06. Lower class houses

___ 07. Commercial--downtown proper

___ 08. Commercial--other

___ 09. Mixed commercial and residential boarding houses, bars, shops, etc.

___ 10. Transitional or run-down mixed area

___ 11. Industrial--factories, warehouses

___ 12. Other [Specify: _____]

7. Specific setting of situation:

a. Within dwelling-unit:

___ 01. One-room apartment

___ 02. Living-room

___ 03. Kitchen

___ 04. Hall or vestibule

___ 07. Other [Specify: _____]

b. Near and relevant to dwelling-unit:

___ 10. On landing, hall or stairway (i.e., inside an apartment building, but outside an apartment)

___ 11. In lobby

___ 12. On porch

___ 13. In yard, driveway or parking area

___ 14. Alley, sidewalk or street

___ 17. Other [Specify: _____]

7. (Continued)

c. In or relevant to business place:

___ 20. Business area or place where transactions with public take place

___ 21. Office or private area of employees, i.e., back-stage from public, e.g., storeroom

___ 22. Near business place, e.g., street, alley, parking area

___ 27. Other [Specify: _____]

d. In or relevant to public institution:

___ 30. Medical setting, front stage-where transactions with public take place

___ 31. Medical setting, backstage--e.g., patient or employee area or consulting room

___ 32. Non-medical setting, e.g., school, park, front-stage where official or employee involved

___ 33. Non-medical setting, backstage, non-public part of institution--e.g., principal's office or employee area

___ 35. Open park or playground, perhaps sometimes supervised, but no official or employee present or relevant at the time

___ 37. Other [Specify: _____]

e. ___ 40. Public place--street, alley, etc., but not relevant to other setting [Specify: _____]

___ 50. Inapplicable (setting was not located)

223

8. What was the condition of the specific setting?

____ 1. Run down, dirty, etc.

____ 2. Reasonably well-kept, clean, etc.

____ 3. Inappropriate (i.e., the above conditions do not help in characterizing the setting, e.g., a busy inter-section) [Specify: _____]

9. Address of setting [Use address from incident log.] _____

10. Arrival of police at designated setting:

____ 1. Police entered into situation which was seen by either citizens or officers as requiring police attention. (Note: Citizens may or may not have been present, e.g., abandoned auto.) [CONTINUE WITH ITEM #11]

____ 2. Police were unable to locate the designated setting (e.g., insufficient directions or non-existent addresses)--police left setting. [SKIP TO ITEM #28]

____ 3. No one answered--police left setting. [SKIP TO ITEM #28]

____ 4. Citizen denied that police were called--police left setting. [SKIP TO ITEM #28]

____ 5. Citizen said that there was no longer a desire or a need for the police--police left setting. [SKIP TO ITEM #28]

____ 6. Police found that other officers were handling the incident and needed no assistance--police left setting. [SKIP TO ITEM #28]

____ 7. Other--police left setting. [Specify: _____] [SKIP TO ITEM #28]

11. Did situation involve police interaction with citizens?

____ 1. Yes [CONTINUE WITH ITEM #12]

____ 2. No [GO TO ITEM #19]

12. Characteristics of the primary citizen participants in the situation: [Use one column for each participant. Place the most central person first, the second most central person second, etc.]

	#1			#2			#3			#4			#5		
Name, if given															
Sex	M	F	O	M	F	O	M	F	O	M	F	O	M	F	O
Race	W	N	O	W	N	O	W	N	O	W	N	O	W	N	O
Age-check: 0-10 Child															
10-18 Yg person															
18-25 Yg adult															
25-45 Adult															
45-60 Middle-aged															
60+ Old person															
Citizen's general role in the situation: Private citizen															
Business manager, proprietor															
Business employee															
Public official															
Public employee															
Client or customer															
Don't know															
Citizen's class: White collar															
Blue collar															
Don't know															
Citizen's income: High income															
Middle income															
Low income															
Don't know															
Citizen's speech: Ordinary or middle class															
Foreign or ethnic accent															
Lower class															

Specify any other distinguishing features of speech, e.g., impediment, affectation, unusual vulgarity, comprehensibility: _____

13. Manner of the primary citizen participants in the situation:

	#1	#2	#3	#4	#5
General State:					
Agitated					
Calm					
Very detached					
Don't know					
Toward Police:					
Very deferential					
Civil					
Antagonistic					
Don't know					
Sobriety:					
Sober					
Some signs of drinking					
Drunk					
Don't know					
Does citizen make special, particularistic appeal to officers	Yes No	Yes No	Yes No	Yes No	Yes No
Write out:					

14. Specific roles of the primary citizen participants in the situation:

	#1	#2	#3	#4	#5
Complainant					
Offender-- suspected or alleged offender					
Victim--e.g., sick person, parent of missing child					
Member of complainant group					
Member of offender group					
Member of victim group					
Informant					
Bystander					
Don't know					

15. (Continued)

225

226

15. Characteristics of other citizens in the situation: [This item will be used only if there are more than five (5) citizens in the situation. They should be described in aggregates depending upon their specific roles (as laid out in Item #14) in the situation.]

Top table

	Complainant Group			Offender Group			Victim Group			Informant			Bystander			Don't know		
	M	F	B	M	F	B	M	F	B	M	F	B	M	F	B	M	F	B
	J	A	B	J	A	B	J	A	B	J	A	B	J	A	B	J	A	B
Total Number																		
Sex: Male, Female, Both																		
Age: Juvenile, Adult, Both																		
Income:																		
High income																		
Middle income																		
Low income																		
Mixed																		
Don't know																		
Manner-- General State:																		
Agitated																		
Calm																		
Very detached																		
Mixed																		
Don't know																		
Toward Police:																		
Very deferential																		
Civil																		
Antagonistic																		
Mixed																		
Don't know																		
Other Pertinent Information: [Specify]																		

Bottom table

	Complainant Group			Offender Group			Victim Group			Informant			Bystander			Don't Know		
	M	F	B	M	F	B	M	F	B	M	F	B	M	F	B	M	F	B
	J	A	B	J	A	B	J	A	B	J	A	B	J	A	B	J	A	B
Total Number																		
Sex: Male, Female, Both																		
Age: Juvenile, Adult, Both																		
General Roles in the Situation:																		
Private citizen																		
Businessman																		
Business employee																		
Public official																		
Public employee																		
Client or customer																		
Mixed																		
Don't know																		
Class:																		
White collar																		
Blue collar																		
Mixed																		
Don't know																		

16. Were there any special difficulties in the assignment of roles to either the primary or other citizen participants in the situation? (E.g., a dispute over who the offender was.)

___ 1. Yes   ___ 2. No

If "yes"--specify: _____

_____

_____

_____

_____

_____

17. Relationships between the citizens in the situation: [Specify the pre-existent relationships between the incumbents of the various roles--use the following code:]

Code

1. family

2. friend(s) or acquaintance(s)

3. neighbor(s)

4. mixed--#1-#4

5. business relationship

6. other formal relationship (e.g., teacher-pupil)

7. no apparent relationship

8. don't know

9. mixed--#1-#8

0. inapplicable

	Complainant	Offender	Victim	Complainant group	Offender group	Victim group	Informant	Bystander	Don't know
Complainant									
Offender									
Victim									
Complainant group									
Offender group									
Victim group									
Informant									
Bystander									
Don't know									

227

18. Witnesses:

Was there an "incident" which was or might have been "witnessed"?

_____ 1. Yes   _____ 2. No   (e.g., sick person)

a. If "yes": How many witnesses were there? _____

b. If an incident was witnessed:

<u>Witness(es)</u> was:
- _____ 1. cooperative toward police
- _____ 2. uncooperative toward police
- _____ 3. detached or "stand-offish"
- _____ 4. mixed--#1-#3
- _____ 9. don't know

<u>Non-witness(es)</u> was:
- _____ 1. cooperative toward police
- _____ 2. uncooperative toward police
- _____ 3. detached
- _____ 4. mixed--#1-#3
- _____ 9. don't know

c. Elaborate on the above if necessary: _____
_____
_____
_____

19. Number of police and citizens present:

a. Total number of citizens related to the situation: [Do not count guides, bystanders or unidentified persons] _____

b. Total number of guides, bystanders, and unidentified persons _____

c. Total number of citizens [add "a" and "b"] _____

d. Total number of police officers present _____

20. Write out capsule description of situation at its outset: (e.g., specify the nature of any kind of "disturbance" that the police entered into) _____
_____
_____
_____
_____

21a. Definition of the situation after arrival of police: [Check the citizens' specification of the problem. If citizens are not present or cannot communicate, check the officers' definition.]

Part I--Usually Felonies

___ 01. Assault, aggravated or "serious" (e.g., knifing or shooting)
___ 02. Auto theft
___ 03. Burglary--breaking or entering, business place
___ 04. Burglary--breaking or entering, residence
___ 05. Burglary--breaking or entering, unspecified or other [Write out: ___]
___ 06. Homicide, criminal
___ 07. Larceny--theft, auto accessory
___ 08. Larceny--theft, bicycle
___ 09. Larceny--theft, from auto (i.e., from inside auto)
___ 10. Larceny--theft, shoplifting
___ 11. Larceny--theft, unspecified or other [Write out: ___]
___ 12. Rape, attempt
___ 13. Rape, forcible
___ 14. Robbery--business place
___ 15. Robbery--street (include purse-snatching)
___ 16. Robbery--unspecified or other [Write out: ___]

Part II--Other Complaints

___ 17. Abandoned auto
___ 18. Assault, simple or minor (e.g., assault and battery, threat, etc.)
___ 19. Burglar alarm ringing
___ 20. Disturbance or dispute, bar-room
___ 21. Disturbance or dispute, domestic ("family trouble")
___ 22. Disturbance or dispute, landlord-tenant
___ 23. Disturbance or dispute, "neighbor trouble"
___ 24. Disturbance or dispute, noisiness or "disturbing the peace"

21. (Continued)
___ 25. Disturbance or dispute, rowdy party
___ 26. Disturbance or dispute, unspecified or other [Write out: ___]
___ 27. Drunken person(s)
___ 28. Fight, gang
___ 29. Fight, juvenile or "kids"
___ 30. Fight, unspecified or other [Write out: ___]
___ 31. Gambling
___ 32. Juveniles--trouble with teenagers and children (e.g., "trouble with boys") [Write out: ___]
___ 33. Liquor law violation, underage drinking
___ 34. Liquor law violation, unspecified or other [Write out: ___]
___ 35. Loitering
___ 36. "Peeping Tom"
___ 37. Property, stolen or "suspicious" (e.g., police check for suspicion of stolen property, buying and receiving, etc.) [Write out: ___]
___ 38. Prostitution
___ 39. "Prowler"
___ 40. Sex offense (e.g., indecent exposure) [Write out: ___]
___ 41. "Suspect"--a person suspected as offender [Write out: ___]
___ 42. "Suspicious person(s)" or "suspicious situation" [Write out: ___]
___ 43. Traffic violation, moving (e.g., speeding) [Write out: ___]
___ 44. Traffic violation, standing (e.g., parking) [Write out: ___]
___ 45. Traffic violation, unspecified or other [Write out: ___]
___ 46. Vagrancy

21. (Continued)
___ 47. Vandalism--malicious destruction of property, juvenile
___ 48. Vandalism--malicious destruction of property, unspecified or other
    [Write out: ____]
___ 49. "Wanted person" or possible wanted person
    [Write out: ____]
___ 50. Weapon, carrying, possessing, etc.

___ 51. Unspecified or other complaint
    [Write out: ____]

Part III--Miscellaneous Incidents and Problems
___ 52. Animal trouble--dogbite
___ 53. Animal trouble, unspecified or other
    [Write out: ____]
___ 54. Auto accident, hit and run
___ 55. Auto accident, injuries
___ 56. Auto accident, unspecified or other
    [Write out: ____]
___ 57. Fire
___ 58. Injured person (except traffic or dogbite injuries)
___ 59. Information request
___ 60. Information for police
___ 61. Lost person
___ 62. "A man down" (or woman)
___ 63. Missing juvenile
___ 64. Missing person, unspecified or other
    [Write out: ____]
___ 65. Police escort request
___ 66. Police surveillance request
___ 67. Sick person (include maternity but not mental cases)
___ 68. Traffic or safety hazard
___ 69. Transportation of mental patient

21. (Continued)
___ 70. Transportation of person(s), other (e.g., juvenile to detention home)
    [Write out: ____]

___ 71. Unspecified or other request or incident
    [Write out: ____]

b. If any criminal damage or loss of property or money was involved, specify the approximate value of the damage or loss: $ ____

22. Did citizen verbally specify a particular service he wanted?
   ___ 1. Yes   ___ 2. No   ___ 0. Inapplicable

If "yes"--check or write out:
___ 1. transportation to medical setting
___ 2. an arrest
___ 3. settlement of an argument or dispute
___ 4. advice or counselling
___ 5. special police surveillance or attention

___ 7. other--specify: ____

23. Was there anything unusual about how the citizens related to the police? (e.g., with hysteria, like boss to employee, etc.)
   ___ 1. Yes   ___ 2. No

If "yes"--specify: ____

24. Was there any noteworthy disagreement among the citizens as to the proper definition of the situation?

___ 1. Yes ___ 2. No ___ 9. Don't know ___ 0. Inapplicable

If "yes"--specify: _____

25. What was the general police response to the prevailing definition of the situation?

___ 1. agreed and proceeded to take some kind of action (verbal or otherwise)

___ 2. disagreed but proceeded to take police action--
specify the disagreement: _____

___ 3. saw as "unfounded" (without basis)

___ 4. saw as civil matter or "not police business"

___ 7. other--specify: _____

___ 9. don't know

26. Did the location of the situation change significantly during the progress of the encounter? [Do not include a movement to a medical setting or to the station.]

___ 1. Yes ___ 2. No

If "yes"--specify the nature of the change and the consequences of the change for the handling of the incident:

_____
_____
_____
_____

27. Did any new participants enter the situation during the progress of the encounter? [These persons should have been in earlier items.]

___ 1. Yes ___ 2. No

If "yes"--specify how many, what roles they played (complainant, informant, etc.), and how their entrance had consequences for the handling of the situation: _____

_____
_____

28. Police actions: [Check all that apply]

a. formal or official action

___ 1. made arrest [specify charge:]

___ 2. made arrest on suspicion or investigation [specify charge:]

___ 3. gave traffic ticket [specify:]

___ 4. gave other ticket [specify:]

___ 5. made official report [specify:]

___ 6. took to station

___ 7. other in this area [specify:]

b. informal use of power

___ 8. used physical force against person

___ 9. threatened with physical force

___ 10. threatened with arrest

___ 11. traffic warning [specify:]

___ 12. other threat or warning (e.g., unspecific warning) [specify:]

___ 13. admonished or moralized

___ 14. other in this area (e.g., other kind of degradation process) [specify:]

231

28. (Continued)

c. informal police action

___ 15. undertook investigation at setting
___ 16. undertook investigation outside of setting
___ 17. interrogated suspect(s) at setting
___ 18. interrogated suspect(s) outside of setting
___ 19. searched property at setting
___ 20. searched property outside of setting
___ 21. searched or "shook down" person(s) at setting
___ 22. searched or "shook down" person(s) outside of setting
___ 23. gave special surveillance or attention after leaving setting
___ 24. other in this area [specify: _____]

d. preparation or suggestion of future action

___ 25. called for more police at setting
___ 26. referred to other police unit [specify: _____]
___ 27. suggested further use of police service [specify: _____]
___ 28. referred to a non-police agency [specify: _____]
___ 29. suggested use of non-police services [specify: _____]
___ 30. encouraged citizen who wanted to sign a complaint [specify: _____]
___ 31. asked citizen if he would sign a complaint--citizen agreed [specify: _____]
___ 32. asked citizen if he would sign a complaint--citizen refused [specify: _____]
___ 33. offered or promised an investigation
___ 34. offered or promised special surveillance or attention
___ 35. other in this area [specify: _____]

e. physical service

___ 36. transported to medical setting
___ 37. transported--other [specify: _____]
___ 38. escorted to medical setting

___ 39. escorted--other [specify: _____]
___ 40. gave first aid or other physical assistance
___ 41. performed other physical service (e.g., removed dead dog) [specify: _____]

f. social service or "cool out"

___ 42. arbitrated in dispute (made judgment)
___ 43. mediated in dispute (acted as referee or "go-between")
___ 44. gave advice or counselling
___ 45. gave consolation or emotional support
___ 46. talked or "cooled" person into handling his problem himself
___ 47. talked or "cooled" person into seeing police action as undesirable because of its consequences
___ 48. talked or "cooled" person into denying that a problem existed in the first place
___ 49. talked or "cooled" person into seeing a problem as solved or taken care of after the fact of police action
___ 50. talked or "cooled" person into postponing his concern or demand by suggesting that he "wait and see" (e.g., "I'd suggest you let it ride for awhile...")
___ 51. used other "cool out" technique or gave other social service [specify: _____]

g. other

___ 52. took information and encounter was terminated [specify: _____]
___ 53. gave or exchanged information and encounter was terminated [specify: _____]
___ 54. continued to other business without having taken any action whatsoever [specify original definition of the situation _____]
___ 55. other action taken--not categorized in above sections [specify: _____]

232

29. Did the police comply with the central request or demand
that was made in the situation?

___ 1. Yes   ___ 2. No   ___ 9. Don't know   ___ 0. Inapplicable

If "no"--specify the discrepancy: _____

_____

30. Manner of police behavior toward the primary and other
citizen participants in the situation: [Use the same
numbering system for primary citizens as was used in Items
#12-14. For officers, use the same numbers as those used
in the general (white) packet. Fill in the boxes with
numbers from the appropriate codes.]

a. control of citizen [use one number per box]

Code

1. took firm control
2. maintained control
3. acted subordinate

primary citizens

	#1	#2	#3	#4	#5
officers					
#1					
#2					
#3					
#4					

b. control of self [use one number per box]

Code

1. had firm self control
2. maintained self control
3. lost self control

primary citizens

	#1	#2	#3	#4	#5
officers					
#1					
#2					
#3					
#4					

30. (continued)

c. manipulative techniques [use as many numbers as necessary]

Code

1. made particularistic appeal (e.g., "I'm Irish, too.")
2. used humor and jolliness
3. used subtle threats
4. used silence
5. attempted to redirect citizen's focal concern to something else (red herring technique)
6. used reasoning or problem-solving technique
7. other manipulative technique used

primary citizens

	#1	#2	#3	#4	#5
officers					
#1					
#2					
#3					
#4					

30. (continued)

d. general manner [use as many numbers as necessary]

Code

1. was hostile, nasty, provocative
2. was brusque, bossy, authoritarian
3. openly ridiculed or belittled
4. subtly ridiculed or belittled
5. was business-like, routinized, impersonal
6. was good humored, playful, jovial

primary citizens

	#1	#2	#3	#4	#5
officers					
#1					
#2					
#3					
#4					

e. prejudice [use one number per box]

Code

1. obviously prejudiced
2. showed signs of prejudice
3. showed no signs of prejudice

primary citizens

officers	#1	#2	#3	#4	#5
#1					
#2					
#3					
#4					

OTHER CITIZENS

[Use if more than five (5) citizens; same as those characterized in Item #15]

f. control of citizens [use one number per box]

Code

1. took firm control
2. maintained control
3. acted subordinate

other citizens

officers	complain-ant group	offender group	victim group	informant	bystander	don't know
#1						
#2						
#3						
#4						

30. (continued)

h. manipulative techniques [use as many numbers as necessary]

Code

1. made particularistic appeal (e.g., "I'm Irish, too.")
2. used humor and jolliness
3. used subtle threats
4. used silence
5. attempted to redirect citizen's focal concern to something else (red herring technique)
6. used reasoning or problem-solving technique
7. other manipulative technique used

officers	complain-ant group	offender group	victim group	informant	bystander	don't know
#1						
#2						
#3						
#4						

(other citizens span: victim group, informant, bystander)

30. (continued)

g. control of self [use one number per box]

Code

1. had firm self control
2. maintained self control
3. lost self control

officers	complain-ant group	offender group	victim group	informant	bystander	don't know
#1						
#2						
#3						
#4						

(other citizens span: victim group, informant, bystander)

236

i. general manner [use as many numbers as necessary]

Code

1. was hostile, nasty, provocative
2. was brusque, bossy, authoritarian
3. openly ridiculed or belittled
4. subtly ridiculed or belittled
5. was business-like, routinized, impersonal
6. was good humored, playful, jovial

officers	complain-ant group	offender group	victim group	informant	bystander	don't know
				other citizens		
#1						
#2						
#3						
#4						

j. prejudice [use one number per box]

Code

1. obviously prejudiced
2. showed signs of prejudice
3. showed no signs of prejudice

officers	complain-ant group	offender group	victim group	informant	bystander	don't know
				other citizens		
#1						
#2						
#3						
#4						

31. Were any participants viewed as possible offenders or members of an offender group during the course of the entire incident?

   ___ 1. Yes   ___ 2. No [Go to Item #37]

32. Was a personal and/or property search attempted or conducted by the police?

   ___ 1. Yes   ___ 2. No [Go to Item #33]   ___ 3. Don't know

If "yes":

a. What kind of search was attempted or conducted?

   ___ 1. personal ("frisk") [Go to "b"]
   ___ 2. property (e.g., auto or house) [Go to "c"]
   ___ 3. both personal and property [Continue with "b" and "c"]

b. If "personal":

  (A.) Would observer say this "frisk" was necessary for the protection of the officer(s)?

     ___ 1. yes
     ___ 2. no
     ___ 9. don't know

  (B.) Did the police ask the possible offender's permission before this "frisk" was conducted?

     ___ 1. yes
     ___ 2. no
     ___ 9. don't know

  (C.) Did the possible offender(s) object to being "frisked"?

     ___ 1. yes [Specify what was said by both parties: _____]
     ___ 2. no

32. (continued)

  (D.) Was the "frisk" conducted?

     ___ 1. yes
     ___ 2. no

  (E.) Was a weapon or other possible evidence found?

     ___ 1. yes [What? _____]
     ___ 2. no
     ___ 0. inapplicable (no "frisk" conducted)

c. If "property":

  (A.) Was this attempted or made prior to an arrest?

     ___ 1. yes
     ___ 2. no
     ___ 9. don't know

  (B.) How did the police attempt or manage to gain entrance?

     ___ 1. simply entered without asking permission
     ___ 2. asked and were granted permission [What was said by both parties: _____]
     ___ 3. asked permission and were refused--did not enter
     ___ 4. asked permission and were refused--entered anyway (Do not include use of search warrant) [What took place between the parties? _____]
     ___ 5. gained entrance with search warrant
     ___ 7. other [Specify: _____]
     ___ 9. don't know

32. (continued)

(C.) Were there any objections to the search?

_____ 1. yes [Specify what was said by both parties: _____]

_____ 2. no
_____ 9. don't know

(D.) Was a weapon or other possible evidence found?

_____ 1. yes [What? _____]

_____ 2. no
_____ 0. inapplicable

(E.) If a property search of a vehicle was attempted or conducted:

(a.) Was a vehicle search attempted or conducted at or near the scene of a possible crime?

_____ 1. yes
_____ 2. no [Where was it? _____]

_____ 9. don't know
_____ 0. inapplicable

(b.) Did the police look closely at the vehicle's interior without actually reaching or climbing into it?

_____ 1. yes
_____ 2. no
_____ 9. don't know
_____ 0. inapplicable

(c.) Did the police enter the vehicle and search it?

_____ 1. yes
_____ 2. no
_____ 9. don't know
_____ 0. inapplicable

33. Was a possible offender(s) interrogated by the police?

_____ 1. Yes   _____ 2. No   [Go to Item #34]

If "yes":

a. Where did the interrogation take place?   [Check as many as necessary.]

	possible offenders		
	#1	#2	#3
1. at the setting	_____	_____	_____
2. on the way to the station	_____	_____	_____
3. at the station	_____	_____	_____
4. other [Specify by writing in]	_____	_____	_____

b. How did the police approach the person(s)?

	possible offenders		
	#1	#2	#3
1. simply began questioning	_____	_____	_____
2. polite request	_____	_____	_____
3. impersonal summons	_____	_____	_____
4. brusque or nasty command	_____	_____	_____
5. other [Specify by writing in]	_____	_____	_____

c. Why was the person(s) interrogated?

#1: _____
_____

#2: _____
_____

#3: _____
_____

33. (continued)

d. Did the person(s) object to being interrogated?

___ 1. Yes ___ 2. No

If "yes", specify what was said by both parties:

#1 _____

#2 _____

#3 _____

e. What kind of constraints were placed on the person(s)?
[Check as many as apply.]

	#1	#2	#3
1. taken to station			
2. seated in car			
3. other physical constraint (e.g., holding of arm)			
4. verbal constraint (e.g., "you're not going anywhere")			
5. no verbalized constraint			
7. other [Specify]			

33. (continued)

f. Did the person(s) object to any of the constraints?

___ 1. Yes ___ 2. No

If "yes", specify what was said by both parties:

#1 _____

#2 _____

#3 _____

g. How long was the person(s) required to remain in the officer's company before arrest or release? [Specify in minutes]

#1 ___ #2 ___ #3 ___

h. Was this person(s) released without being taken to the station? [Check]

	#1	#2	#3
1. Yes			
2. No			

i. Was this person taken to the station but not arrested? [Check]

	#1	#2	#3
1. Yes			
2. No			
3. Don't know			

33. (continued)

   j. Did the person(s) <u>confess</u> to any offense?

      _____ 1. Yes   _____ 2. No   _____ 9. Don't know

   If "yes"

     (A.) When did he confess?

                                 #1   #2   #3

        1. at the beginning--voluntarily   _____   _____   _____

        2. after interrogation [Specify   _____   _____   _____
           how long:]

     (B.) At what specific point in the process did this occur?

                                   #1   #2   #3

        1. before the interrogation   _____   _____   _____

        2. before a personal search   _____   _____   _____

        3. before a property search   _____   _____   _____

        4. at the time of an arrest in   _____   _____   _____
           the field

        5. at the time of an arrest **or**   _____   _____   _____
           booking at the station

        7. other [Specify:]   _____   _____   _____

   k. Specify any other pertinent information concerning the
      interrogation: (e.g., the amount of pressure applied by
      the officers, the relationship between a charge and a
      confession, etc.)

      _____

      _____

      _____

      _____

      _____

      _____

34. Was arrest, detainment, or a trip to the station used as a
    threat?

      _____ 1. Yes   _____ 2. No

   If "yes", specify, quoting if possible: _____

   _____

   _____

35. Was the person(s) apprised of his rights while the observer
    was present?

      _____ 1. Yes   _____ 2. No   _____ 9. Don't know

   If "yes":

     a. <u>Where</u> was the person apprised?

       _____ 1. at the setting

       _____ 2. on the way to the station

       _____ 3. at the station [Specify how long after arriving: _____]

       _____ 7. other [Specify: _____]

     b. At what point in the process did this occur? [Check as
       many as apply.]

       _____ 1. before an interrogation

       _____ 2. before a personal search ("frisk")

       _____ 3. before a property search

       _____ 4. at the time of an arrest in the field

       _____ 5. at the time of an arrest or booking at the station

       _____ 6. at the time of a confession

       _____ 7. other [Specify: _____]

35. (continued)

   c. What did the officer say? [Quote if possible.]

      _____

      _____

      _____

      _____

36. Did the person(s) express a desire to consult an attorney or other third party?

    ____ 1. Yes   ____ 2. No   ____ 9. Don't know

If "yes":

   a. Whom did he want to consult?

	#1	#2	#3
1. attorney			
2. family member			
3. friend			
7. other [Specify]			

   b. At what point in the process did this occur? [Check as many as apply.]

	#1	#2	#3
1. before an interrogation			
2. before a personal search			
3. before a property search			
4. at the time of an arrest in the field			
5. at the time of an arrest or booking at the station			
6. at the time of a confession			
7. other [Specify]			

36. (continued)

   c. What was said between the police and the offender(s)?

     #1 _____

     #2 _____

     #3 _____

37. Was anyone taken or directed to the police station during the progress of this encounter?

    ____ 1. Yes   ____ 2. No [Go to Item #43]

If "yes", specify the total number of persons in the various roles. Then add together all persons and give overall total:

complainant and/or complainant group	_____
offender and/or offender group	_____
victim and/or victim group	_____
informant	_____
bystander	_____
don't know	_____
overall total	_____

38. Was an offender and/or offender group taken to the station?

    ____ 1. Yes   ____ 2. No [Go to Item #43]

If "yes", specify the following: [Give information on three (3) persons, then aggregate the remainder under "others".]

38. (continued)   possible or alleged offenders

	#1 M	F	#2 M	F	#3 M	F	others M	F
Sex								
Race: white, Negro, other	W N O mixed		W N O mixed		W N O mixed		W N O mixed	
Age								
0-10 Child								
10-18 Yg person								
18-25 Yg adult								
25-45 Adult								
45-60 Middle-aged								
60+ Old person								
Degree of force used against offender [Check as many as necessary]								
gross force								
firm handling								
allowed freedom								
Behavior of police [Check as many as necessary]								
were nasty or ridiculed								
moralized								
business-like and impersonal								
friendly								
Behavior of offender								
violent, aggressive								
disgruntled, sullen								
passive, unexpressive								
cooperative								
Verbal behavior of offender								
insulting, explosive								
argued								
passive, quiet								
good-natured, jovial								

	#1	#2	#3	others
Was he arrested?	No / Yes	No / Yes	No / Yes	No / Yes
Was he arrested on suspicion or investigation?	No / Yes	No / Yes	No / Yes	No / Yes
Specify the nature of the charge:	Inapp.	Inapp.	Inapp.	Inapp.

39. Was it made clear to the person(s) whether he was or was not under arrest?

____ 1. Yes   ____ 2. No   ____ 9. Don't know

40. Was anyone arrested or arrested on suspicion or investigation?

____ 1. Yes   ____ 2. No   [Go to Item #41]

If "yes", specify for more than one person if necessary.

a. Who made the decision to arrest?

____ 1. patrolman who picked him up
____ 2. an officer at the station [Specify his rank: _____]

____ 9. don't know

b. At what point was he notified that he was under arrest?

____ 1. at setting [Specify how long after encounter began; _____]
____ 2. on the way to the station
____ 3. at the station [Specify how long after arriving: _____]

c. How much time passed between the point when he was apprehended by the police and the time he was booked at the station?

Specify in minutes _____

d. How much time passed at the station before he was booked?

Specify in minutes _____

e. Other relevant information on the arrest: _____
_____
_____
_____

41. How was the decision made to take offender(s) to the station?

____ 1. call to station or other police agency
____ 2. another officer on the scene
____ 3. officer's own decision
____ 9. don't know

42. Specify the number of offenders who were observed receiving the following:

a. interrogation _____
b. fingerprinting _____
c. booking _____
d. incarceration _____
e. referral to youth or women's division _____
f. rough physical handling _____
g. Specify any other processing or relevant events that were observed at the station: _____
_____
_____
_____
_____
_____
_____
_____
_____

244

43. Was any kind of log entry or memo made by police after the encounter?

    ___ 1. Yes   ___ 2. No   ___ 9. Don't know

If "yes"

a. Specify how situation was characterized: _____

b. Does observer disagree with that characterization?

    ___ 1. Yes   ___ 2. No

If "yes", specify the discrepancy: _____

44. What was the general state of the citizen(s) when the police were leaving?

a. Complainant/complainant group Victim/victim group

    ___ 1. very grateful
    ___ 2. satisfied
    ___ 3. indifferent
    ___ 4. a little dissatisfied
    ___ 5. very dissatisfied
    ___ 9. don't know
    ___ 0. inapplicable

b. Offender/offender group

    ___ 1. very grateful
    ___ 2. satisfied
    ___ 3. indifferent
    ___ 4. frightened
    ___ 5. a little unhappy
    ___ 6. very unhappy
    ___ 9. don't know
    ___ 0. inapplicable

c. Elaborate if necessary: _____

45. If the police verbally characterized the situation after its termination, specify: _____

46. Did officer informally specify any actions he wanted to take or should have been able to take but which he saw as prohibited or improper?

    ___ 1. Yes   ___ 2. No   ___ 0. Inapplicable

If "yes", specify in detail: _____

47. If police characterized any of the persons who took part in the encounter, specify and identify persons by the roles they played in the situation (complainant, victim, etc.):

a. in terms of police informal categories, e.g., "He's a regular" _____

b. in terms of racial stereotypes, e.g., "a worthless black-ass" _____

c. in terms of social class stereotypes, e.g., "a rich bitch" _____

d. in terms of other social categories or identities, e.g., "whore", "neighborhood grouch", etc. _____

48. Write out any other information about the situation or what was said about it that might aid in its overall portrayal:

_____

_____

_____

_____

_____

_____

_____

_____

_____

_____

_____

_____

_____

References

Alexander, Christopher
  1967   "The city as a mechanism for sustaining human contact." Pages 60–102 in *Environment for Man: The Next Fifty Years,* edited by William R. Ewald, Jr. Bloomington: Indiana University Press.

Andenaes, Johannes
  1966   "The general preventive effects of punishment." *University of Pennsylvania Law Review* 114 (May):949–983.

Angel, Shlomo
  1968   "Discouraging crime through city planning." A report prepared for the National Aeronautics and Space Administration. Space Sciences Laboratory and Center for Planning and Development Research, Working Paper Number 75. Berkeley: University of California.

Anonymous
  1972   "The women in blue." *Time* 99 (May 1):60.
  1974   "Cops and couples." *Newsweek* 84 (July 8):79.
  1977   "Citizen dispute resolution: whose property?" *The Mooter* 1 (Fall):2–4.

Arrow, Kenneth J.
  1972   "Gifts and exchanges." *Philosophy and Public Affairs* 1 (Summer):343–362.

Aubert, Vilhelm
  1967   "Courts and conflict resolution." *Journal of Conflict Resolution* 11 (March):40–51.

Bacon, Seldon D.
  1939   The Early Development of American Municipal Police: A Study of the Evolution of Formal Controls in a Changing Society. Unpublished doctoral dissertation, Department of Political Science, Yale University.

Banton, Michael
  1964   *The Policeman in the Community.* London: Tavistock.

Bard, Morton, and Joseph Zacker
  1976   "How police handle explosive squabbles." *Psychology Today* 10 (November):71ff.

Barton, Roy Franklin
  1919   *Ifugao Law.* Berkeley: University of California Press, 1969.

247

Bateson, Gregory, Don D. Jackson, Jay Haley, and John H. Weakland
1956   "Toward a theory of schizophrenia." Pages 201–227 in *Steps to an Ecology of Mind,* by Gregory Bateson. New York: Ballantine Books, 1972.
Baumgartner, M. P.
1980a   "Aspects of social control in a suburban town." Paper presented at the annual meeting of the American Sociological Association, New York, August, 1980.
1980b   "Law and the middle class: evidence from a suburban town." Paper presented at the annual meeting of the Law and Society Association, Madison, June, 1980.
1981a   "Social control and culture." Forthcoming in *Toward a General Theory of Social Control,* edited by Donald Black. New York: Academic Press.
1981b   Social Control in a Suburban Town: An Ethnographic Study. Unpublished doctoral dissertation, Department of Sociology, Yale University.
Baumgartner, M. P., and Donald Black
1981   "Toward a theory of the third party." Forthcoming in *Empirical Theories about Courts,* edited by Lynn Mather and Keith Boyum. New York: Longman.
Bayley, David H.
1971   "The police and political change in comparative perspective." *Law and Society Review* 6 (August):91–112.
1976   *Forces of Order: Police Behavior in Japan and the United States.* Berkeley: University of California Press.
Beaumont, Gustave de, and Alexis de Tocqueville
1833   *On the Penitentiary System in the United States and Its Application in France.* Carbondale: Southern Illinois University Press, 1964.
Becker, Howard S.
1963   *Outsiders: Studies in the Sociology of Deviance.* New York: Free Press.
Bennis, Warren G., and Philip Slater
1968   *The Temporary Society.* New York: Harper and Row.
Bercal, Thomas E.
1970   "Calls for police assistance: consumer demands for governmental service." *American Behavioral Scientist* 13 (May –August):681–691.
Beresford, M. W.
1957   "The common informer, the penal statutes and economic regulation." *Economic History Review* 10 (December):221–238.
Berger, Morroe
1967   *Equality by Statute: The Revolution in Civil Rights.* Garden City: Doubleday (second edition; first edition, 1952).
Bergesen, Albert
1977   "Political witch hunts: the sacred and the subversive in cross-cultural perspective." *American Sociological Review* 42 (April):220–233.
1980   "Official violence during the Watts, Newark, and Detroit race riots of the 1960s." Pages 138–174 in *A Political Analysis of Deviance,* edited by Pat Lauderdale. Minneapolis: University of Minnesota Press.
Berk, Richard A., Harold Brackman, and Selma Lesser
1977   *A Measure of Justice: An Empirical Study of Changes in the California Penal Code, 1955–1971.* New York: Academic Press.
Berman, Harold J.
1963   *Justice in the U.S.S.R.: An Interpretation of Soviet Law.* New York: Random House (second edition; first edition, 1950).
Berman, Jesse
1969   "The Cuban popular tribunals." *Columbia Law Review* 69 (December):1317–1354.

Best, Arthur, and Alan R. Andreasen
1977 "Consumer response to unsatisfactory purchases: a survey of perceiving defects, voicing complaints, and obtaining redress." *Law and Society Review* 11 (Spring):701–742.

Bickman, Leonard
1971 "The effect of another bystander's ability to help on bystander intervention in an emergency." *Journal of Experimental Social Psychology* 7 (May):361–379.

Biderman, Albert D.
1967 "Surveys of population samples for estimating crime incidence." *The Annals of the American Academy of Political and Social Science* 374 (November):16–33.

Biderman, Albert D., and Albert J. Reiss, Jr.
1967 "On exploring the 'dark figure' of crime." *The Annals of the American Academy of Political and Social Science* 374 (November):1–15.

Bittner, Egon
1967a "Police discretion in emergency apprehension of mentally ill persons." *Social Problems* 14 (Winter):278–292.
1967b "The police on skid-row: a study of peace keeping." *American Sociological Review* 32 (October):699–715.
1974 "Florence Nightingale in pursuit of Willie Sutton: a theory of the police." Pages 17–44 in *Sage Criminal Justice System Annuals*, Volume 3: *The Potential for Reform of Criminal Justice*, edited by Herbert Jacob. Beverly Hills: Sage.
1976 "Policing juveniles: the social context of common practice." Pages 69–93 in *Pursuing Justice for the Child*, edited by Margaret Rosenheim. Chicago: University of Chicago Press.

Bittner, Egon, and Sheldon L. Messinger
1966 "Some reflections on the police and 'professional crime' in West City." Unpublished paper, Center for the Study of Law and Society, University of California, Berkeley.

Black, Donald
1968 Police Encounters and Social Organization: An Observation Study. Unpublished doctoral dissertation, Department of Sociology, University of Michigan.
1970 "Production of crime rates." *American Sociological Review* 35 (August):733–748. *Reprinted as Chapter 3 of the present volume.*
1971 "The social organization of arrest." *Stanford Law Review* 23 (June):1087–1111. *Reprinted as Chapter 4 of the present volume.*
1972 "The boundaries of legal sociology." *Yale Law Journal* 81 (May):1086–1100.
1973 "The mobilization of law." *Journal of Legal Studies* 2 (January):125–149. *Reprinted as Chapter 2 of the present volume.*
1976 *The Behavior of Law.* New York: Academic Press.
1979a "Common sense in the sociology of law." *American Sociological Review* 44 (February):18–27.
1979b "A note on the measurement of law." *Informationsbrief für Rechtssoziologie*, Sonderheft 2 (April):92–106. *Reprinted as Appendix A of the present volume.*
1979c "A strategy of pure sociology." Pages 149–168 in *Theoretical Perspectives in Sociology*, edited by Scott G. McNall. New York: St. Martin's Press.

Black, Donald, and M. P. Baumgartner
1981 "On self-help in modern society." *Dialectical Anthropology* 5: forthcoming. *Reprinted as Chapter 6 of the present volume.*

Black, Donald, and Albert J. Reiss, Jr.
1967 "Patterns of behavior in police and citizen transactions." Pages 1–139 in U.S. President's Commission on Law Enforcement and Administration of Justice, *Studies in Crime and Law Enforcement in Major Metropolitan Areas*, Field Surveys III, Volume 2. Washington, D.C.: U.S. Government Printing Office.

1970 "Police control of juveniles." *American Sociological Review* 35 (February):63–77.

Bohannan, Paul
1965 "The differing realms of the law." Pages 33–42 in *The Ethnography of Law*, edited by Laura Nader. Published as supplement to *American Anthropologist*, Volume 67, December.

Bordua, David J., and Albert J. Reiss, Jr.
1967 "Law enforcement." Pages 275–303 in *The Uses of Sociology*, edited by Paul F. Lazarsfeld, William Sewell, and Harold Wilensky. New York: Basic Books.

Brown, Michael E.
1969 "The condemnation and persecution of hippies." *Trans-Action* 6 (September):33–46.

Brown, Richard Maxwell
1969 "The American vigilante tradition." Pages 154–226 in *Violence in America: Historical and Comparative Perspectives*, edited by Hugh Davis Graham and Ted Robert Gurr. A report submitted to the National Commission on the Causes and Prevention of Violence. New York: Bantam Books.

Bryan, James H., and Mary Ann Test
1967 "Models and helping: naturalistic studies in aiding behavior." *Journal of Personality and Social Psychology* 6 (August):400–407.

Buxbaum, David C.
1971 "Some aspects of civil procedure and practice at the trial level in Tanshui and Hsinchu from 1789 to 1895." *Journal of Asian Studies* 30 (February):255–279.

Cardozo, Benjamin N.
1921 *The Nature of the Judicial Process*. New Haven: Yale University Press.
1924 *The Growth of the Law*. New Haven: Yale University Press.

Carpenter, Edmund, and Marshall McLuhan
1960 "Introduction." Pages ix–xii in *Explorations in Communication: An Anthology*, edited by E. Carpenter and M. McLuhan. Boston: Beacon Press.

Carroll, Leo, and Pamela Irving Jackson
1979 "On the behavior of law: determinants of the size of municipal police forces." Paper presented at the annual meeting of the Eastern Sociological Society, New York City, March, 1979.

Chambliss, William J.
1967 "Types of deviance and the effectiveness of legal sanctions." *Wisconsin Law Review* 1967 (Summer):703–719.

Chan, Janet
1980 "A multivariate analysis of the behavior of law." Paper presented at the annual meeting of the American Sociological Association, New York City, August, 1980.

Chevigny, Paul
1969 *Police Power: Police Abuses in New York City*. New York: Vintage Press.

Christie, Nils
1977 "Conflicts as property." *British Journal of Criminology* 17 (January):1–15.

Cicourel, Aaron V.
1968 *The Social Organization of Juvenile Justice*. New York: John Wiley.

Clébert, Jean-Paul
1963 *The Gypsies*. Baltimore: Penguin Books, 1967.

Coates, Robert B., and Alden D. Miller
1974 "Patrolmen and addicts: a study of police perception and police–citizen interaction." *Journal of Police Science and Administration* 2 (September):308–321.

Cohen, Jerome Alan
1966 "Chinese mediation on the eve of modernization." *California Law Review* 54 (August):1201–1226.

Cohn, Bernard S.
1959 "Some notes on law and change in North India." *Economic Development and Cultural Change* 8 (October):79–93.
Colson, Elizabeth
1953 "Social control and vengeance in Plateau Tonga society." *Africa* 23 (July):199–212.
1974 *Tradition and Contract: The Problem of Order.* Chicago: Aldine Press.
Cottrell, Fred
1955 *Energy and Society: The Relation between Energy, Social Change, and Economic Development.* New York: McGraw-Hill.
Cumming, Elaine, Ian Cumming, and Laura Edell
1965 "Policeman as philosopher, guide and friend." *Social Problems* 12 (Winter):276–286.
Dahrendorf, Ralf
1968 "Homo sociologicus: on the history, significance, and limits of the category of social role." Pages 19–87 in *Essays in the Theory of Society.* Stanford: Stanford University Press (revised version; original version, 1958).
Dannefer, W. Dale, and Nicholas Poushinsky
1979 "The C.B. phenomenon, a sociological appraisal." *Journal of Popular Culture* 12 (Spring): 611–619.
Danzig, Richard
1973 "Toward the creation of a complementary, decentralized system of criminal justice." *Stanford Law Review* 26 (November):1–54.
Darley, John M.
1967 "The sharing of responsibility." Paper presented at the annual meeting of the American Psychological Association, Washington, D.C., September, 1967.
Darley, John M., and Bibb Latané
1968 "Bystander intervention in emergencies: diffusion of responsibility." *Journal of Personality and Social Psychology* 8 (April):377–383.
Davis, Kenneth Culp
1969 *Discretionary Justice: A Preliminary Inquiry.* Baton Rouge: Louisiana State University Press.
Deutscher, Irwin
1966 "Words and deeds: social science and social policy." *Social Problems* 13 (Winter):235–254.
Diamond, Stanley
1971 "The rule of law versus the order of custom." Pages 115–144 in *The Rule of Law,* edited by Robert Paul Wolff. New York: Simon and Schuster.
Doo, Leigh-Wai
1973 "Dispute settlement in Chinese-American communities." *American Journal of Comparative Law* 21 (Fall):627–663.
Durkheim, Emile
1893 *The Division of Labor in Society.* New York: Free Press, 1964.
Ellsworth, Phoebe C., and Ellen J. Langer
1976 "Staring and approach: an interpretation of the stare as a non-specific activator." *Journal of Personality and Social Psychology* 33 (January):117–122.
Engels, Friedrich
1884 *The Origin of the Family, Private Property and the State: In the Light of the Researches of Lewis H. Morgan.* New York: International Publishers, 1942.
Enloe, Cynthia H.
1977 "Police and military in the resolution of ethnic conflict." *The Annals of the American Academy of Political and Social Science* 433 (September):137–149.
Erikson, Kai T.
1966 *Wayward Puritans: A Study in the Sociology of Deviance.* New York: John Wiley.

Evans-Pritchard, E. E.
1940   *The Nuer: A Description of the Modes of Livelihood and Political Institutions of a Nilotic People.* London: Oxford University Press.

Farley, Reynolds, and Albert I. Hermalin
1971   "Family stability: a comparison of trends between blacks and whites." *American Sociological Review* 36 (February):1–17.

Felstiner, William L. F.
1974   "Influences of social organization on dispute processsing." *Law and Society Review* 9 (Fall): 63–94.

Finestone, Harold
1957   "Cats, kicks, and color." *Social Problems* 5 (July):3–13.

Fortes, M., and E. E. Evans-Pritchard
1940   "Introduction." Pages 1–23 in *African Political Systems,* edited by M. Fortes and E. E. Evans-Pritchard. London: Oxford University Press.

Frazier, E. Franklin
1948   *The Negro Family in the United States.* New York: Citadel Press (revised and abridged edition; first edition, 1939).

Friedrich, Robert James
        The Impact of Organizational, Individual, and Situational Factors on Police Behavior. Unpublished doctoral dissertation, Department of Political Science, University of Michigan.

Fuller, Lon L.
1940   *The Law in Quest of Itself.* Boston: Beacon Press, 1966.
1969   "Two principles of human association." Pages 3–23 in *Voluntary Associations (Nomos, Volume 11),* edited by J. Rolland Pennock and John W. Chapman. New York: Atherton Press.
1971   "Mediation—its forms and functions." *Southern California Law Review* 44 (Winter): 305–339.

Fürer-Haimendorf, Christoph von
1967   *Morals and Merit: A Study of Values and Social Controls in South Asian Societies.* Chicago: University of Chicago Press.

Gaertner, Samuel, and Leonard Bickman
1971   "Effects of race on the elicitation of helping behavior: the wrong number technique." *Journal of Personality and Social Psychology* 20 (November):218–222.

Gardiner, John A.
1969   *Traffic and the Police: Variations in Law-Enforcement Policy.* Cambridge: Harvard University Press.

Garfinkel, Harold
1956   "Conditions of successful degradation ceremonies." *American Journal of Sociology* 61 (March):420–424.

Gelles, Richard J.
1972   *The Violent Home: A Study of Physical Aggression between Husbands and Wives.* Beverly Hills: Sage.

Gibbs, James L., Jr.
1963   "The Kpelle moot: a therapeutic model for the informal settlement of disputes." *Africa* 33 (January):1–10.

Gluckman, Max
1967   *The Judicial Process among the Barotse of Northern Rhodesia.* Manchester: Manchester University Press (second edition; first edition, 1955).

Goffman, Erving
1956a   "Embarrassment and social organization." *American Journal of Sociology* 62 (November): 264–271.

1956b   "The nature of deference and demeanor." *American Anthropologist* 58 (June):473–502.
1961   *Asylums: Essays on the Social Situation of Mental Patients and Other Inmates.* Garden City: Anchor Books (enlarged version; first version, 1957).
1963   *Behavior in Public Places: Notes on the Social Organization of Gatherings.* New York: Free Press.

Goldman, Nathan
1963   *The Differential Selection of Juvenile Offenders for Court Appearance.* New York: National Council on Crime and Delinquency.

Goldstein, Joseph
1960   "Police discretion not to invoke the criminal process: low-visibility decisions in the administration of justice." *Yale Law Journal* 69 (March):543–594.

Gottfredson, Michael R., and Michael J. Hindelang
1979   "A study of *The Behavior of Law.*" *American Sociological Review* 44 (February):3–18.

Gould, Leroy C., Andrew L. Walker, Lansing E. Crane, and Charles W. Lidz
1974   *Connections: Notes from the Heroin World.* New Haven: Yale University Press.

Grace, Roger
1970   "Justice, Chinese style." *Case and Comment* 75 (January–February):50–51.

Green, Edward
1970   "Race, social status, and criminal arrest." *American Sociological Review* 35 (June):476–490.

Gross, Jan Tomasz
1979   *Polish Society under German Occupation: The Generalgouvernement, 1939–1944.* Princeton: Princeton University Press.

Gulliver, P. H.
1963   *Social Control in an African Society: A Study of the Arusha, Agricultural Masai of Northern Tanganyika.* Boston: Boston University Press.
1969   "Dispute settlement without courts: the Ndendeuli of southern Tanzania." Pages 24–68 in *Law in Culture and Society*, edited by Laura Nader. Chicago: Aldine Press.
1977   "On mediators." Pages 15–52 in *Social Anthropology and Law*, edited by Ian Hamnet. New York: Academic Press.
1979   *Disputes and Negotiations: A Cross-Cultural Perspective.* New York: Academic Press.

Gusfield, Joseph R.
1963   *Symbolic Crusade: Status Politics and the American Temperance Movement.* Urbana: University of Illinois Press.

Hackler, James C., Kwai-Yiu Ho, and Carol Urquhart-Ross
1974   "The willingness to intervene: differing community characteristics." *Social Problems* 21 (Number 3):328–344.

Hagan, William T.
1966   *Indian Police and Judges: Experiments in Acculturation and Control.* New Haven: Yale University Press.

Hall, Jerome
1952   *Theft, Law, and Society.* Indianapolis: Bobbs-Merrill (second edition; first edition, 1935).

Hannerz, Ulf
1970   "What ghetto males are like: another look." Pages 313–325 in *Afro-American Anthropology: Contemporary Perspectives*, edited by Norman E. Whitten, Jr., and John F. Szwed. New York: Free Press.

Haskins, George Lee
1960   *Law and Authority in Early Massachusetts: A Study in Tradition and Design.* Hamden: Archon Books, 1968.

Hasluck, Margaret
1954   *The Unwritten Law in Albania.* Cambridge: Cambridge University Press.

Hayden, Tom
1967   *Rebellion in Newark: Official Violence and Ghetto Response.* New York: Random House.
Henderson, Dan Fenno
1965   *Conciliation and Japanese Law: Tokugawa and Modern.* Seattle: University of Washington Press. Two volumes.
Hepburn, John R.
1978   "Race and the decision to arrest: an analysis of warrants issued." *Journal of Research in Crime and Delinquency* 15 (January):54–73.
Heussenstamm, F. K.
1971   "Bumper stickers and the cops." *Trans-Action* 8 (February):32–33.
Hirschi, Travis
1969   *Causes of Delinquency.* Berkeley: University of California Press.
Hobhouse, L. T.
1951   *Morals in Evolution: A Study in Comparative Ethics.* London: Chapman and Hall.
Hoebel, E. Adamson
1954   *The Law of Primitive Man: A Study in Comparative Legal Dynamics.* Cambridge: Harvard University Press.
Hollingshead, August B.
1941   "The concept of social control." *American Sociological Review* 6 (April):217–224.
Holmes, Oliver Wendell
1881   *The Common Law.* Boston: Little, Brown.
Hornstein, Harvey A.
1970   "The influence of social models on helping." Pages 29–41 in *Altruism and Helping Behavior: Social Psychological Studies of Some Antecedents and Consequences,* edited by J. Macaulay and L. Berkowitz. New York: Academic Press.
Hutchison, Ira W.
1975   "Police intervention in family conflict." Paper presented at the annual meeting of the American Sociological Association, San Francisco, September, 1975.
Jacobs, Jane
1961   *The Death and Life of Great American Cities.* New York: Vintage Books.
Jakubs, Deborah L.
1977   "Police violence in times of political tension: the case of Brazil, 1968–1971." Pages 85–106 in *Police and Society,* edited by David H. Bayley. Beverly Hills: Sage.
Jeffery, C. Ray
1971   *Crime Prevention through Environmental Design.* Beverly Hills: Sage.
Jhering, Rudolph von
1877   *The Struggle for Law.* Chicago: Callaghan, 1879 (fifth edition; first edition, 1872).
Johnson, Weldon T., Robert E. Petersen, and L. Edward Wells
1977   "Arrest probabilities for marijuana users as indicators of selective law enforcement." *American Journal of Sociology* 83 (November):681–699.
Jones, Harry W.
1969   *The Efficacy of Law.* Evanston: Northwestern University Press.
Kaplan, Irving
1965   "Courts as catalysts of change: a Chagga case." *Southwestern Journal of Anthropology* 21 (Summer):79–96.
Karsten, Rafael
1923   *Blood Revenge, War, and Victory Feasts among the Jibaro Indians of Eastern Ecuador.* Bureau of American Ethnology, Bulletin 79. Washington, D.C.: U.S. Government Printing Office.
Kawashima, Takeyoshi
1963   "Dispute resolution in contemporary Japan." Pages 41–72 in *Law in Japan: The Legal*

Order in a Changing Society, edited by Arthur Taylor von Mehren. Cambridge: Harvard University Press.

Kelling, George L., Tony Pate, Duane Dieckman, and Charles E. Brown
1974   *The Kansas City Preventive Patrol Experiment: A Technical Report.* Washington, D.C.: Police Foundation.

Kerbo, Harold R., Karrie Marshall, and Philip Holley
1978   "Reestablishing 'Gemeinschaft'? An examination of the CB radio fad." *Urban Life* 7 (October):337–358.

Kinberg, Olof
1935   *Basic Problems of Criminology.* Copenhagen: Levin and Munksgaard.

Kitsuse, John I., and Aaron V. Cicourel
1963   "A note on the uses of official statistics." *Social Problems* 11 (Fall):131–139.

Knoohuizen, Ralph, Richard P. Fahey, and Deborah J. Palmer
1972   The Police and Their Use of Fatal Force in Chicago. A Report of the Chicago Law Enforcement Study Group, Evanston.

Koch, Klaus-Friedrich
1974   *War and Peace in Jalémó: The Management of Conflict in Highland New Guinea.* Cambridge: Harvard University Press.
1981   "Toward a general theory of liability." Forthcoming in *Toward a General Theory of Social Control*, edited by Donald Black. New York: Academic Press.

Komarovsky, Mirra
1940   *The Unemployed Man and His Family—The Effect of Unemployment upon the Status of the Man in Fifty-Nine Families.* New York: Dryden Press.

Kropotkin, Peter
1914   *Mutual Aid: A Factor of Evolution.* Boston: Extending Horizons Books, 1955 (second edition; first edition, 1902).

Kruttschnitt, Candace Marie
1979   The Social Control of Women Offenders: A Study of Sentencing in a Criminal Court. Unpublished doctoral dissertation, Department of Sociology, Yale University.

La Fave, Wayne R.
1965   *Arrest: The Decision to Take a Suspect into Custody.* Boston: Little, Brown.

Lasswell, Harold
1956   *The Decision Process: Seven Categories of Functional Analysis.* College Park: Bureau of Governmental Research, College of Business and Public Administration, University of Maryland.

Latané, Bibb, and Judith Rodin
1969   "A lady in distress: inhibiting effects of friends and strangers on bystander intervention." *Journal of Experimental Social Psychology* 5 (April):189–202.

Lemert, Edwin M.
1967   "The concept of secondary deviation." Pages 40–64 in *Human Deviance, Social Problems, and Social Control.* Englewood Cliffs: Prentice-Hall.
1970   *Social Action and Legal Change: Revolution within the Juvenile Court.* Chicago: Aldine Press.

Lev, Daniel S.
1971   "Judicial institutions and legal change in Indonesia." Unpublished paper, Department of Political Science, University of Washington.

Levi, Edward H.
1948   *An Introduction to Legal Reasoning.* Chicago: University of Chicago Press.

Lewis, I. M.
1961   *A Pastoral Democracy: A Study of Pastoralism and Politics among the Northern Somali of the Horn of Africa.* London: Oxford University Press.

Liebman, Donald A., and Jeffrey A. Schwartz
   1973   "Police programs in domestic crisis intervention: a review." Pages 421–472 in *The Urban Policeman in Transition: A Psychological and Sociological Review.* Springfield: Charles C Thomas.
Liebow, Elliot
   1967   *Tally's Corner: A Study of Negro Streetcorner Men.* Boston: Little, Brown.
Lintott, A. W.
   1968   *Violence in Republican Rome.* London: Oxford University Press.
Llewellyn, Karl N., and E. Adamson Hoebel
   1941   *The Cheyenne Way: Conflict and Case Law in Primitive Jurisprudence.* Norman: University of Oklahoma Press.
Lobenthal, Joseph S., Jr.
   1970   "Buying out, selling out, copping out: law in the city." *Antioch Review* 30 (Summer):195–221.
Loevinger, Lee
   1949   "Jurimetrics: the next step forward." *Minnesota Law Review* 33 (April):455–493.
Lofland, John
   1969   *Deviance and Identity.* Englewood Cliffs: Prentice-Hall.
Lowie, Robert H.
   1948   "Some aspects of political organization among the American aborigines." *Journal of the Royal Anthropological Institute of Great Britain and Ireland* 78:11–24.
Lowy, Michael J.
   1973   "Modernizing the American legal system: an example of the peaceful use of anthropology." *Human Organization* 32 (Summer):205–209.
Lundman, Richard J.
   1974a   "Domestic police–citizen encounters." *Journal of Police Science and Administration* 2 (March):22–27.
   1974b   "Routine police arrest practices: a commonweal perspective." *Social Problems* 22 (October):127–141.
   1979   "Organizational norms and police discretion: an observational study of police work with traffic law violators." *Criminology* 17 (August):159–171.
Lundman, Richard J., Richard E. Sykes, and John P. Clark
   1978   "Police control of juveniles: a replication." *Journal of Research in Crime and Delinquency* 15 (January):74–91.
Macaulay, Stewart
   1963   "Non-contractual relations in business: a preliminary study." *American Sociological Review* 28 (February):55–67.
MacCormack, Geoffrey
   1976   "Procedures for the settlement of disputes in 'simple societies.' " *The Irish Jurist* 11 (new series):175–188.
MacDonald, John Stuart, and Leatrice MacDonald
   1978   "The black family in the Americas: a review of the literature." *Sage Race Relations Abstracts* 3 (February):1–42.
Macfarlane, Alan
   1970   *Witchcraft in Tudor and Stuart England: A Regional and Comparative Study.* New York: Harper and Row.
MacLeod, William Christie
   1937   "Police and punishment among native Americans of the Plains." *Journal of the American Institute of Criminal Law and Criminology* 28 (July–August):181–201.
Maine, Henry Sumner
   1861   *Ancient Law: Its Connection with the Early History of Society and Its Relation to Modern Ideas.* Boston: Beacon Press, 1963.

Malinowski, Bronislaw
    1925   "Magic, science and religion." Pages 17–92 in *Magic, Science and Religion and Other Essays*. Garden City: Doubleday, 1954.
    1926   *Crime and Custom in Savage Society*. Paterson: Littlefield, Adams, 1962.
    1942   "A new instrument for the interpretation of law—especially primitive." *Yale Law Journal* 51 (June):1237–1254.

Mannheim, Karl
    1940   *Man and Society in an Age of Reconstruction: Studies in Modern Social Structure*. New York: Harcourt, Brace, and World (revised edition; first edition, 1935).

Manning, Peter K.
    1972   "Observing the police: deviants, respectables, and the law." Pages 213–268 in *Research on Deviance*, edited by Jack Douglas. New York: Random House.
    1974   "Police lying." *Urban Life and Culture* 3 (October):283–306.
    1977   *Police Work: The Social Organization of Policing*. Cambridge: MIT Press.
    1980a   *The Narcs' Game: Organizational and Informational Constraints on Drug Law Enforcement*. Cambridge: MIT Press.
    1980b   "Organization and environment: influences on police work." Pages 98–123 in *The Effectiveness of Policing*, edited by R. V. G. Clarke and J. M. Hough. Farnborough: Gower.

Manning, Peter K., and John Van Maanen (editors)
    1978   *Policing: A View from the Street*. Santa Monica: Goodyear.

Marx, Gary T.
    1974   "Thoughts on a neglected category of social movement participant: the *agent provocateur* and the informant." *American Journal of Sociology* 80 (September):402–442.
    1980   "The new police undercover work." *Urban Life* 8(January):399–446.
    1981   "Ironies of social control: authorities as contributors to deviance through escalation, non-enforcement, and covert facilitation." Forthcoming in *Unanticipated Consequences of Social Action: Variations on a Sociological Theme*, edited by Robert K. Merton. New York: Academic Press.

Marx, Gary T., and Dane Archer
    1971   "Citizen involvement in the law enforcement process." *American Behavioral Scientist* 15 (September-October):52–72.

Marx, Karl
    1956   *Selected Writings in Sociology and Social Philosophy*, edited by T. B. Bottomore and Maximilien Rubel. London: Watts.

Massell, Gregory J.
    1968   "Law as an instrument of revolutionary change in a traditional milieu: the case of Soviet Central Asia." *Law and Society Review* 2 (February):179–211.

Mayhew, Leon H.
    1968   *Law and Equal Opportunity: A Study of the Massachusetts Commission Against Discrimination*. Cambridge: Harvard University Press.

McCall, George J.
    1978   *Observing the Law: Field Methods in the Study of Crime and the Criminal Justice System*. New York: Free Press.

McLuhan, Marshall
    1964   *Understanding Media: The Extensions of Man*. New York: New American Library.

Merry, Sally Engle
    1979   "Going to court: strategies of dispute management in an American urban neighborhood." *Law and Society Review* 13 (Summer):891–925.

Mileski, Maureen
    1971a   "Courtroom encounters: an observation study of a lower criminal court." *Law and Society Review* 5 (May):473–538.

1971b Policing Slum Landlords: An Observation Study of Administrative Control. Unpublished doctoral dissertation, Department of Sociology, Yale University.

Mileti, Dennis S., Thomas E. Drabek, and J. Eugene Haas

1975 *Human Systems in Extreme Environments: A Sociological Perspective.* Boulder: Institute of Behavioral Science, University of Colorado. Program on Technology, Environment and Man, Monograph Number 21.

Moore, Sally Falk

1970 "Politics, procedures, and norms in changing Chagga law." *Africa* 40 (October):321–344.

1972 "Legal liability and evolutionary interpretation: some aspects of strict liability, self-help and collective responsibility." Pages 51–107 in *The Allocation of Responsibility,* edited by Max Gluckman. Manchester: Manchester University Press.

Morrison, William Douglas

1897 "The interpretation of criminal statistics." *Journal of the Royal Statistical Society* 60 (March):1–24.

Muir, William Ker, Jr.

1977 *Police: Streetcorner Politicians.* Chicago: University of Chicago Press.

Murray, Henry A.

1951 "Toward a classification of interactions." Pages 434–464 in *Toward a General Theory of Action,* edited by Talcott Parsons and Edward A. Shils. Cambridge: Harvard University Press.

Nader, Laura

1964 "An analysis of Zapotec law cases." *Ethnology* 3 (October):404–419.

1978 "The direction of law and the development of extra-judicial processes in nation state societies." Pages 78–95 in *Cross-Examinations: Essays in Memory of Max Gluckman,* edited by P. H. Gulliver. Leiden: E. J. Brill.

Nader, Laura, and Duane Metzger

1963 "Conflict resolution in two Mexican communities." *American Anthropologist* 65 (June): 584–592.

Nader, Laura, and Harry F. Todd, Jr.

1978 "Introduction." Pages 1–40 in *The Disputing Process—Law in Ten Societies,* edited by L. Nader and H. F. Todd, Jr. New York: Columbia University Press.

Nader, Laura, and Barbara Yngvesson

1973 "On studying the ethnography of law and its consequences." Pages 883–921 in *Handbook of Social and Cultural Anthropology,* edited by John J. Honigmann. Chicago: Rand McNally.

Newman, Oscar

1972 *Defensible Space: Crime Prevention through Urban Design.* New York: Macmillan.

Northrop, F. S. C.

1958 "The mediational approval theory of law in American legal realism." *Virginia Law Review* 44 (April):347–363.

Ogburn, William F.

1964 *On Culture and Social Change: Selected Papers,* edited by Otis Dudley Duncan. Chicago: University of Chicago Press.

Olson, Mancur, Jr.

1965 *The Logic of Collective Action: Public Goods and the Theory of Groups.* New York: Schocken Books, 1968.

Osmond, Humphrey

1957 "Function as the basis of psychiatric ward design." *Mental Hospitals* 8 (April):23–29.

Parnas, Raymond I.

1967 "The police response to the domestic disturbance." *Wisconsin Law Review* 1967 (Fall): 914–960.

1970   "Judicial response to intra-family violence." *Minnesota Law Review* 54 (January):585–644.
Parsons, Talcott
1954   "A sociologist looks at the legal profession." Pages 370–385 in *Essays in Sociological Theory.* New York: Free Press (revised edition; first edition, 1949).
Pashukanis, E. B.
1927   "The general theory of law and Marxism." Pages 111–225 in *Soviet Legal Philosophy,* edited by Hugh W. Babb. Cambridge: Harvard University Press, 1951 (third edition; first edition, 1924).
Pastor, Paul A., Jr.
1978   "Mobilization in public drunkenness control: a comparison of legal and medical approaches." *Social Problems* 25 (April):373–384.
Peabody, Robert L.
1964   *Organizational Authority: Superior–Subordinate Relationships in Three Public Service Organizations.* New York: Atherton Press.
Peattie, Lisa Redfield
1968   *The View from the Barrio.* Ann Arbor: University of Michigan Press.
Pepinsky, Harold E.
1976a   *Crime and Conflict: A Study of Law and Society.* New York: Academic Press.
1976b   "Police patrolmen's offense-reporting behavior." *Journal of Crime and Delinquency* 13 (January):33–47.
Peters, E. L.
1967   "Some structural aspects of the feud among the camel-herding Bedouin of Cyrenaica." *Africa* 37 (July):261–282.
Petersen, David M.
1971   "Informal norms and police practice: the traffic ticket quota system." *Sociology and Social Research* 55 (April):354–362.
Piliavin, Irving M., and Scott Briar
1964   "Police encounters with juveniles." *American Journal of Sociology* 70 (September):206–214.
Piliavin, Irving M., Judith Rodin, and Jane Allyn Piliavin
1969   "Good Samaritanism: an underground phenomenon?" *Journal of Personality and Social Psychology* 13 (December):289–299.
Pollock, Frederick, and Frederic William Maitland
1898   *The History of English Law: Before the Time of Edward I.* Cambridge: Cambridge University Press (second edition; first edition, 1895). Two volumes.
Posner, Richard A.
1972   "A theory of negligence." *Journal of Legal Studies* 1 (January):29–96.
Pospisil, Leopold
1971   *Anthropology of Law: A Comparative Theory.* New York: Harper and Row.
Pound, Roscoe
1917   "The limits of effective legal action." *International Journal of Ethics* 27 (January):150–167.
1942   *Social Control through Law.* New Haven: Yale University Press.
Preiss, Jack J., and Howard J. Ehrlich
1966   *An Examination of Role Theory: The Case of the State Police.* Lincoln: University of Nebraska Press.
Prucha, Francis Paul
1962   *American Indian Policy in the Formative Years: The Indian Trade and Intercourse Acts, 1790–1834.* Lincoln: University of Nebraska Press.
Radcliffe-Brown, A. R.
1965   *Structure and Function in Primitive Society: Essays and Addresses.* New York: Free Press.

Rainwater, Lee
1966 "Work and identity in the lower class." Pages 105–123 in *Planning for a Nation of Cities,* edited by Sam Bass Warner, Jr. Cambridge: MIT Press.
1970 *Behind Ghetto Walls: Black Families in a Federal Slum.*Chicago: Aldine Press.
Ranulf, Svend
1938 *Moral Indignation and Middle Class Psychology: A Sociological Study.* New York: Schocken Books, 1964.
Reiss, Albert J., Jr.
1967 "Measurement of the nature and amount of crime." Pages 1–183 in U.S. President's Commission on Law Enforcement and Adminstration of Justice, *Studies in Crime and Law Enforcement in Major Metropolitan Areas,* Field Surveys III, Volume 1. Washington, D.C.: U.S. Government Printing Office.
1968a "Police brutality—answers to key questions." *Trans-Action* 5 (July–August):10–19.
1968b "Stuff and nonsense about social surveys and observation." Pages 351–367 in *Institutions and the Person: Papers Presented to Everett C. Hughes,* edited by Howard S. Becker, Blanche Geer, David Riesman, and Robert S. Weiss. Chicago: Aldine Press.
1971a *The Police and the Public.* New Haven: Yale University Press.
1971b "Systematic observation of natural social phenomena." Pages 3–33 in *Sociological Methodology: 1971,* edited by Herbert L. Costner. San Francisco: Jossey-Bass.
Reiss, Albert J., Jr., and Donald Black
1967 "Interrogation and the criminal process." *The Annals of the American Academy of Political and Social Science* 374 (November):47–57.
Reiss, Albert J., Jr., and David J. Bordua
1967 "Environment and organization: a perspective on the police." Pages 25–55 in *The Police: Six Sociological Essays,* edited by David J. Bordua. New York: John Wiley
Rickett, W. Allyn
1971 "Voluntary surrender and confession in Chinese law: the problem of continuity." *Journal of Asian Studies* 30 (August):797–814.
Roberts, Simon
1979 *Order and Dispute: An Introduction to Legal Anthropology.* New York: Penguin Books.
Rockwell International, Space Division
1977 *Industries in Space to Benefit Mankind: A View Over the Next 30 Years.* Los Angeles: A report prepared for the National Aeronautics and Space Administration.
Rokeach, Milton, Martin G. Miller, and John A. Snyder
1977 "The value gap between police and policed." Pages 149–157 in *Law, Justice, and the Individual in Society: Psychological and Legal Issues,* edited by June Louin Tapp and Felice J. Levine. New York: Holt, Rinehart and Winston.
Ross, Edward Alsworth
1901 *Social Control: A Survey of the Foundations of Order.* New York: Macmillan.
Ross, H. Laurence
1960 "Traffic law violation: a folk crime." *Social Problems* 8 (Winter):231–241.
Rotenberg, Daniel L.
1967 "Encouragement and entrapment." Pages 207–202 in *Detection of Crime: Stopping and Questioning, Search and Seizure, Encouragement and Entrapment,* by Lawrence P. Tiffany, Donald M. McIntyre, Jr., and Daniel L. Rotenberg. Boston: Little, Brown.
Rubinstein, Jonathan
1973 *City Police.* New York: Farrar, Straus and Giroux.
Russell, Francis
1975 *A City in Terror:1919—The Boston Police Strike.* New York: Viking Press.

Sacks, Harvey
1972   "Notes on police assessment of moral character." Pages 280–293 in *Studies in Social Interaction*, edited by David Sudnow. New York: Free Press.
Sanders, William B.
1977   *Detective Work: A Study of Criminal Investigations.* New York: Free Press.
Scheff, Thomas J.
1966   *Being Mentally Ill: A Sociological Theory.* Chicago: Aldine Press.
Schulz, David A.
1969   "Some aspects of the policeman's role as it impinges upon family life in a Negro ghetto." *Sociological Focus* 2 (Spring):63–72.
Schumann, Karl
1968   *Zeichen der Unfreiheit: Zur Theorie und Messung sozialer Sanktiönen.* Freiburg: Verlag Rombach.
Schur, Edwin M.
1965   *Crimes without Victims.* Englewood Cliffs: Prentice-Hall.
1968   *Law and Society: A Sociological View.* New York: Random House.
1971   *Labeling Deviant Behavior: Its Sociological Implications.* New York: Harper and Row.
Schwartz, Barry
1968   "The social psychology of privacy." *American Journal of Sociology* 73 (May):741–752.
Schwartz, Richard D.
1954   "Social factors in the development of legal control: a case study of two Israeli settlements." *Yale Law Journal* 63 (February):471–491.
Schwartz, Richard D., and James C. Miller
1964   "Legal evolution and societal complexity." *American Journal of Sociology* 70 (September):159–169.
Schwartz, Richard D., and Jerome K. Skolnick
1962   "Two studies of legal stigma." *Social Problems* 10 (Fall):133–142.
Sellin, Thorsten
1931   "Crime." Pages 563–569 in *Encyclopaedia of the Social Sciences*, edited by Edwin R. A. Seligman. New York: Macmillan. Volume 4.
Sellin, Thorsten, and Marvin E. Wolfgang
1964   *The Measurement of Delinquency.* New York: John Wiley.
Selznick, Philip
1961   "Sociology and natural law." *Natural Law Forum* 6:84–108.
1963   "Legal institutions and social controls." *Vanderbilt Law Review* 17 (December):79–90.
1968   "The sociology of law." Pages 50–59 in *International Encyclopedia of the Social Sciences*, edited by David L. Sills. New York: Free Press. Volume 9.
Selznick, Philip (with the assistance of Philippe Nonet and Howard M. Vollmer)
1969   *Law, Society, and Industrial Justice.* New York: Russell Sage Foundation.
Sennett, Richard
1970   *The Uses of Disorder: Personal Identity and City Life.* New York: Random House, 1971.
Sherman, Lawrence W.
1978   *Scandal and Reform: Controlling Police Corruption.* Berkeley: University of California Press.
1980a   "Causes of police behavior: the current state of quantitative research." *Journal of Research in Crime and Delinquency* 17 (January):69–100.
1980b   "Execution without trial: police homicide and the Constitution." *Vanderbilt Law Review* 33 (January):71–100.
Silver, Allan
1967   "The demand for order in civil society: a review of some themes in the history of urban

crime, police, and riot." Pages 1–24 in *The Police: Six Sociological Essays,* edited by David J. Bordua. New York: John Wiley.
Simmel, Georg
1908 *The Sociology of Georg Simmel,* edited by Kurt H. Wolff. New York: Free Press, 1960.
Singer, Peter
1973 "Altruism and commerce: a defense of Titmuss against Arrow." *Philosophy and Public Affairs* 2 (Spring):312–320.
Skolnick, Jerome K.
1965 "The sociology of law in America: overview and trends." Pages 4–39 in *Law and Society.* Published as supplement to *Social Problems,* Volume 12.
1966 *Justice without Trial: Law Enforcement in Democratic Society.* New York: John Wiley.
Slater, Philip
1970 *The Pursuit of Loneliness: American Culture at the Breaking Point.* Boston: Beacon Press.
Solzhenitsyn, Aleksandr I.
1973 *The Gulag Archipelago, 1918–1956: An Experiment in Literary Investigation.* New York: Harper and Row. Parts 1–2.
Sommer, Robert
1969 *Personal Space: The Behavioral Basis of Design.* Englewood Cliffs: Prentice-Hall.
Spence, A. Michael
1974 *Market Signaling.* Cambridge: Harvard University Press.
Spitzer, Steven
1979 "Notes toward a theory of punishment and social change." Pages 207–229 in *Research in Law and Sociology: An Annual Compilation of Research,* Volume 2, edited by S. Spitzer. Greenwich: JAI Press.
Spradley, James P.
1970 *You Owe Yourself a Drunk: An Ethnography of Urban Nomads.* Boston: Little, Brown.
Stack, Carol B.
1974 *All Our Kin: Strategies for Survival in a Black Community.* New York: Harper and Row.
Stark, Rodney
1972 *Police Riots: Collective Violence and Law Enforcement.* Belmont: Wadsworth Press.
Starr, June, and Jonathan Pool
1974 "The impact of a legal revolution in rural Turkey." *Law and Society Review* 8 (Summer):533–560.
Stinchcombe, Arthur L.
1963 "Institutions of privacy in the determination of police administrative practice." *American Journal of Sociology* 69 (September):150–160.
Suttles, Gerald D.
1968 *The Social Order of the Slum: Ethnicity and Territory in the Inner City.* Chicago: University of Chicago Press.
Sykes, Richard E., and John P. Clark
1975 "A theory of deference exchange in police–civilian encounters." *American Journal of Sociology* 81 (November):584–600.
Tannenbaum, Frank
1938 *Crime and the Community.* Boston: Ginn and Company.
Taylor, Michael
1976 *Anarchy and Cooperation.* New York: John Wiley.
Terry, Robert M.
1967 "The screening of juvenile offenders." *Journal of Criminal Law, Criminology and Police Science* 58 (June):173–181.
Thoden van Velzen, H. U. E., and W. van Wetering
1960 "Residence, power groups and intra-societal aggression: an enquiry into the conditions

leading to peacefulness within non-stratified societies." *International Archives of Ethnography* 49 (Part 2):169–200.

Tien, James M., Thomas A. Reppetto, and Lewis F. Hanes
  1976 *Elements of CPTED (Crime Prevention through Environmental Design)*. Arlington: National Issues Center, Westinghouse Electric Corporation (second edition; first edition, 1975).

Tiffany, Lawrence P., Donald M. McIntyre, and Daniel L. Rotenberg
  1967 *Detection of Crime: Stopping and Questioning, Search and Seizure, Encouragement and Entrapment*. Boston: Little, Brown.

Titmuss, Richard M.
  1971 *The Gift Relationship: From Human Blood to Social Policy*. New York: Pantheon Books.

Tönnies, Ferdinand
  1887 *Community and Society*. New York: Harper and Row, 1963.

Trubek, David M.
  1971 "Law, planning, and economic development." Unpublished paper, Law and Modernization Program, Yale Law School.

United States Department of Labor, Office of Policy Planning and Research
  1965 *The Negro Family: The Case for National Action*. Washington, D.C.: U.S. Government Printing Office. ("The Moynihan Report.")

United States President's Commission on Law Enforcement and Administration of Justice
  1967 *Crime and Its Impact—An Assessment*. Washington, D.C.: U.S. Government Printing Office.

van der Sprenkel, Sybille
  1962 *Legal Institutions in Manchu China: A Sociological Analysis*. New York: Humanities Press, 1966.

Van Maanen, John
  1974 "Working the street: a developmental view of police behavior." Pages 83–130 in *Sage Criminal Justice System Annuals*, Volume 3: *The Potential for Reform of Criminal Justice*, edited by Herbert Jacob. Beverly Hills: Sage.
  1978 "On watching the watchers." Pages 309–349 in *Policing: A View from the Street*, edited by Peter K. Manning and John Van Maanen. Santa Monica: Goodyear.

van Velsen, J.
  1969 "Procedural informality, reconciliation, and false comparisons." Pages 137–152 in *Ideas and Procedures in African Customary Law*, edited by Max Gluckman. London: Oxford University Press.

Vera Institute of Justice
  1977 *Felony Arrests: Their Prosecution and Disposition in New York City's Courts*. New York: Vera Institute of Justice.

Wahrhaftig, Paul (editor)
  1978 *The Citizen Dispute Resolution Organizer's Handbook*. Pittsburgh: Grassroots Citizen Dispute Resolution Clearinghouse (revised edition; first edition, 1977).

Wallace, Samuel E.
  1965 *Skid Row as a Way of Life*. Totowa: Bedminster Press.

Wambaugh, Joseph
  1970 *The New Centurions*. New York: Dell.

Waskow, Arthur I.
  1966 *From Race Riot to Sit-In, 1919 and the 1960s: A Study in the Connections between Conflict and Violence*. Garden City: Doubleday.

Weber, Max
  1922 *The Theory of Social and Economic Organization*, edited by Talcott Parsons. New York: Free Press, 1964.
  1925 *Max Weber on Law in Economy and Society*, edited by Max Rheinstein. Cambridge: Harvard University Press, 1954 (second edition; first edition, 1922).

Wertheimer, Roger
1975   "Are the police necessary?" Pages 49–60 in *The Police in Society,* edited by Emilio C. Viano and Jeffrey H. Reiman. Lexington: Lexington Books.
Werthman, Carl, and Irving Piliavin
1967   "Gang members and the police." Pages 56–98 in *The Police: Six Sociological Essays,* edited by David J. Bordua. New York: John Wiley.
Westley, William A.
1953   "Violence and the police." *American Journal of Sociology* 59 (August):34–41.
1970   *Violence and the Police: A Study of Law, Custom, and Morality.* Cambridge: MIT Press.
Wheeler, Stanton
1967   "Criminal statistics: a reformulation of the problem." *Journal of Criminal Law, Criminology and Police Science* 58 (September):317–324.
White, Lynn, Jr.
1962   *Medieval Technology and Social Change.* Oxford: Clarendon Press.
Wilson, James Q.
1963   "The police and their problems: a theory." *Public Policy* 12:189–216.
1964   "Generational and ethnic differences among career police officers." *American Journal of Sociology* 69 (March):522–528.
1968   *Varieties of Police Behavior: The Management of Law and Order in Eight Communities.* Cambridge: Harvard University Press.
1974   "The police and crime." Pages 81–97 in *Thinking about Crime.* New York: Basic Books, 1975.
Winick, Charles
1961   "Physician narcotic addicts." *Social Problems* 9 (Fall):174–186.
Wiseman, Jacqueline P.
1970   *Stations of the Lost: The Treatment of Skid Row Alcoholics.* Englewood Cliffs: Prentice-Hall.
Wolosin, Robert J., Steven J. Sherman, and Clifford R. Mynatt
1975   "When self-interest and altruism conflict." *Journal of Personality and Social Psychology* 32 (October):752–760.
Wood, Elizabeth
1961   *Housing Design: A Social Theory.* New York: Citizens' Housing and Planning Council of New York, Inc.
Yale Law Journal Editors
1967a   "Interrogations in New Haven: the impact of *Miranda*." *Yale Law Journal* 76 (July):1519–1648.
1967b   "Program budgeting for police departments." *Yale Law Journal* 76 (March):822–838.
Yngvesson, Barbara
1970   Decision-Making and Dispute Settlement in a Swedish Fishing Village: An Ethnography of Law. Unpublished doctoral dissertation, Department of Anthropology, University of California, Berkeley.
Youngblood, Gene
1970   *Expanded Cinema.* New York: E. P. Dutton.

Author Index

Subject Index